DIVERSITY AND DIFFERENCE IN EARLY CHILDHOOD EDUCATION

DIVERSITY AND DIFFERENCE IN EARLY CHILDHOOD EDUCATION:

ISSUES FOR THEORY AND PRACTICE

KERRY H. ROBINSON AND
CRISS JONES DÍAZ

Open University Press

Open University Press
McGraw-Hill Education
McGraw-Hill House
Shoppenhangers Road
Maidenhead
Berkshire
England
SL6 2QL

email: enquiries@openup.co.uk
world wide web: www.openup.co.uk

and Two Penn Plaza, New York, NY 10121–2289, USA

First published 2006

A catalogue record of this book is available from the British Library

ISBN 10: 0335 216 82 X (pb) 0 335 21683 8 (hb)
ISBN 13: 9780335216826 (pb) 9780335216833 (hb)

Library of Congress Cataloging-in-Publication Data
CIP data applied for

Typeset by YHT Ltd, London, UK
Printed in the UK by Bell and Bain Ltd., Glasgow

Criss would like to dedicate this book to Ramón for his continual support, encouragement, availability and wisdom; to Dominic for imagining the possibilities and potential of the creative spirit; and to Miguel for keeping it real, and always in perspective.

Kerry would like to dedicate this book to Sara and Bridget in the hope of a more equitable and peaceful world in their lifetime; and to Tunni.

Criss and Kerry would also like to dedicate this book to their UWS early childhood diversity students, past and future.

CONTENTS

FOREWORD

This book by Kerry Robinson and Criss Jones Díaz brings a dynamic mix of poststructuralist theory and early childhood classrooms into the present, providing a wonderfully clear and accessible introduction to poststructuralist theory and to its implications for early childhood classroom practice. They take as their central point of departure the rich diversity of modes of being that children bring with them to the preschool in this endlessly changing, globalizing world. It is an important and original innovation in this book that they situate their analysis in the context of that globalized/globalizing world. At its best, that world is one where borders can be crossed and multiple ways of seeing and of being can be honoured and respected, and where pluralism, inclusion and the principles of democracy can be lived out in everyday lives. At its worst that globalized/globalizing world is a neoliberal nightmare, where the world's wealth is skimmed off by major corporations, and ordinary people become useful as consumers and as commodities to be manipulated and disposed of when it suits the market. In this worse form of globalization, ordinary people are made as homogeneous as possible to ensure that diversity and difference do not interrupt the easy substitution of one worker for another, one consumer for another, one commodity for another. In this version of globalization, borders are relaxed when it suits the flow of money to the corporations, and they are fiercely tightened when it comes to the ordinary poor seeking refuge from terror and annihilation (George 2004).

It is rare to find a book on early childhood that situates itself in this wider political context. Neoliberalism is in fact extraordinarily clever at disguising itself, dressing itself up in equal opportunities policies, for example, while actually producing something very far from equality (Lakoff 2004). In a recent review of early childhood texts (Davies 2005a), including those by Fraser *et al.* (2004), Lewis *et al.* (2004), Lareau (2003) and Anning *et al.* (2004), I found that they included no mention of the pervasive effects of globalization and of the neoliberal forms of management that have impacted on educational institutions everywhere and on the subjectivities of our children (Davies 2003, 2005b). But understanding the historical and political contexts inside which current subjectivities are being shaped is important, and Robinson and Jones Díaz make this clear. We live in deeply contradictory times, constituted through deeply contradictory discourses. As early childhood educators, we need this kind of book to enable us to articulate our professional values and to bring them to life in our everyday practice.

Many of us who worked as and with teachers during the late 1960s and 1970s took part in huge social changes. Groups of people who had been excluded from social power could, and did, insist on change. We lived at that time in a kind of Hegelian or Age of Enlightenment ethos, believing that through an ongoing dialectical process, knowledge improves on itself – it works towards the betterment of society and of humanity generally. In this model, government pours resources into education and funds the teleological march of knowledge, believing this will create a more productive and inno-vative workforce, which will in turn accelerate progress and economic growth. In the 1980s and early 1990s this model shifted towards a neoliberal model in which those ideals were undermined and displaced. Neoliberalism has introduced, over the past two decades, increasing government of indivi-duals, including both greatly increased surveillance and accountability *and* a relinquishing of care and responsibility for individuals. Care and responsi-bility are shifted back to individuals themselves. Funds are withdrawn from education, and discourses of choice and privatization are pushed instead. At the same time as responsibility is moved from government to the individual, mechanisms of surveillance are used to compel compliance with neoliberal practices mandated by government. Auditing and accounting discourses thus take on greater power than, and undermine, professional discourses (Davies 2005c; Rose 1997).

The urgent task for those working in the early childhood area is the recuperation of professional discourses such that they are not simply mimicking what neoliberal doctrines require of them – and are not ignorant of those requirements – but have the power to question them. Those domi-nant, neoliberal discourses that homogenize students and instil competitive individualism in students, aggressively undermining strategies of inclusion and the valuing of difference and diversity, currently have enormous power. In this deeply contradictory space of globalization, this book provides a clear map for thinking through the issues that are relevant to early childhood practice and sets out the theoretical frameworks through which readers can make sense of their own insertion into deeply contradictory discourses. The subjectivities of early childhood teachers and of the children they work with, as well as the nature of that work, are constantly being produced in ways that teachers and children are not necessarily aware of. To become reflexively aware of the discourses through which we are formed, moment by moment, is an extraordinarily difficult task (Davies *et al.* 2004).

In their work as early childhood educators these authors work with students who are being formed by discourses to which they are exposed in higher education, by discourses they encounter in schools, by discourses in the media, and by discourses everywhere around them. Kerry and Criss teach them to be reflexively aware and to see the processes of discursive formation at work on them and on others. I believe this book brings to its readers some of the passion, insight and commitment to high standards that is evident in Kerry's and in Criss's teaching. It is a marvellous resource and a very timely contribution to making our way in this globalized/globalizing world.

Bronwyn Davies

References

Anning, A., Cullen, J. and Fleer, M. (2004) *Early Childhood Education. Society and Culture*. London: Sage.

Davies, B. (2003) Death to critique and dissent? The policies and practices of new managerialism and of 'evidence-based practice', *Gender and Education*, 15(1): 89–101.

Davies, B. (2005a) Emerging trends in researching children and youth: a review essay, *British Journal of Sociology of Education*, 26(1): 137–145.

Davies, B. (2005b). The fairy who wouldn't fly: a story of subjection and agency, *Journal of Early Childhood Literacy*, 5(2): 151–174.

Davies, B. (2005c) The impossibility of intellectual work in neoliberal regimes, *Discourse: Studies in the Cultural Politics of Education*, (26)1: 1–14.

Davies, B., Browne, J., Gannon, S., Honan, E., Laws, C., Mueller-Rockstroh, B. and Petersen, E.B. (2004) The ambivalent practices of reflexivity. *Qualitative Inquiry*, 10(3): 360–389.

Fraser, S., Lewis, V., Ding, S., Kellett, M. and Robinson, C. (eds) (2004) *Doing Research with Children and Young People*. London: Sage.

George, S. (2004) *Another World Is Possible If . . .* London: Verso.

Lewis, V., Kellett, M., Robinson, C, Fraser, S. and Ding, S. (2004) *The Reality of Research with Children and Young People*. London: Sage.

Lakoff, G. (2004) *Don't Think of an Elephant*. Melbourne: Scribe.

Lareau, A. (2003) *Unequal Childhoods. Class, Race and Family Life*. Berkeley: University of California Press.

Rose, N. (1997) *The Powers of Freedom*. Cambridge: Cambridge University Press.

ACKNOWLEDGEMENTS

We would like to thank the following people for their thoughtful comments, suggestions and critical understandings in providing us with crucial feedback on the various chapters: Prathyusha Sanagavarapu, Tania Ferfolja and The University of Western Sydney Narrative Discourse and Pedagogy Research Concentration, particularly Bronwyn Davies, Cristyn Davies, Constance Ellwood, Sue Saltmarsh and Jen Skattebol. Kerry would also like to thank Margaret Vickers, Florence McCarthy and Tania Ferfolja for carrying the load on many occasions when this book was in its final stages.

We would especially like to thank Tania Ferfolja for her tireless and careful editing and formatting of the final manuscript. We are also indebted to Bronwyn Davies and Nola Harvey for their comments on the book as a whole. Finally, we would also like to acknowledge the many early childhood educators and preservice teachers we have worked with over the past decade or so; your valuable contributions and voices are always respected and appreciated in our work.

CHANGING PARADIGMS IN EARLY CHILDHOOD EDUCATION:

Critical perspectives on diversity and difference in doing social justice in early childhood education

Introduction

The international field of early childhood education is currently experiencing a major challenge to the authority of many of the long-standing traditional theories and practices that have been utilized in approaches to children and children's learning. This challenge has largely stemmed from the new sociology of childhood, critical psychology and the utilization of post-modernist/poststructuralist frameworks, which call for educators, researchers and others working with children to begin to reconceptualize their under-standings of childhood and their work with young children. Consequently, many of the universalized 'truths' about 'the child' established in modernist perspectives and underpinning taken-for-granted or common-sense assump-tions about childhood and what it means to be a child, are being seriously critiqued and disrupted by these new and different ways of understanding children as subjects. This book has been written in the light of these sig-nificant and exciting social and educational changes and is a contribution to the growing body of work that aims to reconceptualize childhood and early childhood education. These perspectives have particular significance for understandings of diversity and difference, social inequalities and for doing social justice education with children and their families. Utilizing a feminist poststructuralist approach, informed by other social theories, including queer, critical, cultural and **postcolonial** theories, we explore the possibi-lities that these perspectives have for extending understandings of childhood, constructions of **identity**, and the negotiation of power that underpin social relationships and perpetuate social inequalities, as well as for personal, institutional and social transformations.

Since the late 1980s there has been a significant increase in awareness of the importance of early childhood education policies, practices and curriculum positively reflecting the diverse cultural identities of children and their families. Today, this embracing of the pluralism that exists in children's lives is a central feature of the different philosophies that broadly underpin early childhood education in Western countries – for example, those encompassed within the *anti-bias curriculum* that emerged from the United States (Derman-Sparks and the A.B.C. Task Force 1989) and in the perspectives of Reggio Emilia, stemming from Europe (Dahlberg *et al.* 1999). Such philosophies that enhance and foster diversity and difference are critical in a world that is encountering broad social, economic, political and technological shifts that are continually challenging and changing the lives of children, their families and communities at both the global and local levels. In this book we are particularly concerned with how and to what extent these philosophies, founded on concepts of pluralism, inclusion and democracy, are put into practice on a daily basis in early childhood institutions. How diversity and difference are perceived, taken up by individual early childhood educators and included and articulated into everyday policies and practices with children and their families, is critical to the impact and success of such philosophies in addressing social justice and equity issues. To date, there has been limited research on how early childhood educators' perspectives of diversity and difference impact on their pedagogy and how early childhood institutional policies and practices either disrupt or perpetuate the social inequalities that exist broadly in society.

This book is also a reflection of our growing concern with the potential impact that the global movements of neoliberalism, neoconservatism, and the marketization and corporatization of childhood can have on children, families and early childhood education. Of particular concern is the growing homogenization of social, cultural and linguistic identities of children and their families. Discourses of neoliberalism and neoconservatism have the potential to seriously impact on what knowledge is included in programmes, how it is to be taught, the recognition and inclusion of cultural diversity and difference, and the abilities of families, particularly from low socio-economic backgrounds, to meet the financial commitments of their children's early education. The marketization of childhood and early childhood education is about shareholder profits, rather than the quality of service provision. As Apple (2001: 18) argues, 'Neo-liberalism transforms our very idea of democracy, making it only an economic concept, not a political one'.

Hence, within the discourse of neoconservatism, which operates in tandem with neoliberalism, diversity and difference become problematic, as they are perceived to undermine Western values and traditions regarded as essential to the prevention of the social decay that is seen to be operating in society. Consequently, within this discourse, founded on the cultural **binary** opposition of us/them, a fear of the **Other** is maintained and perpetuated. The impact of these discourses is already being felt in early childhood education throughout the world – for example, the vigour with which standardized testing has been taken up in early childhood education, and the economic spin-offs that have been captured by corporate bodies in preparing children to meet the requirements of such testing (Cannella and Viruru 2004); and the recent public outcry from neoconservative politicians in Australia, when the long-running children's television programme *Play School* ran a segment depicting a young girl named Brenna and her friend, being taken to an amusement park by Brenna's two mums (Krien 2004; Nguyen 2004). This event has critical implications for social justice education more broadly, including addressing gay and lesbian issues in the early childhood curriculum.

Writing this book

This book is primarily based on the research we have conducted together and separately around issues of equity and social justice in early childhood education in Australia. It is also based on our experiences as pre-service teacher educators working with early childhood students for the past decade in a metropolitan university in Sydney, in one of the most culturally diverse communities in Australia. Despite the fact that it is Australia-based research, we feel that the issues that we are dealing with are equally relevant to early childhood educators elsewhere in the world. The social, political and economic factors that are impacting on children and their families, as well as the social inequalities that continue to plague the lives of many of these families, are operating on both global and local scales.

Our joint research has focused on exploring early childhood educators' perceptions of diversity and difference and the impact these have on pedagogy, polices and practices. Through the utilization of surveys and individual interviews we have focused on early childhood educators' perceptions and practices around issues of gender, multiculturalism, bilingualism, sexuality, Aboriginality, family and social class issues, as well as how early childhood institutions incorporate these equity issues into their policies and organizational practices. Unfortunately, a book of this scope that critically examines difference and diversity within a social justice agenda in education cannot adequately deal with all the relevant social, political and economic issues facing children and their families. Consequently, the different foci of the chapters are a representation of our combined and separate areas of research expertise, particularly in the areas of bilingualism, multiculturalism, gender, sexuality, family and social class issues. It is these areas that we feel that have particular international relevance and significance.

It is also important to highlight that early childhood educators are a heterogeneous group from a variety of backgrounds, with a multiplicity of perspectives and voices based on their different locations within social discourses that operate around diversity and difference. Consequently, the perspectives and voices present in this book do not speak for all early childhood educators, but rather they represent the dominant discourses prevailing among those educators, other staff, resource workers, children and their families, and pre-service teachers with whom we have worked in Australia in recent years.

Children's perceptions of difference

The early childhood years (from birth to age 8) are formidable years in the growth and development of cognition, language, social, emotional and physical competence. This development takes place within different social contexts where issues related to human diversity and difference impact significantly on children's understandings of and ways of being in the world. Over the past twenty years research has increased educators' awareness of the bias and discrimination that young children can hold and perpetuate towards those who are perceived as different from the dominant culture and those who engage in social practices different from their own. This research highlights that by the time children enter primary schooling their perceptions of difference largely reflect and perpetuate the dominant racialized, gendered, sexualized, classed and body **stereotypes** and prejudices that prevail in the broader society (Palmer 1990; Glover 1991; Troyna and Hatcher 1992; Mac-Naughton 1993, 2000; Alloway 1995; Makin *et al.* 1995).

Children do not enter early childhood programmes as empty slates but rather bring with them a myriad of perceptions of difference that they have taken up from their families, peers, the media and other social sources and negotiated in the representations of their own identities. Glover (1991) in the early 1990s found that as 2- and 3-year-old children become aware of differences they simultaneously develop positive or negative feelings about the differences they observe. For example, racial awareness is developed early in young children, impacting on their perceptions of skin colour and on their preferences in the social relationships they initiate and foster with other children (Aboud 1988; Katz 1982; Palmer 1990; Averhart and Bigler 1997). Glover (1991) reports that children frequently exhibited negative behaviours towards children from different racial backgrounds: refusing to hold their hands, never choosing to play with dolls from different racial backgrounds and always picking same-'race' pictures for collages. An Australian study by Palmer (1990) clearly illustrated how preschool children were able to make negative evaluative judgements based on racial characteristics. In Palmer's study, the non-Aboriginal children made negative comments such as 'Blackfellas dirty' and children were reported as saying 'You're the colour of poo ... Did your Mum drop you in the poo?' and 'Rack off wog. We don't want to play with you' (cited in Glover 1991: 5). Kutner (1958) found that racial prejudice in young children affects their ability to make sound judgements and often their perception of reality is distorted. By age 3–4 years they are becoming more aware of ability and other differences and are developing critical understandings of their own identities, as well as the diversity and differences of others. Bredekamp and Rosegrant (1991) pointed out that 2-year-olds are already aware of and curious about differences and similarities among people, and they construct 'theories' about diversity congruent with their cognitive stages of development and life experiences.

As children grow older, other differences such as language variation and linguistic diversity become obvious. By 3 years of age, children are aware that speakers use different language codes in different contexts and bilingual children are highly aware of contextual differences in language use (Genesee

1989; Lanza 1992; Makin *et al.* 1995). Lanza (1992) investigated the language use of her bilingual 2-year-old and found that the child was able to separate the two languages or mix them according to the social expectations and context of the language used. Non-bilingual children also demonstrate an awareness of language differences and comments such as 'he speaks funny' or 'I don't understand her' are not uncommon.

Early childhood educators in our research largely perceive children's prejudice more as the passive reflections and expressions of adults' values towards difference, rather than as representations of the narratives and perceptions of the world that children, as individual agents, own themselves. This perspective is reflected in the following remarks: 'Children aren't aware of these things unless it is pointed out to them by adults'; 'Children's prejudices are just a reflection or a mimicking of what they directly pick up from adults' behaviour'; 'They don't really understand what it means, they just say it'. Dominant discourses of childhood that constitute children as too young to engage in or understand discriminatory practices or power, as naturally blind to differences, and as passive recipients who soak up adults' perceptions and values, are still highly influential in early childhood education.

However, in recent years, primarily with the influence of poststructural perspectives shifting understandings of childhood and constructions of identity, research has highlighted how children play a critical and active role in the constitution and perpetuation of social inequalities through their perceptions of the world and everyday interactions with each other and with adults (Aboud 1988; Alloway 1995; Averhart and Bigler 1997; Kaomea 2000; MacNaughton 2000; Grieshaber 2001; MacNaughton and Davis 2001). Children from early ages constitute, perpetuate and negotiate normalizing discourses around their identities, and are actively regulating not only their own behaviour accordingly, but also that of others around them.

Walkerdine (1990) found that 4-year-old boys were capable of yielding power, based on the way they repositioned their female teacher within the discourse of 'woman as sex object'. They utilized derogatory sexual language and explicit sexual references to undermine her power as an adult and a teacher. Research conducted by Alloway (1995), which studied the construction of gender from preschool to grade 3, consistently reported incidences in which boys employed subtle forms of manipulation to constitute themselves as the dominant gender. Such examples include preschool boys throwing objects at girls as they played on outdoor equipment and harassing them by lifting up their skirts and commenting on their underwear. In MacNaugton and Davis's (2001) study of non-Indigenous children's understandings of Indigenous Australians, their findings revealed how non-Indigenous children drew on processes of colonial 'othering' to position Indigenous Australians as exotic, creating the binary of 'us' and 'them'.

Constructions of childhood

Postmodernist and feminist poststructural perspectives have been extremely influential in challenging modernist thinking that has dominated understandings of childhood and children's learning (for example, see Davies 1989, 1993; James and Prout 1990; Walkerdine 1990; Cannella 1997; Mac-Naughton 2000; Grieshaber 2001; Robinson 2002, 2005b; Cannella and Viruru 2004). These perspectives disrupt and challenge modernist humanist perspectives of the universal child – the notion that there is an innate phase in human development that constitutes childhood, which is universally experienced by all children. Rather, proponents who take up these perspectives view childhood as a social construction – a social process in which understandings of what it means to be a child are constituted within the historical and cultural discourses available. The Piagetian theory of child development, which has dominated understandings of childhood and children's learning, is based on the perspective that children from birth proceed to develop along a biologically predetermined, clearly articulated, linear process towards becoming adults. All children proceed through this process, reaching certain cognitive development stages that correlate with particular chronological ages; adulthood is marked by the ability to engage in abstract and hypothetical thinking.

However, in recent times, theories of child development, like that of Piaget's, have been critiqued for their assumed biologically determined universalism, their generalization from small groups to *all* children, their linearity and their failure to recognize the importance of socio-cultural factors and other issues such as gender, ethnicity and historical contexts (James and Prout 1990; Gittins 1998; James *et al*. 1998). The categorization of children's behaviours within chronological 'ages' and 'stages' reinforces normative understandings about children's developmental pathways, especially if viewed from middle-class, Eurocentric perspectives. The 'idea of stages does not orient us to think in any but normative terms about children whose developmental trajectory might differ' (Lubeck 1998: 301).

Consequently, there has been an increased awareness of the need to view child development within different social, cultural, political and economic contexts of childhood. The child is born into society as an embodied being, who grows and physically matures over time, but the collective notion of 'childhood' and understandings of what this constitutes are primarily socially, culturally and historically variable across ethnicity, class and gender (James and Prout 1990; James *et al*. 1998; Gittins 1998; Jenkins 1998). The dominant discourse of childhood has tended to perpetuate white, Western and middle-class values that have historically been linked to strong religious and moral discourses. Childhood has been romanticized by adults and childhood 'innocence', a discursive construction, has been critical in justifying the way that adults have kept children separate from the public domains of active citizenry. Gittins (1998: 111) points out that 'Images of children are invariably constructed *by adults* to convey messages and meanings *to adults*'.

The discursive construction of childhood across different cultures and historical points in time means that there are multiple and different readings and experiences of what it means to be a child; therefore, understandings of childhood are not fixed. In terms of constructions of childhood, post-structuralists and postmodernists are concerned with several main issues:

challenging the scientific 'truths' that underpin **authoritative knowledge and fix definitions** of childhood; the way that the dominant discourse of childhood is founded within the cultural oppositional binary adult/child that perpetuates hierarchical power relationships between adults and children; how such modernist humanist perspectives have tended to silence children's voices and compromise their positions in society as citizens; and the impact that such discourses of childhood have had on understandings of children's learning.

Dominant images of childhood have been developed around children's dependency on adults, which encompass a myriad of power relationships resulting in inequalities between adults and children. However, this construction of children's dependency has major negative consequences as pointed out by Gittins (1998: 107): 'Children, generally well looked after and protected, are none the less extremely vulnerable as a result of their own dependencies, isolation, silencing and disenfranchisement'.

This perspective of childhood is founded on the cultural oppositional binary adult/child perpetuated through modernist thought. Consequently, children are viewed as being inherently different from adults. This modernist paradigm has been instrumental in defining children in opposition to what it means to be an adult and artificially creating the separate, distinct, and often mutually exclusive spaces which have become known as the 'world of the child' and 'world of adults'. This separation of children and adults, perpetuated within the binary logic underpinning current taken-for-granted or common-sense understandings of childhood and children, continues to dominate and influence how educators work with children in their early years and beyond. This perspective has largely determined what knowledge is accessible to children and expectations of what children are capable of achieving and comprehending. The impact of this dominant discourse of childhood is particularly obvious in the area of doing social justice education with children. Many of the early childhood educators in our research were located within this discourse and presumed that children were 'too young' and 'too innocent' to comprehend or think critically about what they considered to be 'adult issues', such as difference, power, 'race' and sexuality. Many issues are excluded (often perceived as taboo subjects) in children's early education in the name of protecting their 'childhood innocence'; thus, we have the development of an imagined 'world of the child' constructed by adults. Consequently, for many early childhood educators, critical social, political and economic events and issues that are impacting on the lives of children and their families are considered developmentally inappropriate and irrelevant to children's early education. The social construction of young children's identities within the social categories of 'race', class, ethnicity, gender, sexuality, language and so on, tend to be under-theorized by early childhood educators (Robinson and Jones Díaz 1999). There is often little recognition for the broader sociological frameworks, which position children's learning and development within socio-cultural contexts (Alloway 1997). Such Westernized views of childhood effectively silence and marginalize minority socio-cultural groups that may have very different ways of viewing and understanding young children (Alloway 1997).

Hierarchies of difference: early childhood educators, diversity and social justice

Early childhood educators are in an ideal position to make a positive difference in the lives of children and their families. This is possible not only on the broader level of advocating for their rights, but also challenging and disrupting normalizing discourses through the curriculum that we teach, the policies that inform our practice and the pedagogies that we utilize in teaching children. However, the location of early childhood educators within the various discourses of diversity and difference that are available to them will impact on how they perceive these issues and approach them with children and their families. Early childhood educational institutions (like other educational institutions) are a microcosm of the broader society; they constitute and perpetuate many of the normalizing discourses that underpin social inequalities through educational programmes, educators' pedagogies, and the hidden curriculum of everyday interactions and practices. Thus, there is often great ambivalence and contradiction surrounding various forms of diversity and difference that exist in society, resulting in what we have called a hierarchy of differences (or comforts). The existence of this hierarchy is a reflection of the different degrees of commitment given by individuals and institutions to the provision of equity across the spectrum of civil risks or social justice issues that exist (Robinson and Jones Díaz 2000; Robinson and Ferfolja 2001; Robinson 2002). It is also a reflection of the varying levels of comfort experienced by individuals and institutions, associated with different equity issues in society. Contradictory practices around diversity and difference are often based on normative assumptions about people, their social behaviours and their entitlements to justice, especially if they choose to step outside what are widely considered socially acceptable conventions in society. For example, gay and lesbian equity issues are often located at the bottom of the hierarchy of differences. The research of Kobayashi and Ray (2000: 402) echoes the findings in our research: they talk about a 'hierarchy of rights', highlighting that institutions responsible for setting public policy and providing public services, such as health care, social services benefits and education, 'represent a network that also functions ideologically to determine what kinds of risk are more or less acceptable and what levels of risk will be publicly tolerated'. Similarly, these researchers point out that many rights are controversial and not all receive the same support, recognition or priority, acknowledging that a 'spectrum of political ideologies' results in 'varying degrees of commitment to equity provision' (Kobayashi and Ray 2000: 406).

Thus, some early childhood educators, who have strong commitments to social justice and equity issues such as 'race', ethnicity, gender or (dis)ability for example, can ironically uphold homophobic and heterosexist values and practices when it comes to dealing with sexuality (Robinson and Jones Díaz 2000). This slippage or contradiction around doing social justice work is not surprising when individuals are viewed as shifting subjects. Within the feminist poststructural context, subjects are viewed as irrational, contradictory and complex beings that change and shift discursively according to different contexts across periods of time (Weedon 1997; Robinson and Jones Díaz

1999). Individual subjects are constantly negotiating the different power relations operating through the different discourses available to them; therefore their locations can change according to the context in which they are operating. Locations within discourses are primarily influenced by the personal investments that individual subjects have in being positioned in one discourse over another. As Robinson (2002) has previously pointed out, the variation in comfort around diversity issues may be related to a number of factors, including an individual's own identity, their experiences or lack of experiences with difference, their knowledge about difference, their religious and cultural values, their positioning in sexist, heterosexist, homophobic and racist discourses and so on.

The notion of a hierarchy of differences, or of rights, poses some critical questions for early childhood education, in terms of how the field approaches social justice issues. Within the philosophical framework of Reggio Emilia, early childhood institutions are regarded as 'civil forums' (Dahlberg *et al.* 1999). These are spaces where 'children and adults participate together in projects of social, cultural, political and economic significance', providing 'a locus for active citizenship through participation in collective action and the practice of democracy' (Dahlberg *et al.* 1999: 73). The development of early childhood education institutions as civil forums is an important goal in terms of the field contributing to global and local social justice. However, it seems that in order to put this concept into practice, there is still a lot of reflexive work that needs to be done. This is especially so when some social justice issues, for example sexuality, continue to be excluded from programmes and considered, in some contexts, as unworthy of the same respect and demo-cratic principles as privileged to other equity issues. There is still a long way to go from 'tolerance' to respect. Further, the perception of children as critical thinking active citizens in their own right, with valuable contributions to make to families, communities, and society more generally, is often over-shadowed by traditional understandings and constructions of childhood as a period of innocence, powerlessness and incompetence. For many educators in our research, broad social, political and economic factors contributing to social inequalities and significantly impacting on the lives of children and their families, are considered irrelevant to the 'world of children'. Rather they are perceived to be adults' issues from which children, in the name of prolonging their 'innocence', need to be protected.

Early childhood educators are traditionally taught to value families as an important resource and in order to do this they must recognize that their perceptions, values and beliefs about family diversity will directly impact on their work with children. Relationships developed between staff and families will depend on how the educator interacts with diverse and different religious practices, sexual preferences of families, child-rearing practices, language differences, gendered practices, ability levels and socio-economic back-grounds of families. Jones Díaz (2003b) argues that it is crucial that early childhood educators acknowledge the **intersections** between identity and difference in understanding the multiple ways in which children and families negotiate everyday lived realities through which they experience their identity.

As professionals, early childhood educators need to recognize the various power dimensions that operate between themselves, children and the different families using their services. Families placing their children in the care of early childhood staff do so in the trust that their children's needs and interests will be met. Families can often feel alienated, silenced and marginalized when their experiences and perceptions of the world are not included and represented in their children's education.

Shifting paradigms in early childhood education: a historical overview

The following discussion provides an introductory historical overview of the paradigmatic shifts that are currently impacting on early childhood education that we have alluded to so far in this chapter. We have found that many early childhood educators have limited knowledge and experience with social theories, despite a major focus of their roles involving working with and advocating for the rights of families from diverse socio-cultural backgrounds. This discussion identifies the main issues and the critical points of difference between **postmodern** and modernist thinking relevant to our various discussions in this book.

The Enlightenment, humanism and scientific 'truth'

To understand the paradigmatic shift that is impacting on early childhood education in the twenty-first century we have to go back as far as the Enlightenment period which began in Europe in the eighteenth century. The Enlightenment, as the word suggests, was considered to be an awakening from a bleak period of human existence, known as the Dark Ages, which began in medieval times. The Dark Ages represented a time when brutality reigned and dominant knowledge was founded on ancient superstitions and medieval Christianity. The Enlightenment, in contrast, is represented as a period of intellectual awakening sparked by geographical discovery and the scientific revolution in which new knowledge associated with mathematics, astrology, physics, biology and anthropology emerged. Based on scientific 'fact' or 'truths', this new knowledge revolutionized the way the world was viewed, including the position of 'man' within the universe and the role of God. This period also saw the emergence of Western philosophy that extended the Enlightenment from greater understandings of the natural world into the social realm of human relationships and interactions. It was perceived that not only could science discover the natural order of the world and the laws that governed it, but also such knowledge and laws could also be discovered about human beings and what it meant to be human. Thus, the Enlightenment gave way to the notion of a universal human history united by the common ideals of human reason and rationality, progress and perfection, all reinforced by and founded on scientific 'truths' (Erickson and Murphy 2003). It was within this context that positivism emerged, which is an outlook that promoted detached, 'value-free' science as the model for social scientific enquiry; that is, scientific objective truth. The insistence that human beings have the capacity to engage in reason and rationality, leading to moral and intellectual progress and ultimately perfection, became the ideals behind what is known as humanism, as well as the foundation stones of modernist thought. Erickson and Murphy (2003: 40) aptly define these concepts:

> Reason referred to the exercise of human intellect unfettered by authoritarian faith, including faith in religion. Progress referred to the resulting positive direction of historical change, opposite to the direction presupposed by medieval Christianity, which considered humanity degenerate and fallen from the grace of God. Perfectibility referred to the final outcome of reason and progress, which, according to Enlightenment thinkers, would lead to steady improvement of human conditions on Earth.

Thus, many different intellectuals and social and political groups have taken up these humanist principles since the late eighteenth century. They were the rallying cries of the French Revolution and often the slogans of social reform, even today.

Marxism, social class and ideology

The failure of the French Revolution to deliver a new egalitarian world, based on the values of humanism, plunged Europe into a period of conservatism that lasted for many decades. It was a period in which the middle and upper classes of Europe and Britain continued to prosper at the expense of the working classes who grew more unsettled as a result of their exploitation. The Industrial Revolution of the nineteenth century entrenched **capitalism** as an economic and social system throughout the world – a system in which the consequences of the inequitable distribution of wealth and access to resources, including land, which excludes and exploits the majority of the world's people, continue to be seen today. It was within this context of the social and political unrest in nineteenth-century industrial Britain and Europe that Marxism as a political movement found its roots. Marxism, in its various forms, has had a profound impact on the world's politics, particularly in terms of theorizing social inequalities and social change.

Karl Marx (1818–1883) and Friedrich Engels (1820–1895) were the cofounders of Marxism, which basically upheld that true social equality was possible through a workers' revolution in which the capitalist state system would be overthrown and replaced by a communist social and economic system run by the people, for the people. Marxism, an economically based social theory, is considered a grand narrative or a universal theory in which a particular perspective provides a totalizing and universalizing explanation of the events at its focus. For Marx and Engels the structure of reality was embedded in the material base of economics. They considered human thoughts, actions and institutions to be determined by their relationship to the means of production – that is, how one makes a living in the material world (Erickson and Murphy 2003).

Social class was viewed as the organizing principle in modern societies and the primary context in which inequality and relations of power operated. Social class distinction was based on a binary relationship between those who own the means of production (that is, those who own and control the land, factories, businesses, multinational corporations and so on), the ruling class or bourgeoisie, and those who work for them (the ruled workers or proletariat). This relationship is perceived to be one constituted within conflict and exploitation, where the owners of the means of production exploit workers to gain the greatest profit from the resources and/or the goods they produce. Social power is linked to those who have access to and control of the means of production in a capitalist society – that is, the ruling class.

Marxist theorists view power as primarily being repressive, negative and universally and monolithically yielded by the state, which ultimately operates to keep the ruling class in power. State institutions, such as schooling (including early childhood education) perpetuate ruling-class ideologies that reproduce the values and practices that keep them in power. Marxist theory continued to be a major political movement well into the mid-twentieth century, spreading its influence beyond the borders of Britain and Europe into other parts of the world, including North America, South America and Australia. Neo-Marxist perspectives (new versions of Marxist thought) are utilized today by some social theorists to theorize social inequalities in globalizing capitalist economies throughout the world.

Structural functionalism

Another social theory that has been influential, particularly in the early to mid-twentieth century, was structural functionalism; though it can be argued that this perspective still operates today in some guises, especially through the **liberal humanist** philosophies underpinning social policies espoused by conservative governments in Australia, the United States and the United Kingdom since the mid-1990s. Structural functionalism, based primarily on the works of the sociologist Talcott Parsons (1902–1979) in the United States, viewed the structure of society and its inherent power relations as being part of 'the natural order of things'. Parsons considered the structure and nature of society to be similar to the workings of a watch, where each separate component or institution in society operated as an integral part of the whole organization, but had a specialized function that worked to keep the whole system working smoothly. Thus, Parsons viewed society as a harmonious and perfect system, within which power relations were considered to reflect the natural order of things, where some individuals had the right to more power than others; for example, adults naturally had power over children and men naturally had power over women. Thus, hierarchical power was considered natural, normal and necessary for the smooth running of society.

However, Parson's theory of a smoothly running harmonious system in which consensus was the norm, met with much opposition from those who pointed out the inequities and contradictions that operated within the system. Crime and conflict were prevalent throughout society and domestic violence in homes was a problem indicating that in many instances Parson's perspective of the world was not appropriate. Parsons argued that problems arose in the system not because of the system itself, which was perfect, but as a result of deviant individuals, who were problematic. Thus, the system was not seen as being responsible for any of the problems that prevailed, but rather the responsibility of individuals who failed to comply with the rules and regulations, or conform to their naturally allocated lot in life; for example, unemployment was a result of individuals who could not keep a job, rather than a system that failed to provide employment opportunities for all. Inequality was viewed within the 'natural order of things'. It is interesting to point out that this philosophical discourse still operates within welfare and conservative political arenas today.

Feminisms, patriarchy, women's subordination

There are several strands of feminist theory (for example, **liberal**, radical, socialist, poststructuralist) and each provides a different explanation of how gender operates in society to structure broad social power relations between men and women. Most, except for feminist **poststructuralism**, tend to view power as primarily operating through a patriarchal social system where men exploit women, children and some men; thus gendered inequalities need to be addressed through major structural changes in society. Socialist feminists take the perspective that this patriarchal social system works jointly with the economic system of capitalism to exploit women, particularly in the workforce, but also more generally in society. Thus, gender tends to be viewed as the main organizing principle behind power and inequality in society, with other sites of inequality, 'race', ethnicity, social class, sexuality and so on intersecting with gender.

The women's movement in the 1960s began to question the taken-for-granted gender relations in society in which women tended to be viewed as being generally oppressed by a patriarchal system. The workforce was one sphere where women tended to be restricted to low-paid, low-status service positions, did not receive equal pay for the same work, and experienced a glass ceiling in the way of promotion into management positions. The division of society into the feminized private sphere of the family and the masculinized public sphere of the economy and politics was upheld as an artificially constructed division of power between men and women. The private patriarchal nature of the family was challenged as a particular source of women's inequality and **oppression**, especially in terms of widespread domestic violence. Feminisms challenged the view that men's power over women was the natural order of things and that women's lot in life was determined by their biology; that is, that women were naturally mothers and carers of children and family.

The emergence of postmodernism and poststructuralism, anti-humanism and challenges to scientific 'truths'

The social theories outlined above are considered grand narratives; that is, they tend to provide monolithic universal explanations of social relationships and of power. For example, in many feminist perspectives, the oppression of women by men was considered the primary form of power and inequality that women experienced in their lives, and this tended be universalized to all women. Such universalized macro-explanations of power have provided valuable foundations on which to view social inequalities, but they are limited in that they do not provide an adequate means through which to understand micro-relations of power, or power as multifaceted, shifting and contextually changing, and as constitutive of performances of identity. They tend to view power negatively, and individuals as its 'victims', rather than looking at the positive and productive exercise of power in people's lives.

Consequently, there was a need for an explanation of power that theorizes not only how power operates in broader social structures, but also on the complex micro levels in individuals' lives; that provides insights into how individuals negotiate power every day in different contexts. Individuals are not always powerless; indeed, power can change across contexts, where one may have more power in one instance, but less in another. Thus, power is contextually located, shifting and fluid. Intellectuals began to seek out different ways of theorizing social power and inequalities within new social movements.

Social unrest in Europe, epitomized in the student riots in Paris in the late 1960s, marked the emergence of new social movements in Europe, the United States and other parts of the world. These new political movements included feminism, gay and lesbian liberation and black civil rights, which 'emerged in response to the oppressive effects on social and personal life of capitalism, the state, and the pernicious ideologies such as sexism, racism, and **homophobia**' (Best and Kellner 1991: 24). One of the major theoretical shifts to find support among these new political movements at this time was postmodernism, which reflected a growing dissatisfaction with the ability of humanism and universal social theories such as Marxism to adequately explain contemporary society and its diverse modes of power (Best and Kellner 1991).

Many intellectuals and political groups associated with the new social movements rejected Marxism as being 'too dogmatic and narrow a framework' to theorize the diverse modes of power that operated in contemporary society (Best and Kellner 1991: 24). As a social theory, Marxism did not adequately deal with the multiple sources of oppression and relations of power associated with other sites of identity (for example, gender, sexuality and 'race') that were not irreducible to the exploitation of labour; nor did it adequately deal with the micro-politics of everyday interactions, which was considered the essential focus of the success of political struggles by postmodern theorists. Thus, postmodern theorists were drawn to these new social movements, proposing that there needed to be a decentring of political alliances, replaced by a focus on 'difference' and recognition of the various perspectives and experiences among and within social groups; as well as focusing on the micro-political struggles of everyday life. For example, postmodernists were critical of the women's movement's universalized perspective that women's oppression was the sole result of patriarchal oppression, which led to their powerlessness; that is, women's oppression and subordination were the result of a patriarchal social structure or system, in which men had supreme power, as well as controlling access to resources and opportunities, keeping women subordinated and powerless.

Hence, postmodernists challenged the very concept of 'woman' as a universal and unifying term, pointing out that it failed to recognize the differences among women in terms of their 'race', ethnicity, sexuality, social class and so on, that impacted on their diverse experiences of inequality or oppression, as well as their power or powerlessness. Thus, postmodernists presented important new avenues for politicizing social and cultural relations, based on what Best and Kellner (1991: 25) identify as 'radical democracy'.

What is postmodernism?

Postmodernism is an intellectual and cultural movement that has gained prominence since the mid-twentieth century, significantly reconceptualizing how identity, the subject (the self), power and difference are theorized. Postmodernism primarily provides a critique of modernist perspectives, which have dominated since the Enlightenment, producing new models of thought. However, postmodernism is not a homogeneous mode of thought; it incorporates a range of perspectives, with some extreme versions totally severing any intersections with modernism. Some others view the prefix 'post' as misleading as some versions have relationships with modernist views, but operate to disrupt and radicalize what they see as the difficulties and barriers of modernist thinking. According to Best and Kellner (1991: 181), 'The discourse of the postmodern is a borderline discourse between the modern and the postmodern that allows a creative restructuring of modern theory and politics'.

What is poststructuralism?

Poststructuralism is part of the matrix of postmodernism; it is a 'subset of the broad range of theoretical, cultural, and social tendencies, which constitute postmodern discourses' (Best and Kellner 1991: 25). Friedrich Nietzsche (1844–1900), the German philosopher, provided the theoretical premises of many postmodern and poststructuralist critiques. Nietzsche, critical of the modernist humanist and positivist principles that emerged during the Enlightenment, 'attacked philosophical conceptions of the subject, representation, causality, truth, value, and system, replacing Western philosophy with a perspectivist orientation for which there are no facts, only interpretations, and no objective truths, only the constructs of various individuals and groups' (Best and Kellner 1991: 22). In poststructuralist theory (as in postmodernism more generally) primacy is given to discourse theory, which we discuss in depth in Chapter 2. Discourse theorists, such as the French philosopher and historian Michel Foucault (1926–1984), argue that meaning is not simply given, but is socially constructed across a number of institutional sites and practices. Discourse theorists emphasize the material and heterogeneous nature of discourse and analyse the institutional bases of discourse, the viewpoints and positions from which people speak, and the power relations these allow and presuppose. Discourse theory also interprets discourse as a site and object of struggle where different groups strive for **hegemony** and the production of meaning and **ideology** (Best and Kellner 1991: 26). Sawicki (1991: 20) points out the focus of poststructuralism is on the 'myriad of power relations at the micro level of society'. Poststructuralism is primarily concerned with language, signs, images, codes, and signifying systems, which organize the psyche, society and everyday social life, but as Sawicki points out above, this perspective is linked to broader social, political and economic institutions that also make up the social body. This point is also reinforced by Foucault, who views the social body as 'a thoroughly heterogeneous ensemble consisting of discourses, institutions, architectural forms, regulatory decisions, laws, administrative measures, scientific statements, philosophical, moral and philanthropic propositions – in short, the said as much as the unsaid' (Foucault 1980: 184).

A feminist poststructural approach

The emergence of postmodern and poststructuralist perspectives, reflected in the new sociology of childhood and the reconceptualization of early childhood education movement, has created different spaces and lenses through which the production of new knowledge about children as subjects is made possible. Feminist poststructuralism is the main theoretical framework that is utilized in this book and is outlined in depth in the following chapter. This perspective provides an invaluable approach to dealing with diversity and difference with both adults and children, and allows for an understanding of how inequalities are played out differently in different situations. In terms of understanding the social inequities that exist in society, feminist poststructuralist perspectives allow for the following critical analyses and understandings:

- knowledge as being partial and constituted within discourses;
- identities and individual subjectivities as constituted within social discourses and as negotiated, shifting, complex and contradictory;
- power as a process, operating through social discourse that is practised and negotiated by individual subjects at both the macro (institutional) and micro (everyday life) levels in society;
- individual subjects having **agency** in their lives, rather than being passive and powerless 'victims';
- social inequalities as constituted within and perpetuated through the social discourses historically and culturally available to individual subjects;
- childhood as a socially constructed concept that is constituted in the social discourses historically and culturally available to individual subjects;
- how individual subjects perpetuate social inequalities through their everyday interactions and practices;

- how change is possible through the processes of altering citational practices, **deconstruction** and reflexivity.

Consequently, feminist poststructuralist perspectives provide a different critical lens through which to theorize contemporary society, to understand the constructions of individual subjects, to negotiate the politics associated with identity differences, to explore the diverse modes of power that operate in society at both the macro (broad societal and institutional context) and micro (everyday personal interactions) levels that underpin the vast inequalities that exist, and to explore possibilities for individual and social transformations. Further, feminist poststructuralism allows us to effectively develop understandings of the way that individual subjects negotiate and construct their own identities, to challenge normalizing discourses that operate on micro and macro levels in their lives, and to demonstrate how individual subjects are instrumental in the perpetuation of social inequalities.

Critical to feminist poststructuralist perspectives is the process of the construction of **subjectivity**, that is, the 'self'. This process of subjectification is crucial to an understanding of the different perspectives or 'truths' that we take up as our own ways of looking at the world; these 'truths' become the foundations of our judgements of and interactions with others in the world. For educators, an awareness of this process is paramount to a reflexive understanding of the way their perspectives are constructed and impact on the way they interact in the world and, more specifically, interact with other educators, children and their families. As Davies (1994: 3) aptly points out:

> An individual's subjectivity is made possible through the discourse s/he has access to, through a life history of being in the world. It is possible for each of us as teachers and students to research the process of subjectification in order to see its effect on us and on the learning environments we collaboratively produce.

Feminist poststructural perspectives have provided a means through which to move beyond the limitations of modernist perspectives in order to view the complexities, contradictions, contextuality and shifting nature of power and subjectivity, critical to an understanding of difference, political struggle and inequality.

Other social theories influencing this book

Apart from our work being primarily influenced by feminist poststructuralist perspectives, other social theories, and particular social theorists, have also been utilized to inform our various analyses of identity, relations of power and social inequalities. For example, the works of Michel Foucault, Pierre Bourdieu, Judith Butler, Stuart Hall and Michael Apple have been critical to the development of our perspectives and approaches to diversity and difference and doing social justice education. Foucault's concepts of 'regimes of truth', the knowledge/power nexus and discourse are outlined in depth in Chapter 2. Bourdieu's concepts of **cultural capital, habitus, field** and symbolic violence are also important and useful theoretical concepts that inform our discussions of social inequality and have been incorporated across the chapters (see Chapters 5 and 7). Overall, we take an eclectic approach to social theory, supporting the perspective that 'a combination of micro- and macro-theory and politics provides the best framework to explore contemporary society with a view to radical social transformation' (Best and Kellner 1991: 298). The following social theories are particularly relevant to our work.

Cultural studies

Cultural studies come from theoretical tenets of neo-Marxism emphasizing the significance of class and capitalist relations within cultural analysis (Davis 2004). The works of Stuart Hall (1996) and Homi Bhabha (1994, 1998) have contributed significantly to our understandings about how knowledge and representation work to define and construct identities. Cultural studies provide an analysis of representation, examining how knowledge is situated in and applicable to specific immediate political and historical circumstances, particularly in relation to issues of representation. Hall's critical examination of representation through media, texts, imagery, language, discourse and ideology as an instrument of social power is an important principle in cultural studies.

Two important concepts emerge within cultural studies that examine issues of identity and representation. They are **diaspora** and **hybridity**, which articulate our contemporary cultural reality of blended or mixed cultural and racial identities in our society. The term 'diaspora' derives from the Greek *dia*, 'through', and *speirein*, 'to scatter' (Brah 1996). In its historical context, diaspora and the identities through which it is produced were a result of forced displacement, dispersal and reluctant scattering, rather than freely chosen experiences of dispersion (Cohen 1999). The term 'hybridity' denotes a two-way borrowing and lending between cultures. As Young (1995) points out, hybridity involves fusion and creation of a new form, which is set against the old form of which it is partially made up. Hybridity, then, comes into existence at the moment of cultural and social practice, in which meaning is articulated both from within past and present cultural histories and trajectories.

Consequently, in many nation states with diverse populations, the diasporic and hybrid reality of blended cultural, racial and linguistic identities remains a significant contribution to the increased diversity in many local and global communities. Hence, hybridity and diaspora inform our work in helping us understand the complexities in how identity is articulated and represented across a terrain of intersecting and often contradictory points of self and group expression.

Postcolonial theory

Since all postcolonial societies have experienced the full impact of neocolonial domination, this theoretical framework influences our social justice research and equity work in relation to constructions of childhood and identity. It is part of a growing body of literature in the early childhood field that aims to reconceptualize childhood and early childhood education, primarily through the disruption of Western hegemonic modernist assumptions constituted within dominant colonizing discourses. These colonizing discourses continue to perpetuate oppositional thinking associated with 'common-sense' knowledge around cultural binaries such as Western/ non-Western, white/black, civilized/primitive, adult/child.

Postcolonial studies critique the cultural hegemony of European knowledges and centre on the historical fact and consequence of European colonialism (Ashcroft *et al.* 1995). Postcolonial theory is useful for directing attention to the impact and embodiment of Western **imperialism** throughout the world; this includes political and economic domination, as well as power over identity and intellect (Gandhi 1998; Young 2001; Cannella and Viruru 2004). Hence, postcolonial perspectives provide a critique of, as well as innovative interventions, aimed at challenging oppression, objectification, and othering, particularly in relation to the meanings and consequences of the colonial encounter as a result of invasion and colonization (Gandhi 1998; Cannella and Viruru 2004).

Central to a postcolonial perspective is the concept of power and how it is utilized to define and control the lives and silence the voices of the Other, from which colonization has rendered unequal power relations between Indigenous and non-Indigenous people and between children and adults. In terms of social justice education, Cannella and Viruru (2004: 123) point out that 'decolonial possibilities can offer knowledges from the margin, unthought-of perspectives/life experiences, hidden histories, and disqualified voices as positions from which to reconceptualize discourses, individual values, and actions'.

Not only does this perspective provide a framework for understanding the impact of Western imperialism in terms of racialized and ethnicized social inequalities, but it is also relevant and useful to early childhood education with the insights that it can offer in relation to the socio-cultural construction of discourses of childhood and the adult/child dualism that undergird Western relationships between adults and children. Postcolonial perspectives can broaden current understandings of children from diverse socio-cultural backgrounds, challenge the colonizing practices and philosophies of modernist universalized 'truths' that construct children as different from adults and the powerless and less worthy Other, as well as create new and different possibilities and avenues for children.

Queer theory

Queer theory, which stems from poststructuralist theoretical perspectives, reinforces the notion that identities are not fixed or stable, but rather are shifting, contradictory, dynamic and constructed. This perspective holds that all identities are performances and challenges normalizing practices, particularly in terms of sexuality and the heteronormative constructions of gender. Queer theory challenges the unquestionable, natural and normal positioning of heterosexuality as the superior sexuality and the othering of non-heterosexual identities, which is constituted within the cultural binary heterosexual us/homosexual them. The term 'queer' encompasses those who feel 'marginalized by mainstream sexuality' (Morris 2000: 20), including those who see themselves as heterosexual but challenge the conformity constituted and enforced in hegemonic discourses of heterosexuality. Ultimately, queer theory disrupts the notion that one's gender and sexuality are inherently fixed in one's biological sexed body, upholding the pluralities of sexuality and the multiplicity of gender. Thus, this perspective provides a critical theoretical lens through which one can begin to see the everyday processes of **heteronormativity** operating within everyday contexts.

Critical theory

Perspectives of critical theory utilized in this book draw principally from Bourdieu's theory of social practice. Bourdieu (1930–2002), a French sociologist and cultural theorist, examined human potential and interaction using a metaphorical lens of economic systems. He proposed three significant concepts of social practice, which included capital, field and habitus. In education, his work has been applied to the analysis of cultural reproduction of inequality through educational practices that reproduce power and privilege for children whose home and cultural practices are congruent with the pedagogical practices of the school (including early childhood education), at the expense of children whose home and cultural practices differ from mainstream educational pedagogy. Hence, those children from middle-class, heterosexual, monolingual and urban families are likely to experience academic success through the pedagogically congruent experiences between home and the educational setting.

Bourdieu argues that different forms of capital, such as cultural, social, economic and symbolic capital, operate together to accumulate various forms of social power in different social contexts or fields. However, he also argues that capital and field do not exist in isolation. Ways in which individuals take up and make use of the various forms of capital in social contexts are fundamental to his theory. Further, his concept of habitus focuses on the dispositions, perceptions, attitudes generated throughout one's cultural history that can enable or prohibit effective exchange or accumulation of one's capital. Bourdieu has informed our work through his analysis of social practice and inequality, particularly in relation to how social practices are informed by power, politics and self-interest that are constrained by and developed through the rules and conventions of culture (Schirato and Yell 2000).

Chapter overviews

The following chapters in this book cover a wide cross-section of issues relevant to the diverse lives of educators, children and their families. The main issues of the chapters are outlined below:

Chapter 2 provides an in-depth overview of the critical theoretical concepts and tools utilized within a feminist poststructuralist theoretical framework. These tools form the basis of our social justice education with pre-service teachers and with children.

Chapter 3 draws on a variety of social theorists writing in the area of class issues (including, but not limited to, Apple, Bourdieu and Giroux) and examines the production of class relations and inequality in early childhood pedagogy, which produce social and cultural power for some at the expense of others. Intersections of class across social identities of ethnicity, language, gender, sexuality, region and religion are highlighted to explore contemporary frameworks for understanding class in a context of increased globalization and fast capitalism. In the current political, economic and social milieu, both nationally and internationally, we investigate the various economic and political agendas within neoliberal and capitalist economies that have produced contemporary discourses of anti-immigration, homogenization, transnationalism and the corporatization of childhood. The implications of these discourses for educators, families and children are raised.

Chapter 4 focuses on how multiculturalism in early childhood education is mostly promoted at the level of attitudinal tolerance of diverse child-rearing, language and cultural practices in which definitions of culture are conceptualized within fixed and definite boundaries and categories of ethnicity. Drawing on 'whiteness' and cultural studies, the discussion in this chapter provides a critique of liberal pluralism and its articulation in discourses of multiculturalism and Indigeneity in view of educational practice in early childhood. It also critically examines early childhood educators' perceptions of children's understandings of ethnicity and power relations, and contrasts these perceptions with findings of research that has examined children's understandings of racialized identity. An overview of contemporary frameworks for thinking about multiculturalism and Indigeneity from a critical standpoint is given in order to facilitate new understandings for early childhood educators to better inform their approach to diversity and difference in a multicultural society.

Chapter 5 argues that there is an obvious need to begin to reconceptualize the family as performative social spaces in order to include the different family practices and structures that exist. The dominant discourse of the Western nuclear family, which is predominantly white, heterosexual and middle class, continues to powerfully inform the curriculum and practises in many early childhood settings, to the exclusion of other families. However, the traditional nuclear family in reality is not reflective of the experiences of many children. The chapter explores the normalizing discourses of family and how these have been perpetuated in society, as well as the various social theories that have extended understandings of the role of family in society. The social, political and economic issues challenging normalizing discourses of family and changing the performances of family are also explored.

Chapter 6 argues that despite the increasing numbers of bilingual families and the seemingly liberal approaches to linguistic and cultural diversity in Western countries, such as Australia, opportunities for children to access adequate bilingual support in their home languages remain limited. In early childhood education understandings of language and identity are often informed by developmentalist and pluralist frameworks, which sustain discursive pedagogical practices of monolingualism. The chapter critically examines the various theoretical frameworks in studies of bilingualism and language learning that prevailed in our research with early childhood educators. The discussion in this chapter provides an alternative reframing of the various issues and theories associated with bilingualism, language retention, second language learning, identity and difference in early childhood contexts.

Chapter 7 explores early childhood educators' perceptions of gender and how this impacts on their practices with young children. Based on our research with early childhood educators, understandings of gender formation commonly slip between gender as biologically determined and gender perceived as sex role theory that is constructed through socialization theory. It is argued that Butler's (1990) concepts of performativity and the heterosexual matrix provide critical insights to extend understandings of gender construction in early childhood. The discussion points out that this process cannot be fully understood without acknowledging how gender is heteronormalized in the process – that is, without examining how normalizing discourses of masculinity and femininity are heterosexualized. The chapter also explores how early childhood education contributes to the process of heteronormativity in young children's lives through educators' everyday practices and policies.

Chapter 8 examines the discourses that prevail among early childhood educators who perpetuate the perceived irrelevance, invisibility and exclusion of sexuality, or more specifically lesbian and gay issues, in early childhood education. The chapter explores the prevalence of the dominant discourses of childhood and sexuality that intersect to constitute sexuality as irrelevant to children; the pervasiveness of the discourse of compulsory heterosexuality and the assumed absence of gay and lesbian families in settings; and how homophobia and **heterosexism** operate in early childhood education. It is argued that it is important to address gay and lesbian equity issues with young children in order to counteract the extensive homophobia and heterosexism that operates in their lives.

Chapter 9 is a concluding chapter that reiterates the importance of **reflexivity** and community responsibilities in doing equity and social justice work in early childhood education. It is argued that it is critical for early childhood educators to reflexively analyse how their own perceptions and practices could be perpetuating social inequalities through their interactions with children and their families. Consequently, there can be an element of risk-taking personally and professionally when it comes to challenging normalizing discourses that operate to construct powerful points of privilege for some individual subjects and groups in society, while excluding others. Further, several critical issues are raised in this chapter that we feel early childhood educators need to consider when reviewing current approaches to social justice education with children and their families. These issues include: promoting theoretical understandings of children, childhood, diversity and difference; enhancing links between theory and practice; acknowledging how diversity and difference are often located in the discourse of deficit; encouraging children's critical thinking and learning; deconstructing the adult/child binary; increasing communications with families and communities; developing policies and procedures that incorporate social justice perspectives; building supportive networks on all levels of early childhood education; promoting professional development of educators and other staff; and the need for further research into diversity and difference in early childhood education.

The book includes a glossary of critical terms that are used throughout the chapters as a quick reference point for readers.

Recommended reading

Cannella, G.S. and Viruru, R. (2004) *Childhood and Postcolonization: Power, Education, and Contemporary Practice*. New York: RoutledgeFalmer.

Dahlberg, G., Moss, P. and Pence, A. (1999) *Beyond Quality in Early Childhood Education and Care: Postmodern Perspectives*. London: Falmer Press.

Schirato, T. and Yell, S. (2000) *Communication and Cultural Literacy: An Introduction*. St Leonards, NSW: Allen & Unwin.

Young, R.J.C. (2001) *Postcolonialism: An Historical Introduction*. Oxford: Blackwell.

DOING FEMINIST POSTSTRUCTURALIST THEORY WITH EARLY CHILDHOOD EDUCATORS

Introduction

Doing social justice education primarily aims to disrupt the normalizing discourses that constitute and perpetuate social inequalities in society and operate to privilege certain identities and marginalize and silence others. As part of this process, social justice education also endeavours to improve the experiences of those who are othered in some way by the mainstream society. 'Other' is defined as those groups that have been marginalized, silenced, denigrated or violated, in opposition to the privileged and powerful groups that are identified as representing the idealized, mythical norm in society (Kumashiro 2002). For example, groups that have been othered include people of colour, Indigenous people, gays and lesbians (or those perceived to be gay or lesbian), women, single parents, people with disabilities, the unemployed, religious minorities and those from minority language backgrounds.

Doing social justice education with children and their families is not easy work. It often involves negotiating a range of different perceptions and values around 'difficult knowledge' (Britzman 1998), or controversial issues. As pointed out above, it involves challenging understandings of 'normal' and can involve interfering with individual (adult or child) subjects' 'truths', belief systems, or common-sense ways of looking at the world. Primarily, social justice education is work that disrupts individual subjects' locations within social discourses that constitute their understandings of difference. Critical to doing social justice education with children and their families is awareness of how educators themselves perceive difference, and in which social discourses they are located when it comes to issues of equity associated with different sites of identities, such as 'race', ethnicity, gender, sexuality, social class and disability. As pointed out in Chapter 1, educators' perceptions of difference can significantly impact on their practices with children and their families, despite the often made claims that 'We treat everybody the same' (Lundeberg 1997; Robinson and Jones Díaz 1999). Thus, a major premise from which we operate in relation to doing social justice education is that educators need to be willing to do the same difficult and reflexive work around *change* in terms of the way they view the world, as they are attempting to undertake with the children and families with whom they work. It is important that educators are willing to take up the issues they find personally confronting, uncomfortable or even somewhat risky.

The main aim of this chapter is to provide educators with an understanding of doing social justice education that is informed primarily from feminist poststructuralist perspectives (Hollway 1984; Davies 1989, 1993, 1994, 1996; Walkerdine 1990; Weedon 1997), as well as by social theorists, such as Foucault (1977, 1978, 1980), Bourdieu (1990, 1991a, 1991b, 1993), Britzman (1998, 2003) and Butler (1990). An overview is provided of the main theoretical concepts that are critical to an understanding of the processes involved in the construction of identity, difference, power and inequality. These concepts include knowledge/'truth', discourse, power, subjectivity, agency, reflexivity, deconstruction and performativity. However, of particular importance to a feminist poststructuralist perspective is the process of subjectification (that is, the construction of self – who you are), in terms of not only how one comes to view the world, but also understanding potential sites for individual and social change or transformation.

What is feminist poststructuralism?

Feminist poststructuralism, as the name suggests, is a perspective that incorporates aspects of feminism with poststructural understandings, in order to produce a richer version of social theory and cultural analysis that moves beyond some of the limitations found in the original theories of feminism and poststructuralism. Feminism provides important insights into the construction of gendered and sexualized subjects, while poststructuralism (like postmodernism) highlights the need to acknowledge the differences and heterogeneity that exist between individuals, groups and subject positions (Best and Kellner 1991). For example, feminism has been criticized for the way it universalized women's oppression and powerlessness as being solely the result of patriarchy; that is, women's oppression and subordination were perceived to be the result of a patriarchal social structure or system, in which men had supreme power over women, controlling their access to resources and opportunities. Poststructuralists challenged the very concept of 'woman' as a universal and unifying term, pointing out that it failed to recognize the differences among women – in terms of their 'race', ethnicity, sexuality, social class and so on – that impacted on their diverse experiences of inequality or oppression, as well as their power. This critique echoed the concerns of many women of colour, lesbians and women from working-class backgrounds, who had become dissatisfied with the movement and critical of the way the term 'woman' had become synonymous with a middle-class, white, heterosexual perspective of women's experiences in the world. Some women were feeling as oppressed by their white, middle-class heterosexual 'sisters' as by male power. Many women of colour were acknowledging that it was not their gender but their colour or 'race' that was the main cause of their oppression, and that they often had powerful positions within their families and communities (Collins 1990). Consequently, feminists who were critical of the universalizing tendencies of feminism looked to postmodernism and poststructuralism to develop different understandings of the way that women's oppression is experienced differently and changes across intersections of identity, within different contexts and over time. Consequently, feminist poststructuralists criticize the reductive, essentialist and problematic universalizing tendencies of feminism and other such grand narrative theories.

Poststructuralism takes on a feminist perspective when issues associated with gendered and sexualized identities and power relations are central to the analysis at hand. However, the centrality of gender and sexuality are always framed within an analysis of the way that they intersect with other sites of identity such as 'race', ethnicity, social class and disability. As MacNaughton (2001: 122) aptly points out:

> In redefining identity as multiple, contradictory, and dynamic, feminist poststructuralists have politicized identity formation. They have argued that identity is constituted in and by social relations of gender, sexuality, class, and race, and that each of us lives our gendered, sexualized, 'classed', and 'raced' identities in and through the power relations that constitute our daily lives. Their beginning point is that individuals are inseparable from social institutions; they do not simply interact but are interdependent and mutually constituting. Individuals are born into already-existing social worlds consisting of social structures, social processes, and social meanings. The individual does not and cannot exist outside of the social, nor can the social exist over and above the individual.

MacNaughton's comments highlight how individual identities and the meanings that are attached to these (gender, sexuality, class, ethnicity, 'race' and so on) are not fixed in biology, but rather are constituted in and through our everyday social interactions and relations of power operating in our daily lives. Consequently, identities are negotiated, managed and reinvented across the different social contexts in which we operate. The formation of identities is constituted within the process of subjectification, which is the focus of the next sections.

Understanding the 'self': the feminist poststructuralist subject

Feminist poststructuralist understandings of the subject (or the self – who you are) and how it is formed are different from those held in modernist perspectives that have tended to dominate the knowledge in this area. In modernist humanist perspectives (as briefly outlined in Chapter 1) the individual subject is one that is fixed in biology and incorporates an essence of 'humanness' that is shared across all human beings. That is, all human beings are considered to share particular characteristics that are inherent in their humanness; these shared and unchanging characteristics are reason, rationality and coherency, which universalize the human experience and set it apart from that of other species. It is upheld that through the explorations of 'objective' science, the human essence is both discoverable and knowable. Within this framework, the human subject is viewed as sharing a universalized human history that is united by the common ideals of the possibility, through human reason, of progress and ultimately human perfection. The humanist subject is considered to be in control and the author of his or her own experience and meaning. Consequently, individuals are perceived to have an 'essential nature' – that is, where the meanings of experiences originate from within the individual. In other words, each person is perceived to have a unique essence or personality that comes from within them and emerges and develops over the person's lifetime.

In contrast, feminist poststructuralists, like other poststructural theorists, perceive the subject as being socially constructed and define subjectivity as encompassing the unconscious and conscious thoughts and emotions of the individual – or their sense of self and how they relate to the world (Weedon 1997). Thus, subjectivity originates not inherently from inside the person, but from the social realm; consequently, it is not fixed, but rather, is fluid and dynamic. In this perspective, the subject does not share a discoverable or knowable human essence or human history, and the possibility, through scientific progress, of reaching human perfection is rejected. Thus, feminist poststructuralists are anti-humanist in that they are critical of essentialist notions that there is a 'knowable essence' of individuals. In other words, they believe that individuals do not have an innate unique, rational, coherent and fixed personality that emerges from within them over their lifetime. This perspective is quite difficult for some to comprehend, as it has been upheld as a very powerful 'truth' in society, so powerful that it has rarely been questioned, until the introduction of postmodern and poststructuralist perspectives in recent times. It is easier to understand this view when we take the time to look closely at ourselves and notice that we are complex beings, who are, more often than not, irrational and contradictory in the way we look at the world and in the way we behave. How often have you done something knowing full well that it was not really the most logical thing to do, but you did it anyway, for whatever reason(s) at the time? Do you constantly change your mind about a particular issue and feel unsure about what you really believe? Feminist poststructuralists consider that it is more useful to view individual subjects as changing, contradictory, unstable, irrational and shifting across different contexts. Individual subjects are constantly re-inventing themselves as they negotiate the various power relationships that exist in their lives.

The process of subjectification

How do we each come to be the people we are? Why do we look at the world the way we do? In terms of social justice education these are critical questions, especially since much of this work involves negotiating the differing values and belief systems that people have in the world. According to feminist poststructuralist perspectives, individual subjects are constantly in a process of subjectification in which their subjectivity (or self) is formed through the *discourses* that they locate themselves in throughout their lifetime. The following discussions explain the critical concepts involved in this process of the construction of self.

Knowledge and discourse

Feminist poststructuralists, like other theorists that fall into poststructuralist paradigms, reject modernist humanist beliefs that human perfection and enlightenment are possible through the discovery of knowable objective scientific 'truths' about the world. They uphold that knowledge is only partial and that 'truths' are only ever interpretations or perspectives held by various groups or individuals, rather than objective facts or truths. According to Burr (1995: 64), knowledge refers 'to the particular construction or version of a phenomenon that has received the stamp of "truth" in our society'. The knowledge that we take up in our lives is generally upheld as our 'truths' about how we see the world; and as Fuss (1989) points out, truth becomes the authority of experience. We gain knowledge from our everyday social interactions with people and institutions – for example, interactions with family, schools, the church, the government or the law. Our everyday discussions with our friends can contribute to the knowledge that we take up as our own.

However, this knowledge is often based on limited insights into the world, on stereotypes and on 'common sense' beliefs, which work to construct, define and 'essentialize' our understandings about the world and the different groups that live within it. **Essentialism** means that certain characteristics become naturalized and normalized representations of groups, defining and fixing who and what they are; it is also the tendency to see one aspect of a subject's identity (often the visible parts) and make that representative of the whole individual. For example, a lesbian mother is typically reduced to her lesbianism and generally read within the context of the stereotypes that abound about what it means to be lesbian; or an Asian child is similarly reduced to a defining characteristic of 'Asianness'.

This knowledge is largely constituted within cultural binaries that result in oppositional or dualistic thinking, and it is commonly perceived to represent 'common-sense logic'. For example, boy/girl, men/women, white/black, heterosexual/homosexual, Western/non-Western, adult/child are a few of the vast number of binaries that exist; they are perceived to be natural opposites and are thus constructed and defined in opposition to each other. Thus, what it means to be a boy or a man is generally considered to be opposite to what it means to be a girl or a woman. These cultural binaries, which have tended to underpin modernist knowledge, are very powerful in the way that they influence how people look at the world. Boys who are perceived to behave in feminine ways often experience harassment from peers or others, who are making it clear that there has been a serious breach of the social regulations that operate around appropriate gender behaviour; thus, their behaviour is considered 'abnormal' and they are punished for the slippage in their performance of masculinity. Kimmel (1994: 126) points out that 'historically and developmentally, masculinity has been defined as the flight from women, the repudiation of femininity'.

Cultural power relations are constituted in and maintained through these binary relationships, based on hierarchies of power, in which one side of the binary has the power to define and subordinate the Other – for example, whites have had the power to largely define, officially and unofficially, what it means to be non-white in society, and whiteness has had the privileged position of not being viewed as a racialized colour. Another very powerful example of this process is the stud/slut binary – constituted within these two words is a powerful hierarchical relationship (one epitomized by double standards) around gender and (hetero)sexuality.

Michel Foucault developed a theory of discourse which provided a theoretical framework for understanding how the world operated in terms of identity and power. For Foucault (1974), knowledge is constituted within *discourses* operating in society, which are historically and culturally formulated. Foucault (1974: 49) defines discourse as 'practices that systematically form the objects of which they speak'. Others have also defined Foucault's concept of discourse in the following ways – all four definitions combined give a comprehensive overview of what this term encompasses:

> [Discourses are] about what can be said and thought, but also about who can speak, when, and with what authority. Discourses embody meaning and social relationships, they constitute both subjectivity and power. (Ball 1990: 2)

> A system of statements, which constructs an object. (Parker 1992: 5)

> A set of meanings, metaphors, representations, images, stories, statements and so on that in some way together produce a particular version of events. (Burr 1995: 48)

According to Foucault (1974), discourses operate through language and constitute the different knowledge we have available to us about the world and those in it; but they are generally invisible or not part of our everyday conscious awareness. The various discourses (or knowledge) that we take up as our own ways of looking at the world are both constituted in and perpetuated through the language that we use in our daily interactions; when we talk to each other the world gets constructed, objects take on the meanings that we attach to them, and certain knowledge becomes powerful. They are often perpetuated through the common-sense cultural binaries that we rarely critically review or challenge. However, discourses are not only constituted through our verbal language, but, as Burr (1995) highlights above, also operate through representations in images – for example, images in posters or on television can represent very powerful ideas about people or objects; these images can be taken up as a true representation of that group or object, regardless of how 'real' these images are. Discourses are not about what is 'real' – remember that knowledge is only ever partial and we can never know the 'truth' about something. They are only ever perspectives or interpretations of the world; however, the knowledge we take up is often perceived as 'truth' and we can hold on to these perspectives very strongly as the only 'true' and 'correct' way to look at the world or version of events. Through our everyday interactions we speak and perform discourses into existence. However, there are numerous ways of looking at the world and sometimes there are many versions of a single event or phenomenon, reflecting the point that there are different discourses operating simultaneously that are constructing different understandings about objects and of the world and how it operates.

The following are examples of discourses that operate in society. These statements contribute to the constitution of the different knowledge that prevails around the various issues, groups, events or phenomena that they address.

- Families are safe, loving environments in which to raise children.
- Families are microcosms of society and are oppressive institutions which perpetuate inequalities between men and women, adults and children.
- Abortion is a woman's right to choose.
- Abortion is the taking of life.
- Women have natural instincts to nurture and care for others; mothering is instinctual.
- Mothering is learnt, so there is no reason why men cannot mother.
- Heterosexuality is normal, non-heterosexual relations are deviant and abnormal.
- Heterosexuality is only one example of natural and normal sexual relationships in society; homosexuality and lesbianism are other examples.
- Masculinity is naturally aggressive; men are tough and make better leaders.
- There are many ways to do masculinities and not all men are aggressive, and there are different ways in which to manage people without aggression.
- Immunization is crucial for healthy children.
- Immunization compromises children's immune systems, making them even more vulnerable to diseases.
- Domestic violence is a private family matter.
- Domestic violence is a public issue that requires social interventions.
- People with disabilities are helpless and vulnerable.
- People with disabilities are capable and productive.
- All Arabs are Muslims.
- All Muslims are Arabs.
- Children should be seen and not heard.
- Children are critical thinkers who can make valuable contributions to conversations.

Individual subjects will experience a range of different and precarious subject positions within these discourses – for example, they might be taken up as 'truths' that constitute their knowledge and perceptions of the world; or as misconceptions or false statements that do not represent their knowledge or perceptions; or they may shift in and out of them in a contradictory manner, depending on the context in which they are operating.

Why is it that one version of events or certain knowledge is considered more truthful than others? Various discourses coexist, competing to be recognized and accepted as the officially sanctioned knowledge or 'truth'. Discourses govern the way we live our lives but do so in ways that are most often not visible or tangible. The invisibility of discourse works to strengthen the relationships of power operating within discourses. As Foucault (1974: 49) comments, 'For those who speak it, a discourse is a given – it operates "behind their backs", it is an "unthought"'. Discourses only become powerful when they are taken up by social institutions, such as those related to religion, education, the law, the government, and individual subjects, who live and speak them as their 'truth' or official version of events about the world. People can have different 'truths', and this is where conflicts can arise. For example, the discourse that children need to be immunized against diseases is given more credibility and power when it is officially sanctioned by governments and medical associations as the 'truth'. In the process of this discourse being socially sanctioned, other discourses that constitute different perspectives – for example, that immunization compromises children's immune systems, making them more vulnerable to other diseases – find less credibility and support from individual subjects because they do not receive the official stamp of 'truth'. However, if the government and medical associations took up the second perspective, the credibility and power of this discourse could change.

It is important to point out that the discourses that constitute our knowledge of the world are historically and culturally specific; they change across and within cultures and over time. For example, understandings and beliefs about women have changed over time and are different in various cultural contexts. In some Western cultures it was historically upheld that women should not be educated, therefore they were excluded from universities. This perspective was largely based on the discourse that if women spent their energies on learning, rather than on having children, their reproductive capabilities would be eventually compromised or could become defunct (Spender 1983). Obviously this discourse was challenged by women and today finds little support; it has been replaced by different and new knowledge about women – for example, that women are capable of balancing career and family life. Discourses are also culturally specific. For example, understandings of masculinities and representations of what it means to be a man or boy in Anglo-Celtic Australia today may be very different from understandings and representations of masculinities within Balinese cultures or within Brazilian cultures. Discourses are also contextually changing within cultures. Therefore, discourses of masculinities can change across class, 'race', ethnicities, sexual identities and so on.

Subjectivity, discourse and power

Foucault's discourse theory is critical to an understanding of the process of subjectification within a feminist poststructuralist perspective. According to

Foucault, our self or subjectivity is constituted within the discourses that are culturally available to us, which we draw upon in our communications with other people. That is, our unconscious and conscious thoughts and emotions, our sense of self and how we relate to the world, as well as the ways that we become individual subjects, who are gendered, classed, racialized, ethnicized, sexualized and so on, are constituted within the discourses that we locate ourselves in and take up as our own ways of being in the world (Weedon 1997). Foucault (1974) points out that discourses live themselves out through people. Our subjectivity and identity originate not inherently from inside us, but from the social realm in which discourses are constituted and perpetuated, constructing and determining the possibilities of who we can be and what we can think. Consequently, our subjectivity is not fixed, but dynamic and fluid.

Subjectivity is therefore made up of a range of shifting and precarious subject positions as a result of its constitution within the contextual, changing, contradictory discourses that are culturally available; consequently, the subject is no longer in total control, and this is in stark contrast with the modernist perspective. The discourses that form our subjectivity and identity have implications for what we perceive we can and cannot do and what we should do and should not do; for example, how we represent ourselves as sexualized subjects will be constituted within the discourses of sexuality that we have available to us. Once we take up a subject position in discourse, we have available to us a particular limited set of concepts, images, metaphors, ways of speaking, self-narratives and so on that we take on as our own. Individuals make an emotional commitment to the category of person constituted within the discourses they have chosen to take up as their own, as well as to the appropriate system of morals (rules of right and wrong) encompassed within these discourses. However, individuals are confronted with a variety of discourses, each with a different version of what it means to be a sexualized being. As pointed out previously, some of these discourses are socially sanctioned over than others, thus they are given more credibility and power. The dominant discourse that heterosexuality is natural and normal and all other sexualities are abnormal and deviant is very powerful and is socially sanctioned by particular religious faiths, governments and legal and medical institutions. Thus, heterosexuality becomes the normalizing discourse that operates in that society. Those who locate themselves in another alternative or counter discourse that constitutes heterosexuality as only one choice among many natural, normal and acceptable sexualities, and choose to be gay or lesbian, will find this discursive position more difficult to negotiate as it does not carry the same privileges as are offered to those who take up heterosexuality. Feminist poststructuralists uphold that to understand the person you need to look to the social realm, within the linguistic space in which people move and interact, rather than within the individual.

Discourses are constituted in language, and if discourses constitute subjectivity, it follows that language is a critical site in terms of the construction of subjectivity. The person you are, your experience, your identity, your perceptions and knowledge, your ways of being in the world are all the effects of language. As Burr (1995) points out, we can only represent our experiences to ourselves and to others by using concepts embedded in language. Thus, language is fundamentally a social phenomenon, occurring between people. The construction of the person or one's subjectivity takes place in these exchanges. There are many different ways we exchange language, including conversation, reading, writing, visually and so on. Language in this sense is not just spoken and written, but a meaning system in which ideas, thoughts, values and so on are shared. Language is perceived not as a system of signs with fixed meanings upon which everyone agrees, but as a site of variation and potentially conflicting meanings. Conversations, writing and social encounters become sites of political struggle and power. For example, the word 'queer' is contested by different meanings; in recent times it has been reclaimed as a positive signifier of non-conformism particularly in terms of sexuality (both heterosexuality and non-heterosexuality), but also in relation to other aspects of identity. Consequently, our subjectivity is never fixed, but is changeable, contradictory, contextual and in a state of flux and instability. This is reflected in the way that individual subjects can be located within different and contradictory subject positions in discourses. Some early childhood educators indicate that personally they would never choose to put their own children in care, believing that it is more appropriate for mothers to look after their children in the early years. Another example of contradictory subject positions is provided by educators who espouse strong social justice and human rights principles, but are also homophobic and heterosexist.

Individual subjects do not just locate themselves in discourses, but will also read others from their own discursive positions. For example, the father who is positioned in the discourse that normalizes representations of masculinity as heterosexual, a discourse that primarily perpetuates the oppositional thinking that masculinity is everything that femininity is not, will read his son's interest in playing with dolls and women's clothes in 'home corner' as unhealthy, unnatural and abnormal. The father will not only question his son's masculinity, but will also fear his son's potential slippage in terms of his heterosexuality. From a feminist poststructuralist perspective, the son's playing with women's clothing is not problematic, but represents a range of possible experiences open to the child in play. The child will understand such play in shifting and contradictory ways – possibly a feeling of power and exhilaration in challenging the perceived limitations of his gender; or a sense of freedom in being able to do his gender differently; or fear and embarrassment if reprimanded or excluded from such play by adults. The discursive location from which educators read the boy's behaviour will be critical in influencing the boy's perceptions of his own behaviour and feelings and his experiences of power in this context, as well as the possibilities he sees for doing his masculinity in multiple and different ways. We are constantly reading other people from the discourses that we take up, often making judgements about who we perceive them to be; for example, the young woman who performs her femininity in a challenging way, seeing herself as a strong, independent, sexy, outgoing individual, who primarily represents the difference through her dress codes – black, short dresses, tight clothing, make-up – can either be read as powerful and independent, or as 'sluttish' and provocative.

Power is a critical concept in understanding the process of subjectification. According to Foucault, power operates through discourses that prevail in society. Consequently, our power as individual subjects is bound up in the discourses in which we position ourselves, as well as how we are read by others from their discursive locations, as in the above example. We have discussed how particular discourses have more power than others through the way that individuals and social institutions take them up as their own 'truths' and ways of looking at the world. Where individual subjects locate themselves in discourse will be a matter of negotiation around power relations, as well as what personal investments they see themselves as having in locating in one discourse rather than the other (Hollway 1984).

As discussed previously, subjectivity is complex, changing, contradictory and often irrational. This shifting is primarily a result of the way that we negotiate power relations in our daily interactions. For example, a pre-service teacher might be willing to engage in racist or homophobic harassment when out socializing with peers, but express anti-racist and anti-homophobic sentiments in their compulsory social justice class. In this context, the pre-service teacher has to negotiate the various power relations at hand, such as the degree of importance they place on remaining popular with peers; or the fear that they might also be a target of peer harassment if they do not participate; or a concern that they might be failed by the diversity lecturer if they appear to be racist or homophobic. Their decisions will be based on negotiating the power relationships and their own investments in different contexts. This is similar to the way that young children negotiate the discursive power relations in their daily lives. An awareness of this process becomes critical for educators. For example, educators who try to positively intervene in a young boy's bullying behaviour will not necessarily succeed if their strategy is primarily to make the boy feel bad about his behaviour and to feel sympathy for the victim, which is more often than not the pedagogical case. For many young boys, who are positioned in the discourse of hegemonic masculinity, aggressive physical behaviour is part of the performance of their gendered identities. This performance is often about getting their gender performance correct in front of other boys, who are positioned in a similar discourse of masculinity (Butler 1990). Consequently, the boy will continue to engage in this aggressive behaviour, despite the educator's intervention, if his gender performance is being positively acknowledged by his male peers and his position of power remains intact. The young boy will have to negotiate the existing power relations at hand, such as being in trouble with the educator, or with parents, or not getting his gender performance correct in front of his peers. Thus, his behaviour may be contradictory; he may respond to his teacher's reprimands, only to continue the bullying when the teacher is not around.

Ultimately, individual subjects can only change their subjectivity through their relocation into another discourse; but there has to be more investment in the shifting than what is offered through remaining in their current discursive location. As contradictory subjects we are constantly negotiating power relations in our everyday lives, shifting contextually according to how we read and negotiate our daily interactions with others. If we consider that it will be more beneficial and desirable to locate in one discourse rather than another, then we can shift our discursive position in order to gain more power and reap the perceived benefits.

As alluded to previously, a discourse gains a position of power over others in the way it is supported and 'activated' by individuals and institutions in society. Consequently, if powerful institutions in society, such as governments, religious bodies, and the legal and education systems, take up a discourse, its power is reinforced and its ability to persuade individuals that it is the most appropriate view of the world is increased. Those who position themselves in this discourse will share in the privilege, advantage and power that are culturally sanctioned through the dominant culture's support for this 'truth'. Those who locate outside this dominant discourse will frequently experience inequities, diminished power and little or no support from the dominant culture for their perspective. For example, 'abortion is a woman's right to choose' is a discourse about a controversial issue that often divides people. This may be a dominant discourse taken up by feminists and reinforced in some cases through legislation that makes abortion legal. However, it will be a discourse that gets little support in religious and pro-life contexts, or in countries where governments support anti-abortion legislation. In the latter contexts the discourse around abortion that is more powerful and considered more truthful is that abortion is the taking of life. Consequently, if you are a feminist who believes in a woman's right to choose your individual and group power may be compromised if you resided in Ireland, but not necessarily if you lived in the United Kingdom. Thus, the power constituted within the particular discourses that you take up as your own perceptions of the world will contextually shift and change. As can be seen from this example, discourses are not simply abstract ideas, they are intimately linked with the way society is organized and run. To take another example, the discourse of capitalism results in the formation of different subject positions – workers, unemployed, employers – which all have different access to power in this context. Further, access to power in these various subject positions is also linked to gender, class, sexuality, 'race', ethnicity and so on.

According to Foucault, power is knowledge, but it is much more than just gaining more understanding or 'knowing' about the world; it is about which particular discourse one takes up as one's way of looking at the world. The discourses that are officially sanctioned in society are about perpetuating particular social relationships that reaffirm the power and privilege of particular groups over others. For example, officially sanctioning the discourse that defines marriage as being between men and women operates primarily to normalize heterosexuality and to exclude and socially marginalize non-heterosexual relationships. Consequently, our positioning in particular discourses, depending on their status in society, is about the everyday politics of either reaffirming or disrupting social inequalities. As we are well aware, there can be dire consequences for not taking up the socially sanctioned discourses that operate in society. However, as Foucault reminds us, where there is power there is always resistance. How people make sense of their lives is an important starting point for understanding how power relations structure society (Weedon 1997). New modes of subjectivity can become available to individuals, resulting in individual changes in perspectives and different choices, which open up new possibilities for political change and social transformation.

Foucault's definition of power

Living and working as an academic in Paris during the students' and workers' uprisings in the 1960s, Foucault developed a reading of power that challenged the Marxist perspectives on power that were influential during the early to mid-twentieth century in Europe. In contrast to the Marxist approach, Foucault does not see the state/economic structures as the primary and sole locus of power; they are important, but he sees relations of power extending beyond the limits of the state. Foucault argues that power is everywhere and ultimately nowhere in particular. What this means is that power is not located in one central body. Rather, he views power as operating through discourses, as pointed out above. Foucault views the relationship between economics, social structures and discourses as a complex relationship, with none being more dominant than the other. Economic relations of power are only one of a range of power relations. This perspective on power challenges not only Marxist perspectives but also those espoused by other grand narratives. It challenges some feminisms, which centralize power within patriarchy, viewing men as the primary owners/holders of power, which they use to dominate women in society.

In Foucault's perspective, power can be visualized as a network of capillaries, starting at the bottom and moving slowly upwards and sideways and back down; rather than operating from the top down, as it tends to be visualized in more traditional perspectives. Power is primarily a relation rather than a simple imposition; power circulates throughout society, rather than being owned by one individual or group (Mills 2003). Foucault (1978: 86) makes the point that 'Power is tolerable only on condition that it masks a substantial part of itself. Its success is proportional to its ability to hide its own mechanisms'. Of particular importance to Foucault's understanding of power is the critical perspective that where there is power there is always resistance. No power relation is simply one of total domination. He acknowledges that power is not always negative, coercive or repressive, but can be positive and productive. Thus, power produces as well as represses. For example, Foucault explores children's sexuality in his *History of Sexuality Vol. 1* (1978). He argues that the regulation and surveillance of male children's masturbation foregrounded this sexuality, producing a pleasure based on secrecy and guilt that resulted from the enforced need to hide the behaviour. Thus, the repression of acts by those in power does not simply result in the erasure of the behaviour. This is a rather simplistic model of actions and power relations. Rather, power incorporates a negotiation of power relations; for example, parents do not generally have unconditional power to get children to do things, and they often have to negotiate power with children. Forms of subjectivity are produced in negotiation with existing power relations.

Foucault's concept of 'regimes of truth' is useful in terms of understanding how certain discourses gain dominance and power over others. 'Regimes of truth' are depicted by a range of discourses that are sanctioned within particular contexts (or discursive fields, such as the family, the church, education, the law, medicine) that are mutually reinforcing and operate to maintain particular 'truths' and current power relations. The discourses that form our identity are intimately tied to the structures and practices that we live out in society from day to day. It is in the interest of relatively powerful groups that some discourses and not others receive the stamp of 'truth' – for example, dominant discourses of femininity serve to uphold gender power inequalities and the gender binary male/female; education and capitalism as systems of social control and exploitation are less likely to enjoy widespread acceptance as common-sense truths. In terms of social justice, individuals can contribute to producing, sustaining, but also undermining and transforming relations involving domination and subordination. Subject positions in discourse often work on behalf of different social interests; for example the discourse that 'men are born to lead and women are born to breed' has been powerful in perpetuating a particular social system based on gender inequalities.

Foucault provided a perspective on power that shifted from explanations of monolithic sovereign power, to one that focused on disciplinary power, based on surveillance and normalization. Within this perspective, populations were not just normalized through the way they were subjected to the daily surveillance and the scrutiny of other people and official institutions, but individuals also became self-surveillant and self-scrutinizing, thus normalizing their own behaviours. With increases in population numbers it became untenable for one sovereign power to watch over or control large numbers of people. Foucault upheld that the need to control large populations of people resulted in the utilization of surveillance processes in order to regulate and normalize people's behaviours. Foucault theorized disciplinary power particularly in the context of schools and prisons. He argued that power does not always use force or aggression and that it can be self-regulating through its potentiality. That is, the threat of power or the perception that one is being watched can result in individuals regulating or normalizing their own behaviour. In schools the prefect system operates as a surveillance process to regulate and normalize students' behaviours.

Foucault utilized the notion of panopticism to explain how disciplinary power operates. The panopticon was an architectural design developed in the nineteenth century, where prison cells were located around a central watch tower that could view all the cells from that one vantage point. Prisoners tended to regulate their own behaviours under this constant process of surveillance. People could be controlled through self-surveillance and therefore start to regulate their own behaviours through self-discipline. It is interesting to point out that in some early childhood settings in Australia the panopticon design is incorporated into the baby change area and/or toilets. This baby change area is often located within a centralized room made of glass, so that individual workers can be viewed by other workers while changing babies' or young children's nappies or clothes; this surveillance has intensified in recent years with increased concerns around potential sexual abuse of children in child-care institutions. The process of disciplinary power can also be seen in terms of the way that perpetrators of child sexual abuse can regulate young children's behaviours through potential threats of power. Perpetrators do not have to be with children all the time to make them do what they want or to make them remain silent about their abuse; the threat of power (for example, hurting someone dear to the child) is often enough for children to self-regulate their own behaviours. Thus, disciplinary power operates as a form of social control.

Foucault's perspective is a major shift away from the oppressor–victim models of power encapsulated in Marxist and feminist perspectives. However, Foucault's perspective on power has been criticized by some for not adequately dealing with questions of individual agency, or for not fully theorizing resistance – that is, locating, describing and accounting for subjects who resist power (McNay 2000). Consequently, some feminist and post-colonialist theorists have modified Foucault's work to incorporate a more in-depth theorization of resistance and agency (Sawicki 1991; McNay 2000).

Agency

Foucault's process of subjectification, in which subjects are constituted within the discourses available to them, has been criticized for being somewhat deterministic. What this means is that individual subjects do not seem to have any active participatory role in the construction of self. Rather, they are considered to be reduced to 'docile bodies' (to use a Foucauldian term), with control totally residing in the powerful devices of cultural discourses through the process of subjectification (McNay 2000). However, in his later work around 'technologies of self', Foucault provides a more substantive understanding of subjectivity. 'Technologies of self' are understood 'as the practices and techniques through which individuals actively fashion their own identities' (McNay 2000: 8). Through this process of self formation individuals can consciously resist the 'technologies of domination' that operate in society.

To what extent individual subjects have agency in the construction of self and social relationships has been debated throughout history, but it is a significant component of feminist poststructuralist perspectives (Davies 1994; Robinson and Jones Díaz 1999; MacNaughton 2000). Agency is about our ability to act with intent and awareness, and this raises important questions about individual and collective responsibility and culpability (Hall 2004). Burr (1995) points out individuals are capable of critical historical reflection and are able to exercise some choice with respect to the discourses and practices they take up for their use. That is, individual subjects are active *agents* in the construction of their subjectivity. In critically analysing the discourses which constitute their lives, individuals can claim or resist them according to the effects they want to establish and can be creative in this process (Sawicki 1991). Sawicki (1991: 103) highlights that the subject is 'able to reflect upon implications of its choices as they are taken up and transformed in a hierarchical network of power relations'. Hall (2004: 127) points out that 'We are subject to discourse, not simply subjects through discourse with the ability to turn around, contemplate, and rework our subjectivity at will'. Ultimately and critically, individual subjects have to take responsibility for their position in discourse and its implications for the perpetuation of social inequalities and injustices. Consequently, agency is a critical concept in terms of social justice education, and Hall (2004: 124–125) makes the pertinent point that:

> 'Agency', its possibility and practicality, brings us face to face with the political question of how we can motivate ourselves and others to work for social change and economic justice ... Do we respond to injustice and the Machiavellian moves of politicians and business leaders with cynicism or with a belief that human beings, individually and collectively, can change for the better, if they revisit some fundamental decisions about their own priorities and values?

Reflexivity

The theoretical concepts and processes outlined above provide a framework from which educators can start to increase their understandings of the formation of individual subjects (both adults and children). It also provides a critical context in which to analyse the construction of the social order, which is steeped in hierarchies of power that perpetuate social, political and economic social inequalities on both the micro and macro levels of society. As pointed out above, our positions in discourse are paramount to the perpetuation or disruption of these social injustices that operate in society. Consequently, it is important that educators take up a *reflexive* approach to their daily practices and pedagogy.

Reflexivity is the 'critical awareness that arises from a self-conscious relation with the other' (McNay 2000: 5). We started this chapter with a discussion of the Other and the process of othering, which are important to an understanding of social justice education. It is imperative that all educators critically review their perspectives, practices, policies and pedagogies in terms of the way that they may be consciously or unconsciously implicated in the process of othering in their everyday interactions with peers, children and their families. Incorporating a reflexive approach in one's personal and professional lives is not just a matter of being aware of one's prejudice and standpoint, but also 'recognising that through language, discourse and texts, worlds are created and recreated in ways of which we are rarely aware' (Usher and Edwards 1994: 16).

Deconstruction

As discussed previously in this chapter, within a feminist poststructuralist perspective, language is a critical site of the construction of the subject. Consequently, deconstructing the language that we use every day is an important step in understanding how power relations are constructed and operate in our daily lives. It is an important process in doing social justice education from a feminist poststructuralist perspective. Deconstruction, stemming from the works of the French poststructuralist, Jacques Derrida, is a critical pedagogical tool that is utilized to expose the multiplicity of possible meanings, contradictions and assumptions that are perpetuated through texts (Davies 1993; Alloway 1995; MacNaughton 1998). Deconstruction involves identifying the various discourses that are operating through texts (for example, stories, movies, television, images, advertisements, newspapers); acknowledging the various subject positions that these discourses make available to the reader; and analysing the power relations that underpin the knowledge that they are constructing. Davies (1993: 8) points out that 'Deconstruction, or putting a concept under erasure, is a political act. It reveals the generally invisible but repressive politics of any particular form of representation'.

The process of deconstruction seeks primarily to identify the normalizing discourses that constitute common-sense understandings that define, restrict and regulate representations of subjectivities and identities, limiting the subject positions perceived possible to individual subjects. For example, many of the popular texts read by children tend to restrict their gendered subject positions to traditional narrow understandings of what it means to be a boy or a girl. Consequently, deconstruction is primarily about disrupting and destabilizing the cultural binaries that underpin much of the common-sense knowledge that we take up as 'truths' or 'reality'. Cultural binaries such as male/female, adult/child, heterosexual/homosexual and white/black are explicit or implicit in the normalizing discourses that operate in texts; they operate to constitute and perpetuate artificial hierarchical relations of power between the paired concepts, which are perceived as polarized opposites. For example, deconstructing the gender binary male/female would involve exploring the power relations that are inherent within polarized knowledge about boys and girls – boys are tough, loud and physically active, while girls are quiet, softly spoken, and prefer to sit, read or talk with friends.

Thus, the process of deconstruction involves critically unpacking the normalizing discourses that construct knowledge of identities, including those operating in our everyday lives (see MacNaughton 1998). The following steps are involved in this process:

- detecting the cultural binaries underpinning the knowledge operating in the text;
- identifying the discourses perpetuated through the stories or images;
- examining the values and assumptions constituted within these discourses;
- acknowledging the purpose of the discourses;
- exploring how particular subjects are positioned within these discourses, that is, exploring what cultural scripts are implicit and explicit in the texts and how they work to position the reader;
- identifying who benefits from these discourses and who does not;
- examining how these discourses contribute to the policies and practices of broader social, economic and political structures; and
- acknowledging different possible readings of the text, asking different questions that highlight and challenge how particular ways of doing identity are normalized to the point that they become unquestionable.

The process of deconstruction is not just valuable for building children's critical thinking and opening up different possibilities for doing their identities, it is also a useful tool to deconstruct the different knowledge that operates in the daily lives of all of us.

What has all this got to do with teaching children? Implications for practice in early childhood education

The theoretical framework outlined above has significant implications for the way that educators work with staff, children and their families, particularly in the context of doing social justice education. However, it is also invaluable in terms of demonstrating the importance of educators being aware of their own locations within discourses, which will impact, consciously and unconsciously, on their practices and daily interactions with others.

Policy directions and implementation

It is important that early childhood institutions reflexively review their policies around diversity and difference to ascertain if they are inadvertently perpetuating normalizing discourses that continue to other those who are perceived as different. Policies as texts can be deconstructed and reconstructed in order to identify the cultural binaries and the discourses that are operating within them that exclude difference and maintain and perpetuate hierarchical relations of power – for example, the naming of particular groups in policies and excluding others; or assuming and privileging a particular family type. Hence, policies need to be regularly evaluated and critiqued in relation to who is represented and who is left out. As pointed out in Chapter 1, early childhood education is a microcosm of the broader society and will thus reflect the normalizing discourses that prevail to sustain the status quo.

Communicating and negotiating with families

Being reflexively aware of how one perceives difference is important to how one communicates and negotiates with families from a range of diverse sociocultural backgrounds. The location of individual subjects in discourses of diversity and difference will impact on the relations of power that operate around these relationships. Educators may be othering families, children and staff who are different through their everyday practices. For example, educators who are positioned in the discourse that perceives gay and lesbian families as abnormal and immoral may operate, consciously and unconsciously, to exclude and marginalize these families.

Programming and planning

The construction of subjectivity has important implications for pedagogy and the curriculum. Children's subjectivity and identities are constituted in discourses and they too are capable of taking up subject positions in different discourses, depending on their desire and understanding of power relations. Early childhood educators need to observe children's positioning in discourse in their setting and to link their interpretations of these observations to programming and planning – for example, bilingual children's rejection of their home language; or the young boy who bullies other children as a performance of his masculinity. Being aware of how families, educators and other staff are positioned in discourses is also crucial; for example, parents from religious backgrounds may express homophobia as a result of their location in that religion.

However, it is important that observations of children's location in discourse are followed up in a range of different programming and pedagogical strategies; for example, discussions, experiences, the use of resources, and integration across a range of curriculum areas are crucial.

Working with staff, families and children

The subjective positioning of early childhood staff and families in discourses around issues of diversity and difference will be crucial in constructing children's knowledge in this area and influencing their subjective position in discourse. Understanding the construction of one's subjectivity, through the process of subjectification, is crucial to educators in order to see its effects on us and on the learning environments we collaboratively produce (Davies 1994).

Children, like adults, are constantly negotiating power relations with each other and with adults. It is important to observe and identify on a daily basis the dominant and alternative discourses available to children operating in early childhood settings, which are either limiting or extending their knowledge of the world, or limiting the subject positions they have available to them; for example the discourses perpetuated through educators' responses to the young boy who likes to dress up in women's clothing.

As knowledge is socially constructed in discourse, it can be deconstructed and reconstructed. Individual subjects are not fixed but are changing beings. Engaging children in critical thinking and reflection on the normalizing discourses that operate in terms of identities, difference, power relations and inequality can enable racist, sexist, homophobic and classist discourses, among others, to be disrupted and challenged, opening up new and more equitable ways of looking at the world. As pointed out in this chapter, language is the place where identities are constituted, maintained and challenged, so it is an important site of subjective change. Deconstruction of the discourses in which people are positioned to identify the power relations operating is a critical tool for developing critical thinking.

Conclusion

This chapter has provided an overview of the theoretical frameworks that we have utilized in our research and teaching over the past ten years, with a particular focus on feminist poststructuralist perspectives. Our readings of these perspectives have also been significantly influenced by the works of Foucault, especially those around discourse, power and subjectivity. We feel that the process of subjectification is critical to doing social justice work with both adults and children. It provides an invaluable theoretical framework in which to understand how individual subjects become who they are and how they actively participate in the construction of their own subjectivities, and regulate those of others. Feminist poststructural perspectives also remind us that we are flexible, complex and contradictory shifting subjects with multiple identities. This is critical to an understanding of power, identity and social inequality.

Recommended reading

Burr, V. (1995) *An Introduction to Social Constructionism*. London: Routledge.

Davies, B. (1994) *Poststructuralist Theory and Classroom Practice*. Geelong, Victoria: Deakin University Press.

Davies, B. (1996) *Power, Knowledge and Desire: Changing School Organization and Management Practices*. Canberra: Department of Education, Employment, Training and Youth Affairs.

Foucault, M. (1974) *The Archaeology of Knowledge*. London: Tavistock.

Foucault, M. (1978) *The History of Sexuality, Volume 1: An Introduction*. Translated from French by Robert Hurley. New York: Vintage Books.

Foucault, M. (1980) *Power/Knowledge*. Translated by Colin Gordon. New York: Pantheon Books.

Hall, D.E. (2004) *Subjectivity*. New York: Routledge.

Kumashiro, K.K. (2002) Troubling education: Queer activism and antioppressive pedagogy. New York: RoutledgeFalmer.

MacNaughton, G. (1998) *Techniques for Teaching Young Children: Choices in Theory and Practice*. Melbourne: Longman.

Mills, S. (2003) *Discourse*. London: Routledge.

Weedon, C. (1997) *Feminist Practice and Poststructuralist Theory*, 2nd edn. Oxford: Blackwell.

LOCAL AND GLOBAL SOCIAL RELATIONS:
Critical perspectives on class and inequality

Introduction

Within the last twenty years, widespread and rapid changes have occurred in every sphere and level of society (Reay 2003). Our everyday lives are continuously marked by the impact of increased globalization, communication technologies, free markets and increased flows of human and non-human resources and capital. At the centre of these changes, the impact on and intersections of social identities – such as class, 'race', ethnicity, gender, sexuality, (dis)ability and social relations – are significant. Due to increased widening of global markets facilitated by rapid advancements in media and communication technologies in which trade, commerce and the flows of human and non-human capital are readily apparent, social identities, practices and power relations take on new forms of negotiation in which meanings about class and inequality are reframed.

Early childhood educators working with young children and their families, witness every day the impact of globalization in terms of how children's life chances are affected by the declining provision of health care, welfare services and education. In terms of early childhood education, children's access to affordable, high-quality programmes that address issues of equity and social justice is crucial in maximizing children's learning opportunities.

On one level, the impact of globalization is relatively straightforward as its effects can be seen everywhere in almost every aspect of our lives. However, on another level, the social, political and economic implications of globalization are relatively unknown to early childhood educators as there has been very little research in early childhood education that examines this new and emerging field of enquiry.

Hence, this chapter offers a starting point from which issues of class, globalization and neoliberalism can be understood. It begins with an overview of globalization and argues that the economic, political, cultural and social impact of globalization on our lives is powerful. Further, this chapter high-lights the need to reframe traditional theoretical frameworks of class and argues that contemporary understandings of class are needed in order to understand that within a globalized world, the increasing inequalities and complexities facing children and families in negotiating discourses associated with neoliberalism, consumerism and corporate constructions of childhood are significant. As Apple (1999) reminds us, education, including early childhood education, does not exist in isolation from broader social structures in society. Therefore, for educators working with young children, critical understandings of globalization are crucial if we are going to make a difference to children's lives. Thus, this chapter discusses the contemporary phenomena of globalization, neoliberalism, consumerism and immigration issues in relation to how they impact on young children and their families.

What is globalization?

Globalization is the construction of world systems that merge finance, trade, media and communication technologies. It also involves the interconnections of linguistic, cultural and social ideologies across multiple sites of economic, cultural, social and political fields, which are characterized by rapid change, free markets and capitalism at global levels (Marginson 1999). Thus, globalization is part of our social reality, a social construction that impacts on every aspect of our daily life. However, apart from the social impact globalization has on our lives, there are the economic imperatives that shape and constitute political, social and cultural spheres of society. These economic imperatives are not neutral even though globalization claims to be an economic doctrine based on natural and objective reality (Dudley 1998). Through its claims for objectivity and truth, it constitutes power. In other words, 'globalization is what Foucault called a "regime of truth", a form of existing rationality that is more powerful than any other form' (Tierney 2004: 8).

While globalization is often equated with Americanization and cultural imperialism, Tierney (2004) argues that it is more complex than a basic imposition of a homogeneous culture on other cultures. This means that it is evident not only at the surface level of homogenizing cultural and social practices, but also in how societies define and construct political, economic, social and cultural structures and practices that take place at a much more complex level. For example, Tierney (2004: 8) cites Waters who argues that globalization does not necessarily imply that the entire world adopts Westernized cultural discourses and social practices, but rather that 'every set of social arrangements must establish its position in relation to the capitalist West' (Waters 1995: 6, quoted in Tierney 2004). Globalization forces a local culture into a relational mode in which both economic 'for-profit' motives fuse with local cultural and social sensitivities in order to boost marketability and consumer consumption. For example, Western popular music is hybridized to attract the clientele of young children as in the case of one of the world's most popular children's entertainment groups, 'The Wiggles'. This group has recently commenced a Latin American tour in which its songs are performed in Spanish, using local dialectal and cultural meanings to attract the children's market.

Tierney (2004) proposes four assumptions about globalization. First, he argues that the momentum for globalization derives from economic and technological forces that are hard to comprehend and control because they are transnational. Transnationalism is the articulation and mediation of technology, free markets, profits and consumerism across the globe. Globalization takes on a transnational impetus.

The second assumption in Tierney's arguments suggests that there is a cultural logic behind globalization, which maintains that happiness and meaning are to be found in goods and services. This assumption argues that consumerism is necessary for the world and individuals to function. Kasturi (2002) says that globalized consumerism blurs the distinction between fundamental needs and commercially generated needs. She suggests that market economies naturalize consumption as a necessary and fundamental aspect of human existence.

Tierney's third assumption proposes that as a result of globalization there is a widening gap between the wealthy and poor. This increasing gap affords greater access to economic and technological means for the wealthy to buy happiness and meaning. Meanwhile, the poor are left further behind.

Finally, Tierney's fourth assumption argues that 'the public good', defined by the liberal state in the twentieth century, has changed as expectations of the state shrink or evaporate, leaving individuals to sink or swim in a borderless economy. According to Tierney, the role of the state is increasingly seen as not having much to do with equity in a globalized world. He suggests that transnational corporate economies are the engines that drive action; the focus is not on public goods aimed at social justice, such as public schooling, health and welfare. Rather, the state's goals and purpose become focused on ensuring that corporations are competitive. Thus, the principles of the corporate economy take precedence over ensuring appropriate provision and delivery of public services. Subsequently, the profitability and competitiveness of businesses, rather than the creation of jobs and the extension of democracy to all citizens, are the goal of the state. The emphasis is increasingly on profit at the expense of the 'pubic good' as social and communal goals are given less prominence and competition and 'for-profit' agendas become the priority (Tierney 2004).

Thus, for early childhood educators working closely with families raising young children, an appreciation of the economic dimension of globalization is fundamental. The likelihood that early childhood settings comprise of both wealthy and poor families means that educators need to be sensitive to ways in which increased consumerism, the widening gaps between the wealthy and the poor, and the demise of the provision of public services will ultimately impact on working poor and disadvantaged families. Since economic resources for many families are constrained by the increasing costs of raising children, educators need to be cognizant of how their programme may or may not exacerbate discursive inequality and power relations between children, families and staff mediated by financial constraints, material possession and choice. As Apple (1999) argues, in an economy which is increasingly conditioned by lower wages, capitalism and insecurity further intensify parents' concerns for their children's economic and cultural futures.

Class relations and cultural reproduction in a globalized world

Traditional understandings about social class are principally based on the work of Marx (1967) and Engels (1974) in which social inequality was related to material wealth and the ownership of labour. Marxism, a structuralist and modernist theoretical framework, posits class inequality within binary distinctions between the ruling class or bourgeoisie, who owned the factories, business and land, and the working class or proletariat, who worked for the ruling class (see Chapter 1 for an overview of Marxism). Marxism claimed that the only means to attaining equality was through a proletariat class struggle in which workers could use their labour as the bargaining chip to improve working conditions, workers' rights and ultimately redress inequalities between the ruling class and the working class to bring about the collective ownership of the means of production. Karl Marx's work was a response to the massive changes triggered by the Industrial Revolution which saw the growth of secular and democratic institutions, such as the political parties advocating for 'the working man' and the union movement, and increased emphasis on technologies and mass production of goods and services (Kell 2004).

While Marxism was applicable in understanding the relationship between the Industrial Revolution and capitalism in society, Kell (2004) argues that as postindustrial societies globalize due to technology, communication, trade and commerce, Marxist theory has become inadequate in explaining the complexities and contradictions emerging in these societies, particularly when exploring uncertainty and ambiguity. As film, literature, music, the arts and architecture become increasingly important sites of cultural analysis and representation, different ways of knowing and meaning-making provide a platform from which diverse cultural knowledges can provide tools for analysing society (Kell 2004). Further, with increasing mobility of the population across the world, diversity rather than homogeneity is apparent, and social identities, such as class, gender, 'race', ethnicity, sexuality and (dis)ability, are constructed and understood in relational terms to each other, rather than in isolation. In postmodern thinking, the overlaps and intersections between identities across different cultural meaning systems are emphasized. For example, a growing number of studies examining parent–teacher partnerships reveal that for parents the work involved in negotiating and advocating for their children's academic success is mainly gender-related. The gendered practices of child-rearing, homework, school liaison and parent involvement are mostly assigned to mothers. However, these studies also reveal that much of this gendered work operates in the deployment of and access to social, cultural, economic resources in which class is a major factor (Reay 1998; Lareau and McNamara-Horvat 1999; Vincent and Martin 2002). Further, Lareau and McNamara-Horvat (1999) and Reay (1998) also examine the impact of 'race' and ethnicity in view of how women from racial and ethnic minorities mobilize cultural resources (capital) in their relationship to schooling.

Consequently, in this new postmodern period characterized by capitalism and globalization, meanings about class relations and class identity take on new hybrid forms. Hall (1997: 2) points out that by deconstructing traditional assumptions about class relations as a dichotomous struggle between the 'workers' and 'owners', 'we can hope to understand the socially constructed and historically contingent ways in which economic interests are articulated and pursued in the everyday capitalist world'. These economic interests cut across relations of class, 'race', ethnicity, gender, sexuality and (dis)ability. However, dismantling the binary relations between 'workers' and 'owners' does not imply that class is no longer significant. Indeed, there is a negative impact of globalization on the working-class urban poor in terms of job security, the casualization of the labour force, and the volatility of competitive market-driven economies. Globalization does not lack a socio-economic dimension; rather, it sharpens material inequalities due to the creation of new power elites (Marginson 1999).

Questions about equity in a globalized world become even more pertinent as new modes of work practices determine economic security or insecurity, particularly for those minority groups, such as the working poor, marked by gender, ethnicity, 'race', sexuality and (dis)ability. For example, in Australia, the most disadvantaged groups are single parents (mainly women), Indigenous Australians, unemployed youth and sections of the elderly (Way 1997, cited in Greig *et al.* 2003). Further, Long (2000) observes that the Australian workforce is divided between the 'overworked' and the 'out of work', between the 'well paid' and the 'poorly paid' and between 'career jobs' and 'fringe jobs', all of which are a product of global competition and the reduction of full-time jobs (quoted in Greig *et al.* 2003).

Neoliberalism and globalization

Neoliberalism is a world-wide phenomenon. It can be defined as a political and cultural strategy through which policies are designed to devolve the state's responsibility for welfare, education and health services to the community, the family, the individual and private enterprise. Individuals maximize their own personal benefits and agendas, resulting in diminished expectations of the state's responsibilities for their welfare (Apple 1999, 2001; Singh 2002a; Greig *et al.* 2003).

Neoliberalism as both a political and cultural discourse impacts on policies and social practices, which have far-reaching affects on the daily lives of individuals and groups (Carrington 2002). Neoliberalism results in a 'massive increase in social and economic inequality, a marked increase in severe deprivation for the poorest nations and peoples of the world, a disastrous global environment, an unstable global economy and an unprecedented bonanza for the wealthy' (McChesney 1999: 41, quoted in Carrington 2002: 5). Thus, neoliberal technologies are designed to alter work practices towards higher levels of flexibility and productivity, which align with national economic objectives (Davies and Petersen 2005). Davies and Petersen argue that discourses of neoliberalism constitute self-enterprising mechanisms, which combine with management techniques and individual performance. Self-enterprising technologies take up tactics of corporate bullying, coercion and subordination to get workers to comply with managerial agendas. Hence, within this discourse, the emphasis on 'performance' renders our subjectivity as dispensable, compliant and competitive, ultimately leading to normalized and naturalized work practices.

Within a neoliberal discourse there is also an assumption that all social groups will ultimately benefit from the effects of corporate profit, regardless of the fact that it increases the wealth of the already wealthy. Yet, in reality, neoliberal agendas aim to reduce labour costs, decrease public expenditures and make work more flexible (Bourdieu 1998). This decreased public expenditure and the commitment from governments to take less responsibility for social welfare, education, housing and health operate alongside attempts to weaken trade unions and other employee representative bodies. For poor families and the working poor, this means that they are more likely to be exploited as their incomes remain low, and their ability to access services is increasingly compromised. Hence, 'survival of the fittest' becomes the mantra of everyday life, experienced through competitive struggles for social, political and cultural resources (Singh 2002a).

In the end, neoliberalism has implications for the working poor and disadvantaged groups in our society, because they are the ones most likely to be affected by government policies on health, welfare, housing and education. Once these services become enterprising concerns from which 'for-profit' desires operate, economically disadvantaged groups and minorities are positioned at the mercy of market-driven agendas from which they are least likely to benefit.

Relationships between globalization and neoliberalism

Apple (1999) argues that within neoliberal discourses the idea of the consumer is fundamental, and for neoliberals the world is a massive supermarket in which 'consumer choice' is the guarantor of the democratic rights of its citizens. He suggests that by 'selling' education, like cars, television or food, in a for-profit market, it will effectively become self-regulating. Subsequently, as a result of globalization, neoliberal discourses position the state in a subordinate relationship to global corporations as 'the principles of the corporate economy take precedence' (Tierney 2004: 11). Penn (2002) argues that in a neoliberal economy the state is generally seen as an inefficient means of funding and delivery of essential services, and any regulation is often viewed as unwarranted interference. Hence, private enterprise is considered to be the answer. For example, early childhood development (ECD) programmes in the USA have followed a neoliberal economic approach based on private enterprise, which differs from state-funded and state-regulated services in Europe. As a result, state intervention is viewed as not necessary, except on behalf of targeted minorities and the very poor.

Apple's (1999, 2001) notion of neoconservative restoration is a clear example of the connections between neoliberalism and globalization. Neoconservatism is reflected in the right-wing ideologies that are currently gaining ground in the broader society, including early childhood education. This emergence of neoconservative thinking is the result of a successful struggle by the right to form a broad-based alliance between neoliberals, who are guided by visions of the weak state and strong personal and private enterprising technologies, and neoconservatives, who in education call for a return to 'high standards', discipline, testing regimes and a focus on literacy. Together these two forces combine with authoritarian populism in which common normative discourses of masculinity, femininity, heterosexuality, monolingualism, the nuclear family and so on are upheld to construct binaries of 'us' and 'them'. Within this binary, the former are the hard working, who are homogeneous, law abiding and decent, while the latter are lazy, immoral, heterogeneous and permissive (Apple 1999).

Education, globalization and neoliberalism

Apple (1999, 2001) argues that neoliberalism is a powerful element in the current conservative movement in education. Neoliberal agendas view schools and other public institutions as 'black holes' into which money is poured without results. Economic rationalism underpins almost every aspect of this discourse in which there are misguided assumptions that there exist fairness and justice in 'for-profit' markets (Apple 1999). Public funding is measured against economic rationalist criteria limited by 'for-profit' outcomes, rather than by outcomes that indicate quality and equity, which are at odds with economic rationality.

Traditionally, education has been seen as for everyone, not just a privileged few, and **affirmative action** policies, such as those associated with access and equity for minority groups, would be addressed through education. In this sense, education has been seen as a means through which the poor could move out of poverty and as an agent of socialization into citizenship. Educational policies were generally geared towards the public good (Tierney 2004).

In recent years, there have been considerable reforms in addressing issues of inequality in education. These reforms, informed by critical, cultural and feminist poststructural theorists, such as Bourdieu (1990, 1991a, 1991b), Foucault (1974), Apple (1999, 2001) and Walkerdine (1990), have addressed ways in which education operates to reproduce power relations of dominant and privileged groups within society. For example, Apple (1999, 2001) has argued that what is taught in the curriculum and regarded as 'official knowledge' is bound up with struggles and history of class, 'race', ethnicity, gender, sexuality and religious relations. Academics and teachers with a social justice agenda, who have been informed by theorists such as Bourdieu and Foucault, take a critical approach towards pedagogy and curriculum. They question what constitutes 'official knowledge' within the mainstream curriculum in order to reshape and contest the power of dominant groups. Issues of representation of minority groups, such as people of colour, those from minority language backgrounds, women, gays and lesbians, and people with disabilities, who traditionally have been excluded from the mainstream curriculum, have been highlighted to reduce inequality in education. However, Tierney (2004: 15) argues that despite these recent gains in educational reform that incorporate a social justice agenda, in the United States in particular, within a globalized market economy, 'the state no longer has a role as a cultural arbiter and shaper of the public good, so education has lost its purpose as well'. According to Tierney (2004), knowledge and the purpose of education are being reshaped. 'Competence' has become the purpose of education, which is evaluated through the process of 'testing'. This reflects the concerns of Cannella and Viruru (2004), who point out that the new colonialism in early childhood is perpetuated through the process of standardized testing of children from very early ages, particularly in the United States; but this process is also operating in other countries such as Australia and the United Kingdom. What is considered 'official knowledge' is replaced with an emphasis on 'skills' and 'competence', which is being redefined by neoliberal economic agendas as 'cultural codes are equated with the competence one displays on standardized tests' (Tierney 2004: 16).

In recent years, standardized testing regimes have been readily applied to position minority groups as subordinate to dominant groups. In Australia, the United Kingdom and the United States, neoliberal discourses have engineered a renewed emphasis on standardized testing (Henry et al. 1999). Constituted in competitive neoliberal discourses in education, children who succeed are constructed as competent and capable, while those children who fall below standardized average score counts are constructed as deficit. Hence, 'globalization's purpose for education reinscribes a theoretical justification for the dominant to be dominant' (Tierney 2004: 16). Thus, for families with young children, it is no wonder that we have seen an increased anxiety around competence and academic success at school. Parents are increasingly under pressure to ensure that their children succeed and survive the education system. In Australia, the private 'coaching colleges' offering tuition in maths and English are experiencing increased levels of participation from students whose parents are anxious that their children achieve academic success. Further, explicit in the pedagogies of such 'coaching colleges', exam techniques are taught, equipping children with the necessary skills and techniques enabling them to compete for competitive places in various selective schools administered by the Department of Education and Training. Since public education is woefully underfunded, and private schools in Australia are well beyond the financial capacity of many working- and middle-class families, the competition is fierce. Good-quality education becomes a hot commodity despite the public rhetoric of quality public education.

Parental anxiety about their children's academic success begins in the preschool years, well before children reach primary school. A growing number of middle- to upper-class families have their preschoolers enrolled in ballet, music, gymnastics and drama tuition. Parenting magazines and newspapers have abundant advertisements from private ballet, music, coaching schools and colleges, proposing the benefits of such extra curricula activities for intellectual, social and creative development towards a 'good start' to academic success at school. The fees of these private institutions are well beyond the means of many low-income and working families.

Hence, in neoliberal discourses operating in education, time is considered a critical commodity and it is perceived that the investment in our children's education needs to begin in the early years. Starting the process in the early years is perceived necessary in order to procure the skills required to enable children to succeed in education and to develop a competitive disposition to participate in globalized markets. Tierney (2004) suggests that as the emphasis changes from public to private education, so too does inequality; within this process there is an amplification of social differences but fewer public dollars going towards public education. This calls into question the role of teachers within these changing times. Tierney (2004) asserts that discourses of managerialism pervade the education system in which teachers become managers who provide students with the techniques to pass a test. Schools pressure teachers to teach to a test and if students do not pass, teachers are held accountable. This move away from teachers as 'transformative intellectuals' (Giroux 1988, 1997) informed by principles of social justice and equity is lost in a globalized world. Consequently, the equity and social justice potential of education is displaced by a training agent role, as in business, industry and competitive modes of production, which are the fundamentals of neoliberalism and globalization.

Globalization and forced immigration

The globalization of labour, finance, technology, trade, communication, transport and so on has led to massive social changes that have coincided with an increased demand for cheap labour both at the national and international levels. Indeed, as Castles and Miller (1998) point out, the flow of labour throughout the world is a result of growing capital mobility, improved transport facilities and uneven economic development, all of which are produced by globalization. This process brings about a competitive labour market in which the political and social rights of workers are subject to economic exploitation. Mass migration has always been a significant factor in the growth of industrial economies, such as Australia, Britain, Canada, New Zealand and the United States (Castles 2000). However, as a result of globalization, the growing disparities in economic, social and demographic conditions between developing and postindustrial nation states provide a context for future mass migration (Castles 2000).

Castles (2000) highlights that there is an increasing demand for 'rightless' workers evident in the West and in some Asian countries, such as Japan and the Gulf states. However, immigrants are not only one homogeneous group; women make up half the world's migrant population (Sánchez 1998). As women are more vulnerable to abuse and more likely to send money home, deregulated and exploitative female labour markets, which employ women in both domestic services and the sex industry, take full advantage of existing gendered power relations and discourses that operate in both receiving and sending countries (Castles 2000).

Within these expanding, exploitative and competitive labour markets, an endless and abundant supply of workers with minimal political and civil rights sets up local and global tensions. Castles (2000) claims that local workers, who compete with such forms of deregulated globalized labour, can take up racism as a reaction to these changing deregulated labour markets. New racisms emerge targeting new immigrants within a social milieu in which competition for jobs is often intensified. These tensions are often exacerbated through increasing competition for affordable housing and the downgrading of social welfare services and education that are increasingly being privatized due to lack of support from government agencies. In early childhood settings, such racializing discourses may also be evident in families' attitudes towards refugees, asylum seekers and immigrants, particularly in marginalized and low-income communities, where struggles to access social services are apparent.

In Australia in recent times, examples of such new racisms have included attacks on Islamic women wearing the hijab; media commentaries which depict illegal immigrants as potential threats to social cohesion; and asylum seekers who are represented by the media and some politicians as immigration queue jumpers. Further, as a result of the attacks of 11 September 2001, and George Bush's war against terrorism, popular stereotypes that all Muslims are potential terrorists have emerged. Castles (2000) cites further examples of new racism, including the emergence of an Australian anti-immigration movement, spearheaded by Pauline Hanson's One Nation Party; anti-immigrant violence of neo-Nazis and skinheads in post-reunification Germany; and the banning of the headscarf in French schools (just to name a few).

Asylum seekers and refugees

The overwhelming majority of asylum seekers do not fall neatly within the categories of the United Nations definition of refugees, even though many are forced to leave their country due to religious, racial, ethnic persecution, political dissidence, war, famine or economic pressure (Castles 2000). The United Nations estimate of 150,000 refugees and asylum seekers, compared to Castles' estimate of 15 million, calls into question the viability of the United Nations definition of asylum and refugees status. Human Rights Watch has estimated that a further 22 million internally displaced persons have been uprooted and forced to leave their country (www.hrw.org). Indeed, there is a pressing need for new international policies that adequately take account of recent political, economic, social and environment upheaval across the world (Castles 2000).

Refugees are constructed through transnational forces, and while they are by no means a heterogeneous group, their experiences transcend national origins through a myriad of geographic, linguistic, religious, political and legal boundaries (Pickering 2001; Lacroix 2003). Notwithstanding these transnational experiences, the universal experience of forced migration renders a definition of what it means to be a refugee. Hence, Human Rights Watch (2004) defines a refugee as:

... someone with a well-founded fear of persecution on the basis of his or her race, religion, nationality, membership in a particular social group or political opinion, who is outside of his or her country of nationality and unable or unwilling to return. Refugees are forced from their countries by war, civil conflict, political strife or gross human rights abuses.

This growing refugee crisis affects all countries around the world, not just postindustrial developing states of the West as often depicted in the media. It is estimated that in 2001, 78 per cent of refugees came from Afghanistan, Angola, Burma, Burundi, Congo-Kinshasa, Eritrea, Iraq, the Palestinian territories, Somalia and Sudan. Contrary to widespread belief that is primarily constructed in the Western media, Asia hosts 45 per cent of all refugees, followed by Africa with 30 per cent and Europe with 19 per cent (Human Rights Watch 2004). Australia, on the contrary, by international comparisons, has a relatively small intake of refugee and asylum seekers. For example, Tanzania hosts one refugee for every 76 people; Britain hosts one refugee for every 530 people; while Australia hosts one refugee for every 1583 people (Edmund Rice Centre for Justice and Community Education and the School of Education, Australian Catholic University 2001).

Despite such comparatively small numbers of refugees in Australia, there has been much debate about the treatment of refugees and asylum seekers, particularly in relation to detention centres. For example, of the 600 children in detention centres, 30 are separated from their families. The findings of the recent National Inquiry into Children in Immigration Detention indicated that Australian immigration detention laws are fundamentally at odds with the 1991 United Nation's Convention of the Rights of the Child, which requires detention of children only as a last resort (Human Rights and Equal Opportunity Commission 2004). The inquiry revealed that 'Australia's immigration detention policy creates a fundamental breach of a child's right to be detained as a measure of last resort and for the shortest appropriate period of time'. More specifically, the Human Rights and Equal Opportunity Commission (2004) found that Australia's immigration detention policy has failed to conform to the UN Convention in protecting the mental health of children, providing adequate health care and education, and failing to protect unaccompanied children and children with disabilities.

Meanwhile, as Australia's treatment of children of refugee and asylum seekers has sparked widespread debate in the Australian popular media, Britain's treatment of children of refugees and asylum seekers in the education system is also under scrutiny. Rutter (2004) estimates that 7 per cent of London's schoolchildren are refugees from Somalian, Kurdish and Congolese backgrounds. She reports on research carried out by Save the Children Scotland, which revealed that many refugee children face difficulties at school due to racialized constructions and anti-refugee sentiments, which manifest in bullying and intimidation. Rutter concludes that due to anti-immigration debates fuelled in the popular media in Britain, the need to deal with racism and bullying of refugee children is crucial. Therefore, it is critical for early childhood educators to understand how such media-driven, popularist, racializing discourses directly influence children's relationships with each other and their understanding of difference.

Regardless of whether immigrants voluntarily or forcibly migrate to other countries, the fact remains that the world is increasingly becoming more heterogeneous across the social categories of class, ethnicity, 'race', religion, gender and sexuality. Indeed, Castles (2000) predicts that voluntary and forced migration is likely to continue in a globalized world in which political, religious and ethnic conflicts remain in accordance with the fast pace of capitalist globalizing economies and rapid advancements in communication and travel technologies. As the world globalizes its capital exchange and market economies, the deregulation of border tariffs and trade and workers' rights, there continues to be a steady and abundant flow of human capital. Thus, labour recruitment becomes cheaper, making it easier for not only corporations but also illegal labour markets to take full advantage of those who need to escape from economic hardship and/or social, cultural or religious persecution.

Corporatization of childhood

As a consequence of globalization, traditional Western views of childhood as a time of innocence are slowly being disrupted. Steinberg and Kincheloe (1997) point out that within the past fifty years, due to rapid social, economic and technological changes, childhood is increasingly shaped by media, popular culture, globalization, technology and capitalism. Children are significantly affected by current social, economic and political issues such as family breakdown and restructuring, governments' neoliberal agendas that directly result in their withdrawal from state responsibilities for welfare, the changing roles of women, and increased access to technologies. Therefore, Steinberg and Kincheloe (1997) argue that we can no longer make use of traditional assumptions about childhood as a time of innocence and naïvety. Rather, the postmodern childhood encompasses meanings about children as consumers, who are informed by a variety of sources, such as television, movies, video games, books, toys, friends and popular culture. Through these various sources, they also have access to adult information and 'adults' worlds'. Thus, children are knowing and not necessarily innocent; the binary of 'adults' worlds'/'children's worlds' is being disrupted. Yet, traditional views of childhood are constantly upheld in contrast to the reality that many children have in-depth knowledge about what are generally perceived to be issues relevant to 'adult worlds'.

As children gain greater access to 'adult worlds', it seems that corporate constructions of childhood also position children at the centre of consumerism. The historian Paula Fass (2003: 975) makes the pertinent point that 'it is foolhardy to discuss globalization, the cultural politics of globalization, and the social consequences of globalization without firmly situating children in that discussion'. She argues that children will become greater consumers of play goods as the process of globalization and deregulated market economies increase children's access to these goods. For example, with the increased access to technology, children in the West are exposed to sophisticated digital, electronic and mechanical gadgets in toys, such as computer games, video games and electronic media texts. The computer and electronic gaming industry is a multimillion-dollar project that has in recent years outgrown other industries (Cannella and Kincheloe 2002). Consequently, children are increasingly targeted by global corporations that produce entertainment, food, clothing, toys, books and so on. Kasturi (2002) notes how children have become an increasingly significant consumer group. She argues that children's entertainment is big business, citing the $4.7 billion Disney corporation as an example, with its cross-marketing of films, comics and theme parks, whose icons appear on children's clothing, breakfast cereals, school bags, toiletries, frozen food and so on, influencing childhood and children's consumption of entertainment and toys. It is no wonder that childhood is viewed as an enterprising and profitable industry. Children and childhood are being bought and sold in new ways, coercing children into avid and fervent consumerism.

Kasturi (2002: 51) states that within corporate constructions of childhood, metanarratives generated by these corporations engender in children the 'need' to buy certain products, and coerce parents into thinking that the 'ideal' or 'natural' childhood involves the 'continuous consumption of these corporate promoted products and services'. For children, then, the social and cultural capital accumulated through the consumption of these products and services becomes a driving force in the continual acquisition of such products and services. For example, children's group memberships and social relations with each other are often constituted in their interests around popular culture, as they engage in complex talk about the narratives, moves and characteristics applicable to the various types of popular culture in which they are interested (Jones Díaz et al. 2002).

Fass (2003) argues that a major problem of globalization is the perpetuation of the sexual exploitation of children. She notes that the potential cultural impacts of globalization have produced anxious representations of children's sexuality, rather than concerns for the increasing rates of child prostitution, child labour and sexual abuse occurring in society. Indeed, globalization has facilitated the various technologies through which children as sexual commodities are constructed through child pornography, sex tourism, and the kidnapping and selling of children. These industries of child exploitation operate on globalized levels highly organized through various networks facilitated by communication technologies, such as the Internet.

Further, corporate consumer constructions of childhood defined by Western perspectives, homogenize childhood as white, Western, urban and middle-class. The metanarratives of popular culture found in Disney, Yu-Gi-Oh, Barbie, Bratz and so on, present normative discourses of femininity, masculinity, heterosexuality, whiteness and the nuclear family (just to name a few). Children and adults from diverse socio-cultural groups, such as people of colour, people from Indigenous cultures, gays and lesbians, and people with disabilities, are underrepresented and often constructed as social problems. This discourse privileges the perspectives and voices of dominant cultural groups, while silencing minority identities (Jones Díaz *et al.* 2002).

Apart from the homogenizing and commercializing affects of globalization on children, the corporatization of childhood is also reflected in the way that early childhood education in Australia has become a 'hot' commodity on the Australian stock market in recent years. As with other stock market companies, the quality of service can be compromised as shareholder profits become the focus of company philosophies and strategies. How this stock-marketization of early childhood education impacts on the field more broadly remains to be seen, but it has the potential to influence curricula, pedagogies, professional standards, and service costs to families, as decisions are influenced by economic rationalism and shareholders, who may not necessary be those utilizing early childhood services or those with an understanding of children's early educational needs. Poor families may find it increasingly difficult to meet the financial costs of their children's early education. What is particularly alarming is the potential for increased class distinctions across the different types of early childhood services that families can afford to utilize.

Macro-economic policies and their impact on children and childhood

Stephens (1995) highlights the significant impact that political and macro-economic policies have on children. She raises concerns about the effects of globalization on children from the West, whose childhoods have become highly individualized, commodified and stratified, while children from developing nation states are the most vulnerable victims of economic policies (Penn 2002: 118). Penn (2002: 121) argues that as the gap between rich and poor countries is growing and as the world's poor are getting poorer, children are disproportionately affected by poverty and are especially susceptible to cuts in infrastructural services such as health and education. Similarly in the West, the increasing gap between children from middle- to upper-class families and children from working poor families, single-parent families, low-income families and families dependent on welfare are especially vulnerable to cuts in social, welfare and education services. Therefore, macro-economic policies driven by globalization and neoliberal agendas impact on the most disadvantaged and marginalized children in both developing and developed nation states.

Bourdieu (1998) claims that neoliberal discourses gain their strength and resilience through the economic, social and political power of those who dominate economic relations. One such organization that dominates world economies and the policies that drive them is the World Bank. The World Bank is an organization of multinational financial institutions from 181 countries headquartered in the USA. The International Monetary Fund, constructed by and administered through the World Bank, was established after the Second World War with the aim of assisting in the redevelopment and reconstruction of debilitated economies. Today, the World Bank has a monetary interest in almost all 'developing' and 'transnational' countries.

The USA has a major influence on the operations of the World Bank, which is closely tied to the US Treasury. Wade (2001: 127) argues that 'The World Bank has been an especially useful instrument for projecting American influences in developing countries and one over which the US maintains discreet but firm institutional control'. Despite unmanageable and large debts owed by developing countries to the World Bank, it claims to be working to alleviate world poverty. However, according to Penn (2002) the evidence is mounting that the World Bank is not only unsuccessful at addressing poverty and indebtedness, but it is contributing to the massive current debt rise in developing countries. While the World Bank argues that 'its interventions are more, rather than less necessary, as a vehicle for achieving economic stability and progress; and that increased technological expertise can solve global problems' (Penn 2002: 121), there is little evidence to suggest that in developing countries, where such intervention has taken place, there has been greater economic benefit to local communities. For example, in Guatemala, with the aim of alleviating poverty, the World Bank has funded dams that have displaced up to 10 million people from their homes, communities and land. It has also pushed local people further into debt and has never compensated for the destruction of millions of lives or of the local environments (Imhof 2000). Furthermore, Castles (2000) highlights that the structural adjustments enforced on developing countries from the World Bank and the International Monetary Fund have resulted in governments abandoning policies that protect the living conditions of the people, including children; this has resulted in the dismantling of welfare systems, increased unemployment and erosion of workers' rights. Penn (2002) heavily critiques the benefits of the World Bank's intervention, pointing out that the claim that neoliberal economic development and global progress are neutral, culture-free and inevitable is so flawed that it is untenable. Indeed Bourdieu (1998) confers that neoliberalism is desocialized and dehistoricized and in the process, like all 'regimes of truth', has the power to 'make itself true'.

Penn (2002: 121) asks whether global economic policies as typified by the World Bank damage children. According to Penn, the World Bank acknowledges that education rates are falling and child mortality is increasing worldwide, but rather than seeing this as a failure of neoliberal economic policy, the Bank prefers to continue to refine its current approaches. For example, Penn (2002: 118) argues that the 'World Bank pursues policies that are detrimental to the interest of children while at the same time claiming to promote their interests'. Penn (2002: 118) points out that the 'Bank claims to work for children in ... [developing countries] ... as the "human capital" of the future without whom no economic intervention can truly succeed'. The key to successful intervention is seen to lie in the application of traditional child development theory, based on 'scientific facts' that underpin Developmentally Appropriate Practices. Hence, what is considered appropriate and proven in the USA is considered to be universally applicable to all children. Penn (2002) states that this universalizing approach to childhood is based on certain Western societal assumptions, such as the importance of **individualism** and selfhood; a permanent nuclear household, with a prime carer and a lone dependent child as the focus of adult attention; the need to encourage choice from a wide range of material goods; and various kinds of nature–nurture dualisms. Penn (2002: 125) suggests that 'The practices advocated are neither neutral nor scientifically established (even if this were possible), but rooted in specific assumptions about childhood and society. Developmentally Appropriate Practice might be more accurately described as "how to understand and bring up your child as an Anglo-American"'. Intervention programmes are based on the assumption that adult early intervention is the key to successful development in children. A lack of intervention and 'poor parenting' are perceived to be the problems that need to be tackled. Thus, more sophisticated and carefully calibrated intervention is considered to be the key to reducing poor parenting, rather than offsetting the ill effects of poverty (Penn 2002). Parents tend to be viewed as lacking the will power, energy or capability to improve their children's circumstances. These intervention programmes have a limited focus on environmental and structural issues that also produce poverty, indebtedness, violence and so forth. For example, Penn (2002) points out that the World Bank's African early childhood development strategy, while making a token acknowledgement of structural problems such as indebtedness, war and HIV/AIDS, still concludes that child malnourishment is 'largely due to inappropriate child feeding practices, high morbidity, and poor child caring practices' (Penn 2002: 126).

Implications for early childhood education

In working closely with children, families, communities and staff, it is crucial that early childhood educators recognize the impact that globalizaton and neoliberalism have on everyday lived experiences. With increased privatization of preschool settings, and continual downgrading of public education, ways in which teachers ensure that their programmes and pedagogies address issues of equity, affordability, diversity and difference will become pertinent to their work.

The following suggestions may assist early childhood educators address issues of neoliberalism and class with families, children and staff members. The discussion that follows offers a range of implications that early childhood educators can adopt on both personal and professional levels.

Challenging neoliberalism and corporate agendas

It is crucial that early childhood educators develop an informed and critical disposition towards globalization and neoliberalism, particularly in relation to its broader social and cultural impact on social identities, such as class, 'race', ethnicity, gender, sexuality and (dis)ability. Central to a critical disposition is the will to challenge inequality and difference with children, staff and families by highlighting the importance of equity in early childhood education.

Early childhood educators can also develop alliances with local and national lobby groups, such as unions, women's groups and local environmental groups, through different communication technologies or participate in interagency or local community events. These alliances or projects can be integrated into daily experiences at the setting in which children and families take a proactive stance towards local issues affected by global processes, such as promoting environmental sustainability. Through these alliances with both community groups and families they can help build social capital through collaborating and forging links with local schools and community-based services such as playgroups, family support, community language programmes, and other child-care or preschool settings.

Reframing our understanding of class in a globalized world

Early childhood educators need to be sensitive to the increasing costs of education that is becoming privatized. The 'outsourcing' of curriculum in which there is an overdependence on excursions, guest speakers and 'fee paying' activities to 'enhance' the curriculum can often pose additional economic hardship on low-income families. Further, costs associated with purchasing educational resources for children that educators often assume all families can afford, need to be carefully considered in terms of the financial burden they place on family incomes, which are already stretched. It is essential that educators understand that while globalization may have some advantages in providing flexible work practices, these advantages are often exclusive of working-class and working poor families, who bear the brunt of insecurity in employment through the increased emphasis on competition and productivity.

As education becomes more competitive, early childhood educators can develop a critical stance towards the overemphasis on standardized testing, particularly in schools that marginalize children from minority groups and encourage competition between children and parents. Furthermore, early childhood educators can engage in conversations to inform parents of alternative ways about engendering 'school readiness' and cultural capital without having to invest in private tuition.

Working with marginalized families and communities

In working effectively with disadvantaged and marginalized families, such as refugees and asylum seekers, it is vital that early childhood educators understand the impact of trauma and detention. In this way, they become aware of the cultural history of refugees and asylum seekers in terms of their experiences of religious, racial and cultural persecution and oppression. This can be done through researching the political, economic and cultural circumstances that bring about forced migration for many minority groups. Furthermore, early childhood educators can work with other culturally responsive support agencies in the community to provide support to families who are refugees and asylum seekers.

In order to work towards adequate representation and participation of minority groups in decision-making processes of the setting, early childhood educators need to critically examine whose voices are heard at the setting. It is imperative that minority groups are represented on parent and citizen committees, parent management committees and other parent committees. This may mean finding alternative and creative ways of seeking their participation, such as holding meetings at times that are convenient for working families; engaging in ongoing conversation with parents to gain feedback on policy and programming directions; or sending home brief surveys asking parents for comment.

Working critically with children, families, staff and the community

Early childhood educators need to engage in critical discussions and follow up experiences with children to assist them in developing a critical stance towards consumerism and competition. They can do this by providing experiences that enable children to identify, describe, compare and contrast ways in which popular culture is cross-marketed to children to encourage them to buy new products. Through these experiences they encourage children (and other staff) to think critically about how normalizing discursive representations of class, gender, 'race', ethnicity, sexuality and (dis)ability are evident in popular culture, computer and video games, children's literature, toys, films, television and advertising which target children.

Awareness of the digital divide in terms of its impact on children's access to technology in the home is fundamental. Not all children have computers at home, and opportunities to develop competence with technologies associated with computers may be limited. Further, the ever increasing gap between what children know about communication and information technologies and what their parents and teachers do not know needs to be acknowledged. However, it is also important that early childhood educators draw on children's expertise with technology, digital and popular culture, by building on the social and cultural capital that children bring to the setting. This can be done through making connections to different curriculum areas such as literacy, numeracy, technology, science and the social sciences.

Conclusion

This chapter has provided for early childhood educators a starting point for investigation of the impact of globalization on children's and adults' lives. In capitalist societies, neoliberal discourses underpin economic, political, social and cultural relations at both macro and micro levels. The economic and political agendas of globalization have produced homogenized meanings about childhood as a corporate construction in which children are specifically targeted as powerful consumers. Popular culture and digital technologies play a significant part in this process.

Furthermore, this chapter has offered a reframing of class identity in a globalized world in which inequality and life chances of children are affected by the widening divide between the working poor and the wealthy. While globalization may have some advantages in providing flexible work practices, these advantages are often denied to working-class and working poor families who bear the brunt of insecurity in employment through the increased emphasis on competition and productivity. Additionally, as governments take less responsibility for the provision of housing, health and welfare services and quality public education, children and families from disadvantaged backgrounds are most likely to suffer.

Recommended reading

Apple, M.W.A. (1999) *Power, Meaning and Identity: Essays in Critical Educational Studies*. New York: Peter Lang.
Bourdieu, P. (1998) The essence of neoliberalism. www.analitica.com/bitblioteca/bourdieu/neoliberalism.asp.
Cannella, G.S. and Kincheloe, J.L. (eds) (2002) *Kidworld, Childhood Studies, Global Perspectives, and Education*. New York: Peter Lang.
Carrington, V. (2002) *New Times, New Families*. Dordrecht: Kluwer Academic.
Marginson, S. (1999) After globalization: emerging politics of education, *Education Policy*, 14(1): 19–31.
Penn, H. (2002) The World Bank's view of early childhood. *Childhood*, 9(1): 118–132.
Steinberg, S. and Kincheloe, J. L. (1997) *Kinderculture. The Corporate Construction of Childhood*. Boulder, CO: Westview Press.
Tierney, W. (2004) Globalization and educational reform: the challenges ahead, *Journal of Hispanic Higher Education*, 3(1): 5–20.

'IT'S MORE THAN BLACK DOLLS AND BROWN PAINT':

Critical multiculturalism, whiteness
and early childhood education

Introduction

This chapter examines multiculturalism in terms of how it has informed and
shaped early childhood education. It begins with an overview of how multiculturalism has influenced Australian society in the past thirty years and
provides a critique of its limitations in challenging legitimized and institutionalized social inequalities. The discussion then moves from a perspective
of social policy on education to highlight the research and literature, which
locates current practices and pedagogies informed by multiculturalism. Then,
by drawing on frameworks of cultural studies, this chapter aims to critique
current early childhood practices with regard to their limitations in providing
equitable and innovative pedagogies. It also aims to examine 'whiteness' as a
social construction, which operates in many of the dominant cultural practices embedded in early childhood education. Further, a critique of practitioners' perceptions of children's understandings of 'race', ethnicity and
power is offered and contrasted against recent findings of research that has
engaged children in investigating their ideas about these issues. Finally, the
chapter concludes with a range of implications and strategies that can assist
practitioners in implementing contemporary pedagogies that embrace critical
approaches to multiculturalism.

Multiculturalism as policy and practice

In Australia, since the 1970s, an important social policy shift was legislated by
the Whitlam Labor government and put into effect by the then Minister for
Immigration, Al Grassby (Hollinsworth 1998; Greig *et al.* 2003). This important piece of social legislation changed many aspects of Australian life in
which there was a significant move away from assimilationist thinking that

expected all cultural and racial minority groups to take up dominant Anglo-Saxon mainstream social practices and identities; to more liberal discourses of pluralism where cultural, social, language and religious differences coexist. Within this discourse, there is tolerance and acceptance of religious, ethnic and social differences among and between groups. Therefore, in Australia, even though multiculturalism is still somewhat controversial, it is accepted as integral to Australian national and cultural identity, and, up until recently, a centrepiece of official government policy (Stratton and Ang 1998). Hence, most Australians consider themselves to live in a pluralist society where cultural and social diversity is accepted and even appreciated.

Furthermore, in Australia, multiculturalism is a social policy and embraces three significant themes relating to preserving cultural identity, attaining social inequality and maintaining social cohesion (Greig *et al.* 2003). Firstly, the emphasis on cultural identity highlights the importance of maintaining language, cultural and religious practices that pertain to individuals' sense of identity, which is in the best interests of the nation (Galbally 1978). Secondly, an emphasis on social inequality stresses access and equity for migrants in terms of employment, education, health, legal services and so on. The third theme of Australian multiculturalism is maintaining social cohesion, which emphasizes harmony between cultural and social groups, a commitment to Australia and acceptance of the basic legal structures and principles of Australian society (Office of Multicultural Affairs 1989).

These three themes of Australian multiculturalism embrace both structural and cultural pluralism (Hollinsworth 1998). Cultural pluralism pertains to the social, linguistic and cultural practices that express ethnic identity. Hollinsworth (1998) argues that cultural pluralism is overwhelmingly private inasmuch as language, religious, cultural and culinary practices are largely confined to the private space of the home or within local ethnic communities. Structural pluralism, on the other hand, refers to the public domains of the legal, educational, health, welfare and other key state institutions. Hollinsworth (1998) argues that in the public arena monoculturalism remains unchallenged, often viewing the presence of linguistic and cultural difference as a problem rather than an asset. Despite the emphasis on access and equity in the past twenty years, the interrogation of access remains confined to institutional barriers of participation rather than discursive social practices that render cultural minorities as marginal and excluded. For example, there is limited participation of cultural minority groups in the Australian media, and representations of diverse social, cultural and language practices are extremely monocultural (Jakubowicz 1994). As a result, most ethnic communities have developed their own language print media, radio, TV and video outlets and while the state has funded many of these projects through the Special Broadcasting Service (SBS), basic media laws as well as ownership and advertising regulation remain dominated by Anglo-Celtic Australians (Hollinsworth 1998).

Limits to multicultural pluralism

While cultural and structural pluralism are pertinent to the importance of cultural identity, the attainment of social equality and the maintenance of social cohesion, much of the criticism of Australian multiculturalism has centred around its inability to challenge the social, legitimized and institutional inequalities that exist based on 'difference' and the ways in which individuals can become marginalized as a result. Australia is widely perceived to be a society where power is dispersed evenly among various cultural groups, and all groups are assumed to have equal access to social, economic and political resources (Jones Díaz et al. 2001). Yet, as Kincheloe and Steinberg (1997: 15) argue, pluralism has become the mainstream articulation of multiculturalism, which 'typically links "race", gender, language, culture, disability and to a lesser degree sexual preference in the larger effort to celebrate human diversity and equal opportunity'.

Much of the criticism around pluralist multiculturalism highlights the fact that while cultural differences can be appreciated and tolerated, the structural inequalities that marginalize cultural and racial minority groups from institutional and social power are reproduced. As hooks (1997: 166) reminds us, 'evocations of pluralism and diversity act to obscure differences arbitrarily imposed and maintained by white racist domination'. While cultural pluralism embodies recognition of cultural difference, it has a limited commitment to equality of opportunities, and the frameworks for challenging the social, legitimized and institutional inequalities based on 'difference' are also limited (Kincheloe and Steinberg 1997). For example, in Australia, white, middle-class, monolingual Anglo-Saxon values and voices dominate socially, linguistically, politically, economically and educationally (Jones Díaz et al. 2001). In contrast, non-white Australians are clearly underrepresented in political, social and economic managerial class (Hage 1998). As Hage (1998: 130) comments, '[d]iversity is always assumed to be a diversity among employees, among those who need to be managed, those who need to be ruled. It is never conceived as a cultural diversity that needs to be promoted among employers, managers and rulers'.

Furthermore, in discourses of pluralist multiculturalism, identity is conceived as fixed or unchangeable, predetermined and unified. Categories of ethnicity are constructed as homogenized entities, in which social and cultural histories are silenced. Culture and identity are often conceptualized as fixed and static, emphasizing rigid boundaries of values and beliefs, language, lifestyle, religion and cultural practices (Luke and Luke 1998).

In addition, public policy on multiculturalism has made assumptions about the organic solidarity of cultures as singular coherent systems of representation and practice (Luke and Luke 1998). These assumptions are also applied to many cultural minority groups living in Australia, in which the impact of migration, neocolonialism, globalization and neoliberalism has silenced significant cultural histories and biographies of individuals. For example, the Latin American and Caribbean community in Australia is often constructed as a homogenized community. This ignores the impact of postcolonialism in terms of the relationship between Europe and its former colonies (Langer

1998), and the national, political, regional, racial, language and cultural differences between Central, Caribbean and South America. Such homogenization also dismisses the impact of 'globalized political, economic and military domination of Latin America by the USA (Jones Díaz 2003b: 319).

Whiteness and multiculturalism

Since the late 1980s and 1990s, critical work on white identity has emerged originating from the USA and Europe. In the USA white hegemony has been seriously challenged primarily due to the unequal racialized positioning of African, Asian and Latino/a Americans (Larbalestier 1999), but particularly of African Americans, in spite of their inclusion as citizens and despite discourses of liberal pluralism, which continue to discriminate against African Americans (Stratton and Ang 1998).

Sociologists as well as cultural and feminist theorists have begun to examine whiteness as a social construction, its place in the making of subjectivity and its relationship to structural institutions (Frankenberg 1997). The central aim of such work is to examine how 'white dominance is rationalized, legitimized, and made ostensibly normal and natural' (Frankenberg 1997: 3). This means that questions are raised as to how whiteness is normative and authorized in institutional policies, procedures and everyday social practice.

Therefore, critical multiculturalism interrogates the structural and subjective workings of normative whiteness as universal, homogenized and essential. Critical multiculturalists are concerned with white positionality and its relationship with 'race', class and gender inequality (Kincheloe and Steinberg 1998). Whiteness, like other racial categories and social identities, is a socio-historical construction and in this way whiteness is subject not only to political, social, economic and cultural histories but also to contemporary shifts and changes in a globalized world. Consequently, it is not a fixed, stable or biological entity, but rather, as Kincheloe and Steinberg point out, it can be invented, lived, modified and discarded.

However, there is no easy or clear-cut definition of whiteness. As an unmarked identity it constantly evades scrutiny while maintaining social privilege. It is a refusal to acknowledge white power, and those who are white are often unknowingly implicated in social relations of privilege, domination and subordination (McLaren 1998). Frankenberg (1997: 6) argues that there is fundamentally a co-constitution of whiteness and racial domination and it 'makes itself invisible precisely by asserting its normalcy, its transparency, in contrast with the marking of others on which its transparency depends'. McLaren (1998) adds that whiteness functions through normative social practices of **assimilation** and cultural homogenization. He refers to American white capitalism as the institutional means through which white people are successful at maintaining the hegemony of racial dominance.

However, in Australia, the taken-for-granted assumption about what it means to be white is evident in the media; for example, normative and singular representations of families as white, nuclear, middle-class, heterosexual and monolingual. These images imply that whiteness is normative and homogeneous. In contrast, whenever any 'other' families, or non-traditional gendered practices, are represented in the media, they are usually stereotypes. For example the 'happy' Italian family eating pasta, or the 'incompetent' husband attempting to change a baby's nappy. These stereotypes mark others as different, perpetuating a binary of the Anglo-Australians as normal, and other Australians as different. To this end, in the Australian media, discourses of normative whiteness remain unchallenged as relations of social inequality are further entrenched 'through powerful socio-political forms of racialization ... that name white as the standard and not the difference, and classify all that which is not white as different and other' (Luke 1994: 53).

Yet, there are many ways to be white and the intersections between whiteness and other social identities such as class, gender, sexuality and age bring about different subjective locations and 'lived experiences'. According to Frankenberg (1993: 233), 'whiteness, masculinity, and femininity are co-producers of one another, in ways that are, in their turn, crosscut by class and by the histories of racism and colonialism'. A clear example of how whiteness intersects with other social identities is apparent in emerging research into white women's experiences in interracial couples where class, gender, sexuality and 'race' foreground everyday social relations and practices (see, for example, Frankenberg 1993; Luke 1994; Reddy 1994). Luke (1994) reports on published work on interracial families, interracial children and white women's experiences of living in 'mixed' families. She argues that white women in interracial families negotiate gender and sexuality, but are marked with 'race' in their unique experiences of racism by association with persons of colour.

Clearly for white women whose are intimately shaped by 'race' and racism, there is both significant conscious and unconscious awareness of racial inequality experienced through shifting histories of racism and varying material relations constructed by 'race' (Frankenberg 1993). However, for white women, while their whiteness renders them as invisible and unmarked, in reality, through their association with their children and/or partners of colour, issues of 'race' foreground their daily social practices and relationships, power relations and material well being.

As a white woman living in an interracial family, I (Jones Díaz) share experiences of whiteness and racializing practices similar to those described by Luke (1994) and Frankenberg (1993) and the women in their studies. I have often observed my brown-skinned children being overtly scrutinized by shopkeepers to ensure that nothing is stolen. My partner has experienced countless instances of police surveillance while driving in Sydney. During the normal course of daily events, he has been stopped and asked to show personal identification for no apparent reason.

Collins (1990) suggests white women often become the 'front runners' and cultural and racial brokers as 'their identities change from being insiders within their own dominant culture to becoming an "outsider within"' (quoted in Luke 1994: 59). Consequently, my 'in-between' status positions me as the 'front runner' and 'cultural broker' of the family. Bank tellers, government officials, school personnel, doctors, work colleagues and so on, look directly at me, and occasionally glance uncomfortably at my partner, to merely acknowledge his existence. Some have even refused to include my partner in negotiations or transactions. Hence, my negotiation of the insider/outsider nexus is evident in the ways in which my partner and I tenuously deal with these daily encounters. The disapproving looks, glances and ambiguous body language are all just part of the everyday politics of racializing practices that we experience. These strenuous relationships are more often than not constructed within and contextualized against markers of 'race', language and gendered power relations within normalizing discourses of whiteness.

Whiteness and Indigeneity

In Australia, compared to the USA and the UK, there is little scholarly work that has scrutinized whiteness as an unmarked racial category (Larbalestier 1999). However, it was not until Federation in 1901 that whiteness became the official defining racial marker of the Australian nation (Hollinsworth 1998). This is not to suggest that Australia was devoid of racism and racializing practices prior to Federation. On the contrary, Australia's colonial past is rooted in Eurocentric constructions of white supremacy and authorized racism.

The Immigration Restriction Act of 1901 (more commonly known as the White Australia Policy) aimed to restrict non-European immigration and deported immigrants already residing in Australia. For example, many Pacific Islanders and Asians were denied citizenship and deported back to their countries of origin despite having spent many years in Australia working as labourers in the sugar cane and other industries (Hollinsworth 1998). Apart from the fact that this act banned all 'coloured' immigration to Australia, it also excluded Indigenous Australians from citizenship (Greig *et al.* 2003). In this context, racism and nationalism were almost synonymous (Hollinsworth 1998), and constituted in the White Australia Policy. Consequently, in the history of white Australian politics there is a limited view of whiteness as ethnic dynamic, or 'whites' as a racialized group (Singh 2000).

The establishment of missions and reserves, the denial of civic rights and forced removal of children, the control of property, illicit sexual relations, exclusion from schools, swimming pools and other community services, and the exploitation of their labour are just some examples of institutional racism directed at Indigenous Australians. Inscribed and rooted in this history, Australian national identity and constructions of 'race' have aimed at enforcing and policing the marginalization of Indigenous Australians since colonization.

Australia's racialized colonial past has seen social, political, economic and historical domination and oppression of Indigenous communities. For example, European colonization and authorized assimilation have left legacies of dispossession, forced removal, economic and educational disadvantage, language death, high mortality and poor health. Yet, this is barely acknowledged in discourses of multicultural pluralism. Indeed, as Singh (2002a: 225) reminds us, 'Australia has yet to name, let alone initiate, the long project of unlearning and dismantling White Australia politics'. Through this unlearning there is the fundamental recognition that 'race' is constituted in a dynamic set of social relations and is not a stable category but rather contingent on historical, social, institutional and discursive practices (Apple 1999). Such practices are implicit in the relations between Indigenous and non-Indigenous people.

Yet in multicultural pluralism there are tensions and silences in national ideals of cultural diversity in terms of how Indigeneity is addressed. Curthoys (1999: 286) argues that multicultural pluralism subsumes issues of Indigeneity, which has brought about an uneasy tension and silence as Indigenous Australians have 'protested against being incorporated within the "multicultural" and seen as just one ethnicity among many'. As Curthoys reminds us, Indigenous people have stressed that their situation is different from that of immigrant Australians (including Anglo-Australians). Their indigeneity to the Australian landscape has meant a special and unique relationship to the land. Like all Indigenous peoples around the world, Indigenous Australians rightfully demand recognition of their unique status as original owners of the land dispossessed by conquest (Moodley 1999). Yet dispossession and institutionalized racism inflicted upon them have meant that the social, cultural and political histories of Indigenous Australians are central to the construction of Indigenous identities in their everyday realities of racism in Australia (Robinson and Jones Díaz 2000).

Within this tension between pluralist multiculturalism and Aboriginality, there are unanswered questions about the relationship between whiteness and Indigeneity. As May (1999) points out, this tendency to ignore Indigenous voices and concerns is evident in the debates on multiculturalism in Canadian, North American, Australian and New Zealand literature. To this end, it is imperative that examinations of whiteness in multicultural societies acknowledge the complexities of the historically and politically situated specificity of racism as experienced differently by Indigenous peoples from those of immigrant backgrounds.

Ashcroft (2001: 25) argues that 'post-colonial discourses reveal the extent to which the historical condition of colonisation has led to a certain political, intellectual and creative dynamic in the post-colonial societies with which it engages'. Drawing from postcolonial perspectives to examine whiteness is one way of conceptualizing the political and historical specificity of Indigenous Australians. Further, Young (1990) argues that a new politics of difference gives rise to understandings about how modes of thinking and ways of being are constituted within European constructs. For example, social Darwinism, the prevailing European scientific discourse of the late nineteenth century, was obsessed with categorizing and classifying people into racial typologies, which asserted white supremacy based on Eurocentric assumptions that being civilized was Christian, white and European. Further, the eugenics movement that followed (which is based on the perceived inferiority of the 'unfit', poor and Irish), from the 1840s onwards, set about constructing a theory of 'race' aimed at enforcing and policing the differences between Europeans and non-Europeans. Hence, social Darwinism which justified a scientific racism was used by colonizing British and European interests as a convenient and suitable justification for the dispossession of land, slavery, rape, disease and the erosion of languages and cultures, which engendered a theory and practice of human inequality (Young 1995).

Multiculturalism and early childhood education

In early childhood education, pedagogical approaches to cultural, racial and social difference have been informed by broader social and political processes, based on normative understandings of socio-cultural difference. The broader social frameworks of liberal pluralism influence most pedagogical approaches to difference, such as multiculturalism and anti-bias. This is evident in Australian education during the 1970s and 1980s. Multicultural education centred around teaching children about other cultures in an attempt to combat racial prejudice and stereotypes, in order to dispel ignorance which was seen to be the root of intolerance and prejudice (Rizvi 1993). Multicultural models conceptualized intolerance as 'basically as a matter of attitudes, and [were] said to be constituted by prejudice' (Rattansi 1992: 25). This approach most often translated into a tokenistic and superficial respect for cultural differences where cultural and linguistic differences were highly trivialized and manifested into what Castles *et al.* (1988) termed 'spaghetti and polka' understandings about cultural difference, more commonly known to early childhood staff as the 'tourist approach' (Derman-Sparks and the A.B.C. Task Force 1989).

The anti-bias curriculum, primarily developed by Derman-Sparks and the A.B.C. Task Force (1989), was introduced into Australia in the late 1980s and at the time was seen as an innovative pedagogy that aimed to avoid superficial and 'touristic' approaches through everyday and realistic representations of cultural diversity, and was incorporated throughout the curriculum (Hopson 1990; Derman-Sparks and the A.B.C. Task Force 1989; Green 1996). Both multicultural and anti-bias education aim to develop children's positive attitudes towards diversity, through the reflection and acknowledgement of socio-cultural difference, and therefore explanations about difference are often couched in terms of 'celebration' and 'tolerance', harmony and pluralism. Moreover, anti-bias approaches were also seen to provide effective ways of including all types of differences, whether they be racialized, gendered or classed. However, in its attempts to incorporate the complexity of diversity that is presented in early childhood settings, it has relied upon 'add on' conceptual models, which package difference and diversity into fixed social boundaries where notions of double or triple oppressions apply.

'Add on' models of diversity construct difference in linear and hierarchical modes of priority in which strategies of intervention with children around critical issues of equity are confined to what staff perceive as visible differences. This was evident in research conducted by Robinson and Jones Díaz (2000: 100) who investigated staff attitudes, policy and practices with regard to diversity and difference. In their survey of 49 practitioners, they found that in settings with proportionately high levels of children attending from diverse language and cultural groups, there was greater focus on visible difference than when there were less obvious physical differences – for example, children from gay and lesbian families and children appearing 'white' from Indigenous backgrounds. Furthermore, 'add on' models of diversity construct children from socio-cultural minorities as victims of double or triple disadvantage. For example, children from ethnic or racial minorities with disabilities suffer from double disadvantage, and black women suffer from the 'triple oppression' of 'race', class and gender (Anthias and Yuval-Davis 1991; Pettman 1992). In this regard, 'race', gender, ethnicity, class, disability, sexuality and age cannot be tagged mechanically without recognizing how the complexities of social identities are contextually produced and located at the intersections of ethnicized, racialized, sexualized and gendered discourses and discursive practices. As Rattansi (1992) points out, racialized discourses and encounters are suffused with elements of sexual and class difference and dispersed around different axes and identities. Racialized, ethnic and gendered discourses are contradictory and ambivalent in character, and thus produce a multiplicity of subject positions and discourses.

Consequently anti-bias education has yet to fully acknowledge the inter-relationships between social categories and difference in relation to how young children are actively involved in the construction of their own identities and subjectivities. Further, when tolerance and acceptance of difference are emphasized at the expense of critiquing the relationships between difference, power and inequity, our capacity to work towards a pedagogical agenda that addresses the various social inequities based on 'difference' is limited.

As a result, socio-cultural, political and economic inequities based on difference rarely become focal points from which to discuss the principles and goals of anti-bias and multicultural education. Explanations of and conversations about social inequalities with children are limited because interpretations do not go beyond descriptions of particular circumstances and are often confined to staff understandings of children's developmental stages of growth and development. As one respondent commented, 'If issues are dealt with positively and appropriately to children's development, they will understand some issues and have a positive basis for the future' (Robinson and Jones Díaz 2000: 114).

Liberal pluralism in early childhood education

In recent years, in early childhood education, 'diversity' has tended to replace 'multiculturalism' as a popular term for the coexistence of social, cultural and class differences that exist in society. Paralleling the broader social contexts of liberal pluralism, diversity in early childhood education has largely empha-sized tolerance and acceptance of difference, despite pedagogy that has been inherently embedded in monocultural and monolingual Anglo-Australian cultural practices, which until recently have remained unchallenged. From this perspective the term 'diversity' used alone is insufficient in analysing issues related to inequality.

Furthermore, simplistic pluralistic notions about diversity do not give caregivers and teachers the necessary conceptual tools for analysing and understanding how inequalities are constructed and perpetuated by indivi-duals, social groups and social structures. This is particularly significant to the field of early childhood education since the relationships between people, the learning experiences of children and the management practices that operate within it are crucially linked to broader societal processes, policies and practices. Apple (1999) argues that schools (and early childhood settings) are not separate from the political and moral realities of broader society, but are indeed embedded in them. He also points out that any separation between the politics of education and the politics of society is artificial since education is a crucial part of the larger society. He emphasizes that education is precisely the social field where possibilities of critique and interrogation of social inequality are more likely to be explored.

This tendency to separate education from broader societal realities was evident in our research. In this study, there was less attention to and concern for the impact of discrimination, racism and inequality operating in society and in children's and families' lives. Hence, ways in which individuals are marginalized as a result of inequality seemed poorly understood. For example, few respondents acknowledged adults' and children's experiences with racial inequality. While just over half of the respondents did agree that cultural diversity, difference and power were worth critically raising with children, few connections were made between structural inequalities, discrimination and critical thinking.

Furthermore, while many participants expressed positive views about the importance of raising Indigenous issues with children, just under half acknowledged that Indigenous people experience stereotyping and racism. Only a few respondents recognized the possibility that children from Indi-genous backgrounds had experienced discrimination from children, staff and families at their setting. Moreover, this contradiction in respondents' views was also evident in issues associated with children's experiences of racial discrimination and inequality. Respondents ranked children's experiences with discrimination at the lower ends of the scale, perhaps indicating that practitioners' awareness of children's experiences with inequality and dis-crimination is limited. It follows, then, that in this study, educators were largely unaware of the broader socio-political inequities that are prevalent in our society, particularly with regard to how discrimination and racism implicitly and discursively impact on children in their daily lives.

Whiteness and mainstream early childhood curricula

In early childhood education, the predominance of child development theories informed by developmental psychology has had a powerful and significant influence on policy, pedagogy and practice. Understandings about how children learn through growth and development according to specific and predetermined ages and stages are assumed to apply universally to all young children (Cannella 1997). Assumptions about children's learning are principally informed by the work of Jean Piaget (1964, 1968) who emphasized that children's ability to learn depended on their ability to pass through stages of cognitive, linguistic, social, emotional, moral and physical development. Such universalizing approaches to children are highly problematic because they deny the varied and multiple realities of children's lives (Silin 1995).

The fact that children's lives are mediated and constructed within social structures and cultural and discursive practices, bounded by national, regional, economic, political and globalized realities, is denied through the early childhood field's preoccupation with developmental psychology. Indeed, as argued by James *et al.* (1998), developmental psychology capitalizes on unexamined assumptions that view children as natural rather than social phenomena in which this naturalness is embedded in inevitable processes of maturation. Further, discourses of developmentalism are largely informed through middle-class Eurocentric perspectives that promote a singular and linear view of childhood, based on **biological determinism**, with limited regard for the broader socio-cultural contexts which influence learning (Alloway 1997; Jones Díaz and Robinson 2000). Cannella (1997) describes how developmental psychology has consistently paralleled assumptions of children as underdeveloped, irrational and savage to anthropological studies of colonized people as 'primitive' to maintain Eurocentric beliefs of white supremacy. In this sense, developmental psychology colludes with discourses of whiteness through its preoccupation with objective Western science, emphasizing rationality, reason and objectivity.

As Kincheloe and Steinberg (1997: 209) point out, rationalistic modernist whiteness has been shaped by its association with science and the disciplines of psychology and educational psychology. They argue that science constructs and privileges 'mind over body, intellectual over experiential ways of knowing, mental abstractions over passion, bodily sensations and tactile understanding'. Since developmental psychology emerged from the Enlightenment, post-Enlightenment/modernist eras of rational and scientific thought, a view of human beings as rational, objective and individual has emerged (Grieshaber 2001). This view is largely a European and white discourse emanating from the nineteenth and twentieth centuries following the rapid and aggressive European colonization of the world (Hollinsworth 1998). Hence, by the end of the twentieth century, meanings about whiteness representing objectivity and masculinity as the highest expression of white achievement still inform everyday social relations (Kincheloe and Steinberg 1998).

From this standpoint, developmental psychology, aligned with science and preoccupied with reason and rationality, is evident in the grand narratives of theories of child development, which have also informed early childhood understandings of identity as hierarchical, linear and chronological. Identity formation is often understood as a developmentally fixed end product. These understandings, when applied to children from diverse socio-cultural communities, deny the multiplicity and often contradictory realities of social and cultural practice from which children's identities are mediated, transformed and negotiated.

Bhabha (1994, 1998) and Spivak (1999), drawing on the work of Hall (1992, 1996) in relation to identity negotiation, point out that identity is not a fixed end product but rather fluid and transformative, which is always subjected to the 'play of difference' (Hall 1996). This 'play of difference' is socially constructed through the social contexts in which people are situated that in turn influence and shape their identity. As Papastergiadis (1998: 2) reminds us, 'identity is no longer perceived as natural, exclusive or fixed. It is always formed in relation to others'. It is in this relationship to others that children, like adults experience their identity in multiple and often contradictory ways. Hence, they are often marginalized and othered due to their difference.

Processes of othering are apparent in the many discursive representations of Indigenous and non-white Australians apparent in young children's thinking about Aboriginality. This was evident in research conducted by MacNaughton and Davis (2001). Their findings concluded that representations and constructions of Aboriginality expressed traces of colonial othering, defining Aboriginal people through 'their' difference from 'us'. Additionally, their findings revealed that educators' use of resources and curriculum practices was predominately confined to ceremonial and traditional representations of Aboriginality.

Practitioners' responses to children's understandings of 'race', ethnicity and cultural difference

In our research it was clear that while many educators held positive views and attitudes towards the importance of multicultural and anti-racist education, their perceptions of children's experiences of and understandings about 'race', ethnicity and cultural difference appeared to be under-acknowledged. For example, just over half of the respondents claimed that children do not understand Indigenous issues, exemplified by statements such as 'I think that children in the nursery room are too young to be aware'. There appeared to be more emphasis placed on children developing healthy self-esteem and cultural identity than on children's understanding of Indigenous issues, racism and power. Yet, children's capacity to locate themselves in racializing discursive practices ultimately affects their own thinking about themselves. Rizvi (1993) reminds us that children's constructions of 'race' are inherently connected to the broader discursive practices and social relations in which racism is produced in Australian society.

Furthermore, many educators commented that children's ability to understand issues of 'race', ethnicity and cultural difference is largely based on difference in physical, language and cultural practice, as highlighted in the following comment: 'Children realize that children look different but do not fully understand the issues of race and cultural identities as this is an "internal" aspect of multiculturalism'. This assumption that children's understandings are limited to the physical and obvious aspects of racial and ethnic difference denies children's lived experiences of living in families and communities that are affected by normative discourses of whiteness and racializing practices.

Assumed absences and invisible identities

Moreover, assumptions about children's daily interactions and direct experiences with Indigeneity were confined to the adult's knowledge of children at the setting rather than their knowledge of children's experiences outside the setting, in their community or home contexts. Many of the respondents' comments were drawn from their observations of children at the setting based on an assumed absence of Indigenous families and children attending the setting. There were many comments that Indigenous issues were only relevant when there were Indigenous children attending the setting:

> If the children [were] in my group, I would actively incorporate this area into planning and programming but because they aren't [in my group], I only sometimes cover this.

> . . . there are no Aboriginal families in our setting but if there were, then that would be important.

> There are no Aboriginal children at our setting.

> No specific issues related to Aboriginality in [our] setting.

> This is not the majority background at our centre, so it is not incorporated actively.

> We have not got children who belong to Aboriginal and Torres Strait Islander [communities].

> Again, considering all the other 'issues' that we would be incorporating into our daily practice . . ., [it is] not possible to do it [Aboriginal perspectives] all the time.

This assumed absence that there are no Indigenous families and children attending the setting is problematic, particularly since some Aboriginal people appear to be white, or Anglo-Australian. Due to this, their lived realities and experiences of Aboriginality and racism are constantly denied and therefore perceived as not relevant to children's lives. It appears that Indigenous issues were only seen relevant when children and families from 'visible' Indigenous backgrounds were attending the setting. Further, through this denial there are other assumptions that children who do not have

Aboriginal parents also do not have other family members, friends, connections or experiences with Indigeneity.

Children's experiences of whiteness, racism and inequality

Only in recent years in early childhood education has research drawing on postcolonial frameworks and cultural studies been conducted. Such research investigates the crucial relationship between the 'social' and the 'individual' in the social construction of subjectivity and identity in discourse. This research spans a range of areas, including children's interpretations of media representations of 'race' (Tobin 2000), children's writing and representation of 'race' (Kaomea 2000), Anglo-Australian children's understandings of Indigenous Australians (MacNaughton and Davis 2001) and children's negotiation of language and identity in early childhood primary and community based settings (Jones Díaz 2005). Yet within much of this research the voices of children and their experiences of 'race' and whiteness are not the primary focus. Rather, the emphasis is on children's negotiations and responses to racialized, sexualized and gendered discourses. Indeed, there is little research into how children of colour experience 'race' and racializing practices of normative whiteness. Further, the recommendations from the findings of our research suggest that further work needs to be undertaken in order to investigate children's voices as they negotiate aspects of identity and power relations in everyday social practices in early childhood settings.

It is crucial that educators gain contemporary insights into the various ways in which young children negotiate racialized identities within a context of whiteness and dominant early childhood curriculum frameworks. Further, dominant conceptual frameworks that inform early childhood educators in their approach to diversity and difference need to incorporate the voices and experiences of children as they mediate their emerging identities across the various social fields of their daily life, including home and community contexts. With regard to interracial children, their unique experiences of negotiating visible whiteness and meanings of 'race' in their daily lives are unknown to educators (and to some of their parents). The extract below is an attempt to highlight the significance of children's voices in attempting to draw attention to real (and imagined) effects of whiteness for a child from an interracial family. It is based on data from research currently being undertaken by Jones Díaz (2005) in an investigation of language retention and identity in bilingual children and their families.

Rubie and Martín: a case study

The following narrative illustrates an experience I (Jones Díaz) had with my son around issues of 'race' and whiteness and his relationships with other children. As a white mother of Afro-Latino Australian bilingual boys, whose father is an Afro-Latino immigrant from the Caribbean, issues of language and 'race' emerge on a daily basis and form part of the ambience of everyday lived experience in my family. We also have many conversations about 'race', gender and sexuality.

Martín (pseudonym) is 9 years old and attends a primary school situated in the Inner West of Sydney. The families of the children range from disadvantaged working-class to upwardly mobile double-income middle-class professional families. Hence the diversity of class, cultural, racial and linguistic representations at this school is characteristic of many Inner West schools in multicultural Sydney.

Martín has often expressed a liking for a girl in his class. He tells me about his plans to 'get Rubie (pseudonym) to talk to me', 'to get Rubie to sit next to me' and, more importantly, 'to get Rubie to play with me'. However, Martín's progress with Rubie has not gone according to plan. One day, Martín arrives home from school, enters the room in which I am working, and hurls himself down on the chair, sighing:

> Martín: Mummy, I don't want to be brown anymore.
> Criss: Uhh, why not?
> Martín: I'm sick of being brown, it's not working. I can't attract Rubie's attention, and anyway she likes Joseph more than me.
> Criss: Joseph? But isn't that because they are friends outside of school?
> Martín: Yeah, but he's white and Rubie's white and she talks to him a lot.
> Criss: (a long pause of silence and hesitation) But, but ... oh maybe, you know that, you know that, you have beautiful brown skin and oh, Martín, when you say that you don't want to be brown anymore, that really upsets me. I get really sad.
> Martín: But it's true.
> Criss: Yeah but there are lots of black and brown kids in your class and you are not the only one.
> Martín: Yeah but Joseph isn't black and Rubie is starting to like him more than me.

Conversations like the above are not unusual in my family. There are always ambiguities and uncertainties around such issues in which racialized and heteronormative discursive practices arise. However, my subjective realities of being white and living in a black family bring into question my own shifting and transformative location in 'whiteness'. For my family, 'whiteness' is always interrogated and visible, yet, its shifting, contradictory and transparent character with regard to the interplay of the day-to-day social and power relations and experiences is highly ambiguous and often difficult to locate.

My response 'but there are lots of black kids in your class and you are not the only one' could be an attempt to diffuse his concern perhaps (perhaps due to my perceived limitations during the course of this conversation to deal with the power of normative whiteness and racializing discourses in Martín's life). Yet, for Martín it is not about how many other children in his class are black or brown.

Later, Criss asks Martín:

Criss: Martín, can I ask you a question about the Joseph thing and sitting next to Rubie?
Martín: What?
Criss: If Joseph was black or brown, would it still worry you that he gets to sit next to Rubie?
Martín: No.

Martín's firm response to my question is undeniably clear as he perceives Joseph (pseudonym) to have a structural, spacial and temporal advantage of sitting next to Rubie. The structural mechanisms operating here appear to be beyond his control, and for Martín his capacity to access Rubie is dented by his fear that perhaps Joseph's cultural capital accumulated in his whiteness will ultimately prevail. This is even more aggravated due to the spacial and temporal set-up of the seating arrangements in this classroom.[1] While Joseph is in the right place at the right time, his whiteness gives him additional symbolic advantage, despite being among a racially diverse group of children, where he is potentially in the minority: 'yeah but Joseph isn't black and Rubie is starting to like him more than me'.

Towards critical multiculturalism in early childhood education: implications for practice

The extract above raises issues for educators in their work with young children particularly from interracial families but also generally for all children who grapple with conflicting and fluid experiences of identity construction. Critical multiculturalism offers educators a lens through which to interrogate normative practices constituted in discourses of whiteness from a critical standpoint. A recognition of and willingness to interrogate how culture is connected to the discursive frameworks of power and inequality (Giroux 1997) are an effective starting point for educators. This requires educators to recognize that 'pedagogical and institutional practices produce, codify and rewrite disciplinary practices, values and social identities in relation to, rather than outside of, the discourse of history, power and privilege' (Giroux 1992: 9). In this sense, educators need to acknowledge that their contribution in reproducing educational practices in their setting is directly connected to broader social, political, historical and cultural frameworks that influence their work with children and the families with whom they interact.

Going beyond culture as 'celebration'

To this end, early childhood educators are in a position to critically recognize the limitations of multicultural pluralism, which is confined to the celebratory and superficial, and where understandings of identity are fixed. Rather, there needs to be a recognition and appreciation that cultural identities are not fixed in tradition, but are fluid and multiple, and constantly being rearticulated in the modern world (May 1999). Within this context, educators are able to go beyond simplistic understandings of diversity as 'tolerance' and culture as 'celebration', and recognize that cultural differences and ethnicities are situated within a particular place in time that involves cultural experiences that are not necessarily fixed and contained by that experience (Hall 1992).

It is crucial that educators acknowledge the 'multiple, contradictory, and complex subject positions people occupy within different social, cultural, and economic locations' (Giroux 1992: 21). So, rather than constructing children, whose identities are intersected by issues of 'race', class, gender or sexuality, as victims of double or triple oppression, it is more useful to understand how their subjectivities and identities are shaped and mediated against a backdrop of intersecting, often conflicting and multiple discursive identities constructed through discourses of femininity, masculinity, heterosexuality, whiteness and class.

Therefore, the challenges that critical multiculturalism presents to early childhood educators call for new ideas and pedagogical strategies that are capable of constructing a politics of difference that will extend the potential of a cultural democracy (Giroux 1992). New ideas and strategies informed by 'frameworks from post-colonial theory, black theory, cultural studies, critical theory and pedagogy disclose the workings of pedagogies of whiteness: the unspoken learnings and teachings surrounding race and ethnicity' (Rhedding-Jones 2001: 144–145). In practice this means that educators are prepared to recognize the significance of providing opportunities for children to engage in critical thinking or argument in the context of difference, inequalities and power relationships. To do this effectively, educators need to observe children taking up subject positions in discourses of whiteness in order to fully appreciate the complexities and contradictory positions through which many children are positioned.

Adopting a reflexive stance towards cultural and racial differences

These careful observations require early childhood educators to adopt a reflexive and critical stance towards their work with children and their relationships with families and local communities. As Kincheloe and Steinberg (1998) argue, critical multiculturalism draws on traditions of critical pedagogy to analyse the construction of the 'self', in particular the white 'self'. Central in this process is a willingness to engage in the reflexive process of deconstructing whiteness and decentring normalizing practices that privilege white dominance as normal and natural.

Consequently, this process involves a willingness to reflect on preconceived and unexamined discourses of whiteness that operate in institutional policies, procedures and everyday social practices authorized in early childhood settings (and in the community). For example, in early childhood education, educators have many opportunities to reflect on how the routines undertaken in daily practice are directly informed by dominant white Anglo-Australian cultural practices, such as sleeping, eating, feeding, toileting, reading and speaking. As a result, educators need to decentre their location in discourses that pathologize difference as abnormal or deficit, as well as acknowledge and incorporate differences in child-rearing, family and language practices that are represented by the families and children attending the setting.

Spivak (1990, quoted in hooks 1997: 178) points out that 'the holders of hegemonic discourses should de-hegemonize their position and themselves learn how to occupy the subject position of the other'. This is a critical message for early childhood educators. Learning to occupy the subject position of the Other requires educators to locate their own subjectivity to examine how 'the knowledge or "truths" one holds about the world and the ... power one experiences ... in different contexts, are all constituted in discourse' (Robinson and Jones Díaz 1999: 35). This requires white educators to locate their own 'whiteness' as an unmarked identity of invisibility and transparency, particularly with regard to how they are located in discourses of whiteness, which have inscribed much of the collective memories, histories, use of language and cultural practices of Indigenous communities and non-white Australians.

Conclusion

This chapter has examined multiculturalism and constructions of whiteness from a critical perspective to examine how they inform and shape early childhood education. In particular, discourses of multicultural pluralism have been examined to reveal their limitations in challenging racialized and unequal power relations that exist in multicultural diverse societies. The dominant curriculum and pedagogies informed by developmental psychology have also been examined to illustrate the relationship between developmental psychology and discourses of whiteness in early childhood education. Moreover, this chapter has discussed early childhood educators' perceptions of how children understand and experience 'race', ethnicity and power relations. By drawing on recent research into young children's experiences of 'race', the arguments raised highlight the need for further work in this area. The chapter concludes with a range of implications that can assist educators in moving towards a more critical approach drawing on contemporary pedagogies that embrace critical approaches to multiculturalism.

Note

1. In Australia, primary schools with composite classes will often combine children from two year levels. In Martín's class, there are year 2 and year 3 children and the seating arrangements are devised by the teacher. According to Martín, when the children are working at their tables they are assigned to particular areas of the room in which year 2 and year 3 children do not sit together. Consequently, part of Martín's frustration is related to the teacher's seating arrangement and hence his inability to sit closer to Rubie.

Recommended reading

Apple, M.W.A. (1999) *Power, Meaning and Identity: Essays in Critical Educational Studies*. New York: Peter Lang.

Hall, S. (1996) Introduction: who needs 'identity'?, in P. Du Guy (ed.) *Questions of Cultural Identity*. London: Sage Publications.

Kincheloe, J.L. and Steinberg, S.R. (1997) *Changing Multiculturalism*. Buckingham: Open University Press.

Singh, M.G. (2000) Review essay. Changing uses of multiculturalism: Asian-Australian engagement with white Australia politics, *Australian Educational Researcher*, 27(1): 115–130.

FAMILIES AS PERFORMATIVE SOCIAL SPACES:

Reconceptualizing the family for social justice

Introduction

'Family' is a powerful and pervasive word in our culture and represents a highly unstable and contradictory space, in which an individual's sense of belonging and identity can be affirmed on the one hand, or dismissed and denied on the other. Thus, 'family' is a contentious space, which encompasses a variety of social, cultural, economic and symbolic meanings, that shift across socio-economic class, ethnicity, gender, 'race', age and sexuality. How we 'do' family, define families, live in families, and who we live in them with, are all highly contested issues. Despite the diversity in how we 'do' family, normalizing discourses of the traditional nuclear family (that is, heterosexual, married, monogamous, mother and father with children) continue to underpin dominant representations of appropriate and successful family life. This discourse of the nuclear family, which tends to encompass Western, white, middle-class, Christian values and morals, impacts on the way that non-nuclear or Other families are often perceived and judged. For example, the perceived breakdown in social and community values in recent times is often equated to a loss of traditional family values inherent in the nuclear family due to the emergence of Other families considered not to reflect or uphold such values. Rather than embracing the diversity of family that exists, different families, particularly gay- and lesbian-headed families and single parents, are frequently viewed as social problems, destabilizing the foundations of strong and moral family life and social values (Carrington 2002). There is widespread agreement that society is undergoing a process of rapid and radical economic, political, legal and social change, but the political rhetoric of the times, influenced by neoconservative values, upholds that the family should remain unchanged (Silva and Smart 1999). Thus, the traditional nuclear family is often mythically linked to a false expectation that it is the 'natural' foundation of a stable, safe and economically vibrant society and has shifted 'from being a particular family shape to becoming a prescriptive recipe for living' (Carrington 2002: 8).

The field of early childhood education (as well as other educational social institutions) perpetuates the dominant discursive values and practices that operate in the broader society. Thus, despite recognition of the need to encompass family diversity, primarily based on the philosophical position that family is critical to children's positive and successful educational experiences, practices in the early childhood education field still largely represent and perpetuate normal family relations within the discourse of the white, middle-class, heterosexual nuclear family. Consequently, the values and perspectives of different families tend to be othered, marginalized and silenced, rarely receiving the official institutional validation given to the nuclear family.

Consequently, in this chapter it is argued that in order to acknowledge both the rapidly changing nature of family life and the diversity that exists, it is critical that understandings and representations of family shift away from universalized prescribed structures that normalize the nuclear family and exclude others. The nuclear family, although it may be the most prevalent in Western societies, is but one of many different types of family living practices that occur in society. Therefore, incorporating a feminist poststructuralist framework, we argue that it is more useful and inclusive to begin to reconceptualize families as multiple discursive performative social spaces that are fluid and changing across and within different cultural contexts over time. Further, recognizing different family relations in terms of 'localized networks of choice' (Carrington 2002: 140) acknowledges the agency that individual subjects have in making family networks, rather than being perceived to just passively inherit them.

This chapter on family examines a number of critical issues that pose significant challenges for the ways in which early childhood education and educators understand, represent, embrace and include family diversity in their policies, programming and practices. These issues include: perceptions of family; the need to reconceptualize family in order to be more inclusive of diversity and difference; current social, political and economic impacts on doing family; prominent social theoretical understandings of the role of family in society; social constructions of motherhood and fatherhood; families of choice; the impact of globalization on family relations; and the social construction of childhood and the position of children in families. The chapter concludes by highlighting the implications that these issues have for early childhood education.

What is a family?

What seems to be on the surface a rather simple question, 'What is a family?', is far more complex than perhaps many of us would first imagine. As pointed out, this is a highly political and controversial question, where opinions are diverse and contradictory, based on vastly different personal experiences of being in families, or indeed not being in families. Official and social definitions of family can vary greatly according to legal, cultural and religious influences and often exclude many people's 'realities' of family life. This exclusion and lack of recognition can have significant social and economic implications for those individuals living in families that do not 'fit' the discourses of family that are socially sanctioned. For example, the discourse of the single-parent family is primarily one of deficit and dysfunction, in which children's experiences are often viewed as lacking as a result of the absence of the influence of either a mother or father. Consequently, any 'problems' experienced with children from single-parent families are often attributed in the first instance to their perceived dysfunctional family life.

Generally, the family is perceived to be fixed in that it is constructed as a 'natural' expression of human biological relationships. This perception is encompassed within the dominant discourse of family in Western society, represented in the narrative of the nuclear family. Through this discourse, the nuclear family is privileged and normalized through the official stamp of support that it receives from other social institutions such as the church, the law, government and education. It is represented as the social norm and as the only natural, normal and successful family relationship. This normalizing discourse of the nuclear family permeates all aspects of everyday life through individual interactions and institutional practices. Western cultural celebrations around 'Mothers' day' and 'Fathers' day' continue to reinforce the importance of nuclear family relations, despite the complexities around such relationships in many children's lives due to family breakdowns and new family reconfigurations.

In Australia today, the nuclear family makes up approximately 71 per cent of all family types, with the remaining 28 per cent made up of single-parent families (22 per cent) and stepparent or blended families (7 per cent) (Australian Bureau of Statistics 2003). These figures are similar to those found in other Western countries. Interestingly, same-sex families are not recognized as a category within national census data collections on family relationships in Australia, but they make up a significant portion of family types. In the United States it is estimated that 6–10 million children have lesbian or gay parents (Mercier and Harold 2003: 35). The Australian Bureau of Statistics figures above also make it difficult to consider the prevalence of extended family relationships. Consequently, official numerical representations of family do not necessary provide an accurate or 'real' picture of the way family is practised or experienced. However, what these figures do demonstrate is that a large and growing number of families do not fit into the normalizing discourse of the nuclear family. In fact, single-parent families are increasing significantly, primarily as a result of marriage breakdowns in Western societies. There may be greater tolerance for single-parent families on one level in society today, but there is still a sense of silence that operates around their 'private' circumstances that works to exclude them on another level. As pointed out previously, the discourse that constitutes these families as somehow deficient and dysfunctional continues to marginalize them in society.

In answering the question what is a family, it is critical to highlight that there is no one universal way of doing family, despite the prevalence of the normalizing discourse of the nuclear family. How individuals define family and do family is a very subjective process. Personal experiences of growing up in families, what Bourdieu (1990, 1993) calls family habitus, have a fundamental impact on how individuals view family, what they think families should be, and how they do family relations in their own lives. Ultimately, individual subjects' perceptions and practices of family are constituted within the discourses of family that are culturally available to them; this point is taken up further in the next section. Silva and Smart (1999: 4) point out that 'although there is a numerical dominance in the form of two-parent families, this structure no longer defines so exclusively what it is like to live in a family, or what a family *is*'. The increasing diversity of how individuals choose to do family life today is undeniable.

Reconceptualizing family as performative social spaces: a feminist poststructuralist perspective

Feminist poststructuralism, which informs our discussion in this chapter, highlights a very different way of looking at family and is critical of the fixed and rigid structures that operate to normalize the nuclear family. In this perspective families are viewed as discursively constituted social sites in which multiple ways of doing family are possible and real. Consequently, family is not fixed within rigid and static structures, but rather constitutes dynamic and unstable sites that are influenced by individual and social change. When we say that families are discursively constructed, this means that the perceptions or meanings that make up understandings of family come from the different discourses of family that are culturally available. As pointed out above, the nuclear family is the dominant or normalizing discourse of family that operates in Western societies. However, there are other competing discourses of family that allow for different meanings and possibilities of doing family life; but these discourses are not given the same official sanction in society, so are less powerful and therefore less supported by individual subjects. The discourse of the nuclear family, which constitutes this way of doing family as the only normal, stable, successful and Christian way possible, in Foucault's terms, operates as a regime of truth in society, through the way it is supported and normalized by other social institutions and through the practices of individual subjects. It is also normalized within Western modernist dualistic thinking depicted in the cultural binary nuclear family/alternative family. While the nuclear family signifies the normal, alternative families are defined in opposition to this and signified as abnormal, unsuccessful, unstable, dysfunctional and often unchristian. Location in discourses can be influenced by a range of issues, including one's gender, ethnicity, sexuality, religious faith, personal experiences, cultural norms and so on.

Continuing to define 'the family' within homogeneous, rigid and universalized prescribed structures denies the diversity of family life that exists; it also perpetuates the social, legal and economic inequities experienced by alternative families. Consequently, it is critical to begin to reconceptualize family in a more inclusive framework. Feminist poststructuralist perspectives of family provide a useful framework in which to begin to view family as socially constituted within discourse and as dynamic and shifting. Butler's (1990) concept of performativity (see Chapter 7 for an in-depth discussion) is valuable in extending these understandings, highlighting how meanings of family are normalized through the everyday repetitive discursive performances of family life embodied by individual subjects. In terms of Butler's theory of performativity, it is the repetitiveness of the performance that both constitutes the realness of doing family (in that it conforms to regulatory norms), as well as providing a means through which different meanings of family are made possible (Butler 1990, 1993). The taking up of the nuclear family discourse is critical to the performance of heterosexual gendered identities; especially for getting these performances correct in the eyes of others. However, the repetitions of family performances are not stable and within 'different contexts and times a repetition can take on a different meaning, undermining and subverting the dominant norms' (Alsop *et al.* 2002: 103). For example, challenges to rigid family binaries constituted within heteronormative relationships, through gay and lesbian families, have provided a context in which different performances of family are made possible. Thus, family can be viewed as performative social spaces, in which individual subjects take up specific and different performances of family life.

Families also need to be depicted as strategic local and globalized networks of choice rather than founded on biological connections or cultural/racial profiles (Carrington 2002). This perspective not only disrupts the normalizing discourse of the nuclear family, but also the homogenizing and essentializing stereotyped understandings of family, such as the notion that there is a single 'Greek family' or a 'Lebanese family' or a 'Vietnamese family' or even a 'gay and lesbian family' profile. A focus on families as performative social spaces in which similar and different performances of family life are embodied, provides not only an understanding of these social relationships as being fluid, contradictory and contextualized, but also a framework in which individual subjects have agency about how they do family. That is, it shifts understandings away from the perspective of individual subjects passively residing within pre-given structures, to a reading of individual subjects actively in the process of creating and recreating their family life performances. Viewing families not as signifiers for exclusion but as more flexible and fluid allows for the inclusion of other non-nuclear characteristics and processes in understandings of family life.

Changing practices in a changing world: current challenges to families

Families are highly responsive to individual and social changes. Births, divorce, death, migration, wars, political upheavals, geographic mobility, economic shifts, partnering and remarriage, among other factors, can impact significantly on family structures and practices, resulting in different and new ways of doing family life that significantly challenge traditional perspectives of the family. The 'everyday experiments in family practices' (Silva and Smart 1999: 10) which have begun to challenge the normative structures of family life are becoming more common, as individuals take up different discourses of family out of choice. Thus, new and different family formations and performances are reflective of increasingly complex, contradictory and shifting individual subject positions. The following phenomena are examples of major social, economic and political challenges impacting on the normative nuclear discourses of family life:

Increased Westernization. Western influences perpetuated through processes of globalization, technological change, media representations and migration to the West continue to challenge non-Western families and traditional cultural practices. Migration to other countries can result in generational changes in cultural values, as well as in family practices and structures.

Women's liberation movement. Feminism has significantly challenged traditional patriarchal discourses of family life, including strict gender role differentiation. Demands for more equitable partnerships in family relationships and in care for children have in some families resulted in changes in family practices performed by men and women; for example, some men choosing to stay home with children while women work.

Individuals marrying later, divorcing earlier, and remarrying. Romantic discourses of love and marriage often leave individuals (particularly women) frustrated and dissatisfied when the realities of marriage and family life do not match their preconceived expectations. Almost one-third of families end in divorce for various reasons, including domestic violence. Thus, perceptions of marriage are changing, especially for women, who are less likely to remarry as quickly as men.

Cohabitation and children born outside marriage. Changing perceptions of marriage have increased the number of couples who choose to live together and have children outside marriage.

Planned pregnancies, and fewer births at later ages. Contraception has provided many women with the option to plan families around careers, or to choose not to have children at all. Legalized abortion has also been an option for some women. Generally women are having fewer children and are having them later in their lives. Overall, couples are becoming parents at later ages and families are smaller.

Drop in fertility rates. The fertility rate in Western countries has dropped in past decades and is equated with, among other factors, access to contraception, women choosing to have children later in life, or women choosing not to have children at all.

Generational changes. Family practices are changing across generations. This is particularly so in immigrant families, where children take up the dominant cultural practices of their new homeland, often rejecting those that belong to their previous homeland or to the parents' birthplace, resulting in family conflicts.

Unemployment. High levels of unemployment are impacting on families from all ethnic groups and social classes. Poverty and welfare dependency impact on the well-being of family members, their access to resources, and their life choices. The decline of manufacturing in industrialized countries has resulted in the loss of many jobs, particularly those that have been traditionally filled by men. Consequently, many families who have relied heavily on male breadwinners have experienced challenges to traditional gender role differentiation in family practices.

Financial commitments. Large financial commitments, associated with the cost of living and the desire for commodities, have meant that both parents often have to work to meet the family's obligations. Consequently, there has been an increased reliance on women's paid work. Family financial commitments can place great pressure on family members, particularly at times of economic and employment instability. In recent years, there has also been an increase in the role of grandparents in caring for children, while both parents work.

Children's rights. In the past decade there has been a greater focus on the rights of children, which are impacting on parental practices in some instances – for example, disciplining children. An increased awareness of the pre-valence of child abuse has resulted in greater surveillance of families and of adult–child relationships more generally and increased legislation to pro-tect children. This has been accompanied by an increased understanding of children's agency and of their citizenship rights to be consulted and to participate in decision-making processes that affect their lives.

Gay and lesbian rights movement. This movement has challenged the social, political and economic inequities that face non-heterosexuals. A major focus of this movement has been the legal recognition of gay and lesbian marriages and their families and their equal access to resources and rights similar to those experienced by heterosexual parents and families. Thus, gays and lesbians are challenging dominant discourses of marriage and the nuclear family.

Reproductive technology and self-insemination. Reproductive technologies have increased the opportunities for some heterosexual couples to overcome fertility and conception problems in order to have children; they have also given single women and lesbians the option of having children without male partners. Self-insemination is also an option that has been utilized by single women and lesbians.

Ageing population. With an increase in life expectancy in developed and industrialized countries and a decrease in fertility, these countries are experiencing an ageing of their populations. Consequently, governments are being forced to consider the health and well-being, including housing and care, of increasing numbers of elderly people. In many instances, the care of the elderly is seen by governments as the primary responsibility of their immediate families, reducing the extent of welfare provision offered by governments.

Social theories of 'the family'

Historically, the family was neglected as an area of study primarily because it was generally perceived to be a private issue, in which the state was considered to have no role. The family was also regarded as having little importance in relation to the broader social structure of society. However, this perspective has dramatically changed; the family is now seen as playing a crucial role in perpetuating dominant social discourses, in the construction of children's subjectivities, and in perpetuating dominant power relationships that exist in society. Thus, families as performative social spaces are agents of self-reflexivity, actively interacting with the broader society. Families are no longer viewed merely as passive foundations for other social structures, but as sites in which individual subjects are redefining the multiple possibilities of intimate relationships (Giddens 1992; Beck and Beck-Gernsheim 1995). Although we have utilized a feminist poststructuralist framework throughout this discussion, it is important to provide a brief overview of other major social theories that have influenced understandings of family relations and the role of family as a social institution.

Structural functionalist theory and the naturalization of the nuclear family

Structural functionalism, a grand narrative view of family, considers the family as an adaptive unit that mediates between the individual and society, with its main role considered to be that of meeting the needs of individuals for personal growth and for physical and emotional integrity. Apart from this central purpose, the family is considered to have a larger role in relation to meeting the sexual, reproductive, economic and educational (socialization of the young) needs of the society at large. These basic functions are perceived to be the prerequisites for the survival of the society. However, the family is seen as being largely separate from the political processes operating in society, which are perceived to be played out through other public institutions such as the government, law, education and so on. Thus, the family in this perspective is theoretically depoliticized and considered not to have an active role in the public arena of politics and economics. Structural functionalists view the patriarchal nuclear family as the natural primary unit of a stable, harmonious and healthy society. It is a neutral safety zone, a retreat and safe haven for individuals to escape and recuperate from the rigours and demands of their public working lives.

Talcott Parsons was one of the most influential structural functionalist theorists writing during the 1950s and 1960s. He upheld that society was an efficient, harmonious and orderly system, with a common set of shared moral and social values, resulting in consensus among its members. The smooth functioning of society is dependent on members of the society adhering to these 'agreed' values. Individuals and families who do not share these values are considered deviant and dysfunctional and ultimately problematic to society. Their lack of conformity is seen as a result of poor socialization as children, which can lead to social and systemic dysfunction. For example, in the 1950s and 1960s when Parsons was influential, gender role differentiation in the family was considered to be reflective of the natural biological differences between men and women. Women who challenged what was perceived to be their natural lot in life were considered problematic to the stability of the natural order of society.

Parsons upheld that the nuclear family was the natural fundamental social structure of the industrialized modern society. The nuclear family of post-war America he believed was a newly emerging form of family, which was more specialized than previous family structures, evolving to meet the requirements of modern society. The nuclear family was considered ideal for this new industrial landscape as it was highly mobile and free from kinship pressures at work. Carrington (2002) points out that the naturalization of the nuclear family is mythical and is linked to the way that it was reinforced through modernist scientific (for example, social Darwinist) and Christian moralist discourses that polarized nuclear and extended families (that is, mother, father, children, grandparents, aunts, uncles and so on that often lived together). Such discourses were perpetuated by structural functionalist ideologies like those espoused by Parsons. In social Darwinist terms, progress in society was seen as a linear process (similar to that in Darwin's human evolutionary theory) that was associated with Western industrialization. This Western constructed narrative linked the nuclear family to industrialization and Western progress, while on the other hand it constituted non-Western or Eastern society and non-nuclear families, such as extended families, as pre-industrial (remedial) and primitive. In this process, extended families have been stereotyped, racialized and directly associated with primitive and less progressive cultures (Carrington 2002). However, as aptly pointed out by Carrington, the nuclear family is not a prerequisite for industrialization, and the Western framing of the nuclear family 'Cannot be separated from the processes of capitalism or from ideological agendas such as Christian dogma, scientific theory or notions of nation' (Carrington 2002: 18).

There have been major criticisms of structural functionalism, based primarily on the way this perspective depoliticizes and mythologizes the nuclear family; how it is based on misconceptions of society as harmonious and founded on identifiable core values that everybody agrees upon (the prevalence of domestic violence is difficult to explain away in this perspective); how the system is exempted from contributing to the existence of social problems and difference is generally perceived as individual deviance; and how inequities are legitimized as natural through perceived biological differences. Power differences and inequalities are viewed as a reflection of the natural order of things. For example, differences in children's perceived intelligence are considered the natural result of children's genetic make-up, with high intelligence naturally occurring in white, middle- and upper-class professional families.

Although structural functionalism as a social theory was particularly influential during the 1950s and 1960s, the perspectives and values inherent in this approach can be heard in the rhetoric of neoconservatism that is emerging as a political force throughout the world today. The neoconservative call for a return to the 'traditional nuclear family' of the 1950s, and to the mythical core set of social and moral values that it was perceived to be founded upon, is reflective of structural functionalist principles. The dismissal of difference as being problematic and deviant is certainly a central argument that has been utilized against alternative families, who continue to lobby for social and official recognition.

Marxist theories, the family and social reproduction

Marxist perspectives, originating primarily from the works of Karl Marx (1818–1883) have been influential in highlighting the role that the nuclear family plays in the **social reproduction** of power relations in society. Like structural functionalism, it provides a grand narrative view of family in society. These various perspectives stress that the family is an 'ideological state apparatus' through which ideologies upheld by the state are reproduced and perpetuated through family members, generation after generation. In contrast to structural functionalism, Marxist perspectives provide a political view of the family, concerned with identifying and exploring the process of ideological domination in shaping and creating the individual subject. The bourgeois patriarchal nuclear family is seen as the primary site of social and class socialization and reproduction.

Marxist theorists are particularly concerned with how the structure of domestic labour is integral to the system of capitalism. Neo-Marxists, such as those critical theorists who were part of the Frankfurt School in Germany (1923–1950), were interested in the relationship between the nuclear bourgeois family and authority, especially in terms of how dominant patterns of subordination and domination in the family reflected those operating in broader social structures. This resulted in an increased awareness of how gender role differentiation in the family was linked to the needs of the capitalist economy. For example, the role of women in the household was to provide a caring and nurturing environment for men who were considered the major economic providers of the family, as well as the major source of workers for the capitalist system. Contented and loved workers at home were considered to be healthy and productive workers in the capitalist system. Thus, women were seen to play a critical role in the emotional stability of workers, ultimately contributing to the stability and productivity of the workforce. The patriarchal nuclear family, based on strict gender-differentiated roles, was viewed to be critical to the continued success of the capitalist system.

Family social relationships were viewed to operate around a public/private split, in which family, marriage and domestic life became strongly linked to core values of privacy and intimacy, while economics, work and politics were considered public matters. Different gender roles in society were analysed in terms of how they conformed to the public/private split; that is, women and their influence were aligned with the private world of the family, while men dominated public matters. The nuclear family under capitalism was considered to be critical in providing an environment in which individuals could be emotionally supported through the deprivations and alienations they experienced in an advanced capitalist society. Thus, as a result of this process, as Morgan (1996: 7) points out, by default 'the public worlds of business and politics could continue unchallenged'.

Feminist theories and the family

Feminists have been the most influential social theorists in recent times to extend understandings of the role of family in society. However, there are many variations of feminism (for example, liberal feminism, radical feminism, socialist feminism, psychoanalytic feminism, feminist poststructuralism) providing different perspectives on family relations and how they operate to perpetuate gender inequalities. Feminism largely operates as a grand narrative, but feminist poststructuralism, as pointed out previously, has emerged as a different approach that does not take on the perspectives that are inherent in universalizing grand narrative social theories. As feminist poststructuralism has been outlined in depth previously in this chapter, brief overviews of other feminist perspectives are given here. Feminists from various perspectives have been primarily responsible for critiquing the normalization and maintenance of the public/private split in gendered social relationships in society. They have also highlighted the family as a major political institution in which individual subjectivities are constituted and inequalities of power that operate broadly in society, especially those between men and women, adults and children, are maintained.

Marxist feminists uphold that women's oppression is tied primarily to the operations of the capitalist system. Incorporating the principles of Marxist theory into their social critique, they view the family as central in reproducing gendered and class relations in society and in bolstering capitalism through its role in reproducing labour power; that is, reproducing and socializing children to be future workers in the capitalist system. This perspective upholds that women's oppression and inequality in society are primarily linked to their economic dependence on men as a result of their unpaid role in the home, as well as their lack of access to well-paid, full-time employment in the workforce. Thus, the family is generally viewed as an oppressive institution for women. Equality for women, according to Marxist feminists, will only be achieved through the elimination of capitalism.

Socialist feminism largely arose as a result of some Marxist feminists' dissatisfaction with Marxist theory and its failure to adequately deal with gender issues. Marxists tended to view workers' oppression as being more critical than women's oppression. Socialist feminists argue that the lives of women in non-capitalist systems are not substantially different or transformed from those under capitalism; that is, they are still oppressed by patriarchy. Thus, socialist feminists uphold that women's liberation must not be analysed solely in terms of capitalism, but must include an analysis of patriarchy (a system of male dominance and power) and how both systems simultaneously oppress women. The patriarchal nuclear family is considered central to the perpetuation of gender and class inequalities.

Radical feminists linked the nuclear family to women's oppression, but unlike Marxist or socialist feminists, they fundamentally view women's oppression as a result of patriarchy and men's control over women's bodies. The nuclear family is considered to be a primary source of the perpetuation of patriarchal power relations among men and women, with women being largely oppressed and victimized in their homes as well as in public arenas. The patriarchal nuclear family, its intimate links with marriage and strict gender differentiated roles (for example, child care), operate to subordinate and oppress women in society. Radical feminists have been instrumental in highlighting the 'reality' of family life, focusing on the extensiveness of domestic violence, rape in marriage and child sexual abuse occurring in the home.

Psychoanalytic feminists view the family as the primary site of the construction of the gendered subject. Incorporating Freudian psychoanalysis, this perspective focuses on the ways in which our subjectivities and cultures are constructed from our earliest unconscious embodied experiences as children. The 'passionate emotional entanglements' that arise from these experiences in families impact on the way we perceive ourselves and how we interact with others in the world (Alsop *et al.* 2002: 40). These experiences are perceived to be critical in shaping individuals' desires and in constructing the social world. Deleuze and Guattari (1987) utilize psychoanalysis and view the nuclear family as being complicit in the repression and moulding of individual desires. Carrington (2002), incorporating the perspectives of Deleuze and Guattari, and Bourdieu's concept of habitus formation, argues that the desires of individual subjects are shaped primarily through the family in the way they take up, purchase and consume this highly particular architectural form.

Habitus, cultural capital, symbolic violence and family

Bourdieu's concepts of habitus, capital and symbolic violence are useful in helping to understand how the family impacts on individual subjects and on the shaping of the social world. According to Bourdieu, social reality is a construction that is reproduced through the existing power relations operating in society that serve to foster and maintain the position and status of particular groups over others. The family is a critical site of social reproduction. The narrative of the nuclear family is a construction that serves particular ideological visions and political agendas and is normalized through other social institutions, such as education. For example, it reproduces neo-conservative values and morals that maintain heterosexual privilege, such as the exclusive access of heterosexuals to socially and legally sanctioned marriage. Thus, nuclear families have greater cultural capital in society than alternative families.

Bourdieu's concept of symbolic violence, which is 'violence that is exercised upon a social agent with his or her complicity' (Webb *et al.* 2002: 25) provides an explanation of how social inequalities can continue largely unabated. Within this perspective, individual subjects are subjected to various forms of violence, such as being treated unfairly or denied resources, or are limited in their social mobility and aspirations, but they do not tend to see it that way; rather it is misrecognized by individual subjects as the natural order of things. Gender domination in the patriarchal family is an example of symbolic violence in operation. Through habitus formation in this context, women were often confined emotionally, socially, economically and physically and the perception that women were inferior to men in the home and more generally in society was perpetuated. Women's misrecognition of this violence as 'natural' and 'normal' gendered relations in the world led to their being complicit in reinscribing through their daily practices, their own domination (Webb *et al.* 2002).

The social construction of motherhood and fatherhood

Just as the normalizing discourse of the nuclear family operates to maintain a particular social order, so do the normalizing discourses of motherhood and fatherhood that are articulated, particularly within this family formation. Motherhood is often perceived to be the essence of what it means to be a woman, which is perpetuated through the belief that motherhood is a 'natural' and instinctual process in women's lives, due to their biological make-up and reproductive capabilities. However, both motherhood and fatherhood are discursively constructed social practices that are actively negotiated, taken up and recreated by individuals rather than instinctively linked to and fixed in biology. That is, cultural understandings of meanings of motherhood and fatherhood are constituted within the various discourses socially available to individual subjects at particular points in time. Motherhood and fatherhood, as socially constructed practices, are integral to the performance of hegemonic gendered identities. The link that has been socially fostered between motherhood and women's biology has been primarily utilized to maintain a social system of gender inequality based on the 'natural' delegation of women as the sole carers of children and as homemakers. In this respect, motherhood can be seen to be another example of Bourdieu's symbolic violence; that is, the inequities that operate in women's lives associated with being socially delegated the prime and often sole responsibility of mothering and caring for children and other family members, and as homemakers, are often misrecognized as the natural order of things. There is no reason, apart from the way it has been discouraged within dominant socially constructed meanings of masculinity, why men cannot mother.

The dominant discourse of motherhood idealizes, glorifies and romanticizes this role and often demands women to be altruistic; that is, their actions are primarily for the benefit of others, even at the expense of their own needs and wishes. In Australia in recent years, this discourse has emerged in political rhetoric around discussions focusing on the country's critical negative population growth. However, the status of motherhood tends to be diminished quickly within the limited social, political and economic supports provided to mothers once they have children. The 'good mother', as constituted in the dominant discourse of motherhood, is highly attentive and sensitive to the needs of her children, puts her children's needs first, is always there when needed, and provides a stimulating learning environment for her children from the time they are born. Interestingly, the 'good mother' is still often perceived to be one who stays home and cares for her children in their early years; ironically, this is a perspective that is strongly supported by many of the pre-service early childhood educators we have worked with.

The 'good mother' is also perceived to be able to successfully juggle her time and other roles as wife, homemaker and increasingly, paid worker (full-time or part-time). This discourse is responsible for constructing successful 'good' mothers as being 'superwomen' who can efficiently fulfil all these demanding roles simultaneously. There are some mothers who continue to successfully fulfil the superwoman discourse, but for most the 'good' mother benchmark is unattainable, not through any fault of their own, but as a result of the often unrealistic goals that this discourse places on women. Consequently, mothers' behaviours and practices become the focus of public scrutiny; they are continually judged (often judging themselves more harshly than others) as 'good' or 'bad' mothers, depending on how successfully they perform and cope with these multiple roles. For many, it is often an impossible task posing critical implications for their health and well-being. In educational contexts, including early childhood education, judgements are often made about 'good' or 'bad' mothers based on the various criteria raised above; these criteria are largely based on white, Western, middle-class values associated with the nuclear family lifestyle.

'Good fathers', on the other hand, have traditionally been viewed in terms of their abilities to economically provide for their families and as effective disciplinarians. This primary defining role of fatherhood has meant that many men have played a secondary role in the everyday raising of children, becoming more actively involved in family and homemaking activities on a weekend or holiday basis. Motherhood and fatherhood have been primarily constituted within the gendered cultural binary male/female, in which meanings of motherhood have been defined in opposition to meanings of fatherhood, based on gender role differentiation. The dominant discourses of fatherhood and motherhood operate to reinscribe the perceived 'naturalness' of the patriarchal heterosexual nuclear family. Good mothers and good fathers are married and heterosexual, reinforcing the perceived deviance and unnaturalness of non-heterosexual relationships and families. However, increasingly, some men are taking up different performances of masculinity and extending their roles in families to include caring for children on either a shared or full-time basis. However, they can often become the targets of harassment from other men (and some women) for taking up 'women's roles' and stepping outside the boundaries of hegemonic masculinity. Interestingly, fathers do not tend to experience the same public scrutiny that is directed at mothers in relation to raising children; this is most likely associated with their primary responsibilities being viewed as being located largely in the public sphere of work, which limits their time with family.

Families of 'choice': doing family differently

The destabilization of the normative myths around family that we have identified so far in this chapter is opening up spaces and opportunities for individuals to choose different performances of family. The normalizing discourse of the nuclear family is also being disrupted through different performances of gender – for example, as indicated in the previous section, where some men are taking on more responsibilities for caring and nurturing children, either on a full-time or shared basis. As discussed earlier in this chapter, it is important that we begin to reconceptualize families as globalized and localized strategic networks of choice. The following families are examples of how individual subjects are doing family differently through choice.

Gay and lesbian families

Lewin (1998: 25) points out that 'same sex commitments are nothing new; only the demand for equity and recognition has changed the landscape'. Gay- and lesbian-headed families generally have to battle for social and legal recognition, often facing discrimination from both institutional practices and the broader community. The normalizing discourse of the heterosexual nuclear family operates to exclude gay and lesbian families from being viewed as 'real', appropriate or successful families. Neoconservative discourses stemming from particular religious and moral values perpetuate representations of gay and lesbian families as deviant and abnormal. Stereotypes often operating through the media perpetuate homogenizing representations of the lives of gays and lesbians, rather than acknowledging the vast diversity that exist within these different communities. In more recent years, there has been a very active movement on the part of gays and lesbians to access social, political and legal rights as granted to heterosexuals and heterosexual-headed families – for example, the legal recognition of gay and lesbian marriages.

Recent research points out that gay and lesbian families are often silenced and marginalized in the field of early childhood education (Corbett 1993; Wickens 1993; Casper *et al.* 1998; Cahill and Theilheimer 1999; Robinson and Jones Díaz 2000; Robinson 2002; Skattebol and Ferfolja 2005). This research also highlights the importance of including these families within children's broad education of family diversity. This is largely in order to acknowledge the experiences of many young children who come from gay or lesbian families, and to counteract the myths and stereotypes associated with gays and lesbians that children encounter daily. Robinson (2002) points out that gay and lesbian families, or gay and lesbian equity issues more generally, continue to be largely excluded from early childhood curriculum and social justice agendas for several reasons, which include the prevalence of homophobia and heterosexism operating in many early childhood settings; the taboos that exist around children and sexuality; fears around dealing with sexuality due to its controversial status; the perception that these families and equity issues are irrelevant to most children's lives; the assumed absence of significant gay or lesbian adults in children's lives; the pervasiveness of the discourse of compulsory heterosexuality; and the assumed absence of gay and lesbian families in early childhood settings (for an in-depth discussion of these issues see Chapter 8).

There are many concerns that face gay and lesbian families in relation to their children's education. Many gay and lesbian parents are wary about 'coming out' but do so in some circumstances; they fear 'coming out' may result in their children experiencing discrimination from educators and other staff. Many are also concerned that their children will experience discrimination from other children and parents if their children talk openly about their family experiences in schools (Cahill and Theilheimer 1999;

Skattebol and Ferfolja 2005). How early childhood settings approach family diversity can affect how open gay and lesbian parents are with their children's educators. If settings include gay and lesbian families in their social justice agendas, curriculum on family diversity, and organizational policies and practices, it sends a strong message not just to gay and lesbian parents, but to all parents, educators and children that family diversity is recognized and respected.

Interethnic and interracial families

Interethnicity and interraciality are markers of family shifts throughout the Western world, primarily as a result of the impact of globalization, migration, increasingly sophisticated technology and communications, as well as increasingly mobile populations. This has resulted in an increase in ethnically and racially mixed marriages and families, which have brought heterogeneity to mainstream cultures (Carrington 2002). Family hybridity is the bringing together of two different racial and/or ethnic cultures from which new and different family practices emerge. Intermarriage refers to unions that cross class, language, caste, nationality, ethnicity, racial and religious barriers and is an important site in which shifting social values emerge, such as those around child-rearing and gender role expectations. Within these family contexts, tensions in cultural negotiations can arise around family practices, such as child-rearing, which can stem from different cultural constructions of childhood.

Australian research (Carrington 2002) on interethnic families highlights that these families can experience racial discrimination, but they do not see it as a defining characteristic of their experiences. Community attitudes towards interethnic and interracial marriages have significantly changed from earlier generations when these families tended to be viewed as dysfunctional environments in which to raise children and experiences of racism were prevalent (Carrington 2002). However, perceptions of interethnic and inter-racial families and their experiences of discrimination and racism can be influenced by their geographical location, as well as the political climate of the time.

The representation and inclusion of interethnic and interracial families in early childhood curriculum, policies and practices is important in challenging normalizing discourses of family that can operate in early childhood settings. Interestingly, our research with early childhood educators indicates that many educators working in settings that tend to have a more homogeneous family clientele in terms of ethnicity and 'race' often do not consider dealing with equity issues around ethnic and racial difference relevant to their children and families.

Families from non-English-speaking backgrounds

Many of the issues faced by children and their families from non-English-speaking backgrounds are addressed in Chapters 4 and 6, but it is important to briefly highlight some of the main concerns facing families here. People from non-English-speaking backgrounds come from a very diverse range of ethnic and cultural backgrounds and cannot be viewed as a homogeneous group. This diversity is shaped by differences across ethnicity, culture, religion, age, gender, occupation, social class, length of residence in their current country, English proficiency and educational qualifications (Cass 1995). Social and equity issues facing many of these families are associated primarily with: a lack of knowledge about or access to existing services and resources; the inability of services, including early childhood education, to meet the specific needs of these families in culturally appropriate ways; reduced employment opportunities due to levels of English language proficiency; lack of recognition in many instances of overseas qualifications; employment experiences often associated with low-paid service industries; unemployment; and the challenges that face families that have recently arrived in their new countries of residence, including social dislocation, isolation and racism (Cass 1995).

The issues raised above have particular significance for early childhood education in the way that different settings cater for the specific needs of the diverse families from non-English-speaking backgrounds utilizing their services. Encouraging these different families to fully participate in their children's early education will require educators to be aware, sensitive and reflexive about the social equity concerns facing many of these families, in varying degrees.

The impact of globalization on doing family

Globalization is opening up opportunities for different and new family structures and practices and significantly challenging normalizing discourses of family. Carrington (2002) points out that the increasing fluidity of globalizing capitalism has resulted in destabilizing and problematizing normative discourses of family, self and community.

Imagined communities

Globalization has resulted in a shift from place-bound and solid communities within static values and systems of practice to the abstract, imagined community (Albrow *et al.* 1997). **Imagined communities** are those that base themselves around particular constructed identities rather than shared location (Carrington 2002: 118). These communities can coexist in localized areas or spread across the world. Global communities can be maintained largely through Internet connections rather than through physical localized sites. Increasingly, individual subjects are identifying themselves with 'simulated communities' (Carrington 2002) that make use of available technologies to pursue common agendas regardless of their physical locations. Thus, increasing fluidity of culture and individuals has impacted not just on how we perceive the global community and our individual place within it, but also on the local spaces in which we live.

Transnational/satellite families

Globalization has impacted significantly on families in relation to issues associated with global mobility. This is represented through such families where the main financial provider (most often the father/male in these instances) is located in a different geographical location from their family, returning for short visits or on special holidays with the family. This is primarily a result of the need to follow employment opportunities, or employers' expectations that their employees will be mobile and willing to travel to various work locations. The information technology industry is one example where a central parent organization can be located in a different country from many of its workers, who are expected to travel to its location for regular meetings. Technology, communications and air travel make these demands possible. In other cases, families may move constantly with the parent to different employment locations, which can disrupt children's early education. In other cases, it may be difficult for some children when one parent is absent from the family home for prolonged periods of time.

This phenomenon, called 'global labor diasporas' (Appadurai 1996: 44), places immense strain on families and marriages, but women are especially burdened as they are often left alone for long periods of time to keep families together and meet the family needs. They also have to deal with the issues and conflicts that may arise as their family settles into new cultural contexts that often have different cultural values and behaviours. Fitting into new locations and negotiating the normalizing discourses operating among neighbours and peers can be difficult and complicated, posing concerns for both mothers and their children. These relocation issues are similar to those faced by immigrant or refugee families, but pose particular concerns for transnational families. A state of 'cultural flux' occurs for these families resulting from the constant arrival and departure of a parent and the lack of family stability, making it difficult for the family to make critical life decisions and choices (Appadurai 1996). Appadurai (1996: 44) points out: 'It is in this atmosphere that the invention of tradition (and of ethnicity, kinship, and other identity markers) can become slippery, as the search for certainties is regularly frustrated by the fluidities of transnational communities'. Thus, Appadurai (1996: 44) argues, culture becomes less of a habitus and 'more an arena for conscious choice, justification, and representation, the latter often to multiple and spatially dislocated audiences'.

Thus, people are increasingly shifting across multiple locations for varying lengths of time, moving in and out of numerous communities while at the same time maintaining satisfactory social relations across all these sites. Moving populations are not just migrants or guest workers moving from one part of the globe to another, either voluntarily or involuntarily, but rather, people generally are on the move globally and locally, challenging traditional framings of static and homogeneous communities.

Refugee families

As a result of continuing social and political unrest throughout the world there has been an increase in the number of individuals and families seeking asylum in other countries that are seen as more politically stable and economically prosperous. For many refugee families it is about fleeing actual or potential human rights abuses in their home countries. Consequently, refugee families may be experiencing severe personal traumas when they arrive in other countries to resettle; this can be especially the case for young children. This trauma can also be associated with the loss of close relatives and friends. Refugee families often arrive in countries with few resources. Young people and children comprise a significant proportion of Australia's refugee intake (approximately one-third) often coming with one parent only or as unattached minors (Cass 1995).

The various policies on refugees in each country will impact on their refugee status and how successfully they are resettled, if at all, into a new country. In recent times there has been an increase in the rejection of refugees, especially those who seek asylum as 'boat people' and attempt to land 'illegally' on foreign shores. This has been the case in Australia in recent years, resulting in the refusal to take these refugees or recognize their international refugee status. Further, refugees, including children, who do arrive 'illegally' in Australia can experience long periods of mandatory detention while waiting on the investigations of governments to determine their refugee status. However, in July 2005, as a result of increased community and media concern and a political deal struck between the Australian federal government and moderate coalition parliamentarians, the government has begun to release some asylum-seeker families into the community. Consequently, and ironically, the personal traumas experienced by refugees in their home countries can be prolonged by government policies in the various countries in which they seek asylum.

The experiences raised above can pose significant issues for educators working with refugee children and their families once they settle into their new communities. Children's experiences of trauma can significantly affect their health and well-being, their sense of confidence and security, as well as their learning in schools. Different traumatic experiences associated with war, dictatorial regimes, terrorism, torture, famine, poverty, and living in extreme fear can have serious short-term and long-term effects on developing trusting relationships with individuals, particularly those in institutional locations. It can often take a lot of time and effort on the part of educators to build trusting relationships with children to the point that they begin to feel secure in their new environments. There are also issues for refugee children and families associated with settling into new environments away from the familiarity of their home countries and away from the family and friendship groups they have left behind. Finding appropriate, secure and affordable housing, building new networks of support and friendship, language issues, challenging cultural differences, financial and employment concerns, and accessing available government and non-government support services are a few of the concerns that face these families daily. Negotiating language differences will be a particular issue in terms of meeting children's educational needs. Furthermore, refugee children and their families may experience discrimination in their new communities, which can exacerbate many of the fears and insecurities they may already be dealing with.

The position and 'role' of children in families

As performances of family begin to change through the choices of individual subjects, through challenges to normalizing discourses of motherhood and fatherhood and gendered identities, and as a result of broader social, political, economic and technological challenges, it is little wonder that there has been a simultaneous challenge to understandings of childhood and how they are positioned in families. In recent years, the discourses of children's rights and child protection have raised serious concerns about the vulnerability of children to a vast range of abuse, neglect and exploitation in societies throughout the world. Research indicates that child abuse in its various forms is a major social phenomenon that continues to confront different communities and social institutions responsible for children's welfare (Breckenridge and Carmody 1992; Easteal 1994). However, what this research has done in particular is to highlight the vulnerabilities experienced by children in their own families. Much has been written on children's physical, sexual and emotional abuse and neglect in the home and thus, in the context of this book and its limitations on space, we can only acknowledge this critical issue as a major concern in any discussion of the position of children in families.

However, what needs to be reiterated here in relation to this critical social problem is that child abuse and neglect is a direct result of the power differentials between adults and children, and between older children and younger children. In more recent years, there has been a growing awareness of the various forms of abuse (physical, sexual, emotional) that are perpetrated against younger children by older children with more power. In many cases it is also related to differences in power associated with gender, as the greatest percentage of child sexual abuse involves men or boys abusing girls (Breckenridge and Carmody 1992; Easteal 1994). Utilizing a feminist poststructuralist framework, we argue that in order to significantly counteract the vast abuse that occurs, particularly in the home, it is critical to deconstruct the cultural binaries adult/child and male/female that constitute the power relations that exist between adults and children and in gendered relationships. As pointed out in Chapter 1, the oppositional thinking that is constituted in the cultural binary adult/child operates to maintain adults' power and control over children and perpetuates the dominant discourse of childhood that constructs them as 'innocent'. Ironically, Robinson (2005d) argues, in the efforts to protect childhood 'innocence', which is ultimately a cultural construct, children have been simultaneously made more vulnerable. Children in many Western contexts have not been encouraged to become competent individuals, but rather have been denied agency and access to certain knowledge, generally perceived by adults to be inappropriate for children – for example, discussions around sexuality. It is the very 'innocence' and 'purity' constructed around children that can lead to their vulnerability (Kitzinger 1990; Gittins 1998). In terms of sexual abuse, 'childhood innocence' is a commodity exploited in child pornography, where innocence becomes titillation and the perception of 'forbidden fruit' fuels the desire. This image of childhood innocence is not just perpetuated in pornography but is apparent in mainstream media representations of children (Kitzinger 1990; Elliott 1992). Childhood 'innocence' is a viable billion-dollar consumer industry, reflected in the success of international child sex tourism, Internet pedophile rings and the prevalence of child prostitution throughout the world (Tate 1992). Corteen and Scraton (1997: 99) reinforce this concern. They state:

> In protecting their innocence, children's experiences and competencies are neglected – with adults directing and determining their behaviour, choices, opportunities and potential. Denied independence, or the information and experiences necessary to develop their emerging sexualities, children and young people are made vulnerable.

To begin to enhance children's agency and competencies, it is critical to problematize and deconstruct cultural binaries such as adult/child that make children more vulnerable, in order to build different and more equitable relationships between adults and children.

The children's rights movement in particular has highlighted the need to recognize children as subjects with individual identities beyond their relationships with adults, who have their own rights and have a significant contribution to make in society, as active citizens with agency. Thus, there is a slow but steady increase in adult awareness of the importance of including children's voices and perspectives in decisions that directly affect children's lives and the lives of their families more generally. When these issues are discussed with our teacher educators in class, it is interesting to note that many of them feel uneasy, believing that 'giving' children more power to make decisions can only lead to children dismissing the authority of their parents and other adults and result in children just doing what they want. Consequently, for many adults, based on the oppositional 'logical' thinking that stems from cultural binaries like adult/child, 'giving' children more power and voice essentially means that it reduces adults' power and compromises adults' voices. Ultimately, this relationship is considered problematic as it is perceived to lead to a state of chaos and anarchy. Disrupting the cultural binary adult/child is on one level about adults relinquishing their perceived right to power 'over' children, but it is more about thinking differently about the relationships that exist between them and developing ways to 'share' the power more equitably. Along with this process come different ways of actively listening and hearing children's voices and incorporating them into family decisions, developing children's responsibilities, competencies and leadership in and outside the home. This requires adults to take children seriously, as well as a reconceptualization of adults' perceived rights to enforce their wills at all costs on children as a 'rite of passage'; this shift is about facilitating the possibilities of doing relationships with children differently.

Implications for practice in early childhood education

This chapter has raised many important issues associated with family diversity that have critical implications for early childhood educators. The following implications address issues associated with policy, programming and planning, communicating with families, and working with staff, families and children.

Policy direction and implementation

It is important that early childhood educational settings review their organizational practices, policies and philosophies in terms of how realistically they reflect family diversity. It is critical that the inclusion of family diversity is achieved through a whole-setting approach and is monitored and reviewed at regular intervals. In order to be more inclusive, there needs to be a shift from fixed structural concepts that define families in certain ways, to understandings of families as multiple performative social spaces based on strategic local and globalized networks of choice. In practice, for example, this would involve reviewing written materials, such as policies and forms, to check that they use language that is inclusive of single-parent, gay and lesbian, and other non-nuclear families; and using more inclusive terms such as 'parent' rather than mother/father. It is also important to include diversity issues even if there is the perception that they are somehow irrelevant to the current children and families utilizing the setting. For example, policies and practices need to include equity issues associated with gay and lesbian families, even if they are perceived to be absent in the setting. These equity issues are relevant to all children and families as homophobia and heterosexism are primarily practised by heterosexual children, staff and families, whether there are gay or lesbian families present or not.

Communicating and negotiating with families

Educators and early childhood educational services are faced with the challenge of how to support and include the many different families that are part of children's lives. It is important that strategies are developed to include those families that tend to remain on the margins of settings' activities. For example, families from minority cultures and/or different language backgrounds need to be supported and encouraged to participate in setting organizational, social and educational activities. Achieving this may require the development of employment strategies that target staff who are bilingual or multilingual and working with particular cultural community groups that are present in the community near the settings. Reaching out to different families through newsletters and special educational and social events is also a useful strategy. Additionally, it is important not to assume that gay and lesbian families are not using the setting; many choose not to be openly 'out', fearing discrimination.

Programming and planning

Disrupting the normalizing discourse of the nuclear family, constituted within the cultural binary nuclear/non-nuclear that operates to exclude and problematize family diversity, is a critical pedagogical starting point for working with children. Settings need to review their available resources to see if they provide educators and children with a range of different family representations. However, popular culture resources that children tend to read that often perpetuate normalizing discourses of family and gender are also valuable. They can be deconstructed with children to challenge normalizing perspectives of family and of gendered identities, to identify power relations inherent within the narratives, and to recreate new and different storylines that represent multiple performances of family and of gender. The processes of deconstruction and reconstruction are useful pedagogical tools for developing children's critical thinking around normalizing discourses and social inequities, providing children with new and different options in the world.

Working with staff, families and children

Taking a reflexive approach to pedagogy and practice is important in order to examine how the perceptions and everyday interactions of staff, children and families either perpetuate or disrupt normalizing discourses associated with the 'legitimation' of family and gendered relations. This is a critical component of taking a whole-setting approach to dealing with diversity and difference. The perceptions of individual subjects will not always be the same; however, this process gives an important starting point to acknowledge the differences, discuss them openly, and identify possible strategies to begin more effective negotiations across the differences that emerge. It is a process that requires time, commitment and long-term planning; it cannot happen overnight and its focus on personal and professional change makes it potentially 'risky' for some, so this must be respected. Community courage, where individuals share the personal and professional risks in incorporating, upholding and defending policies, philosophies and practices that reflect family differences, is critical for its success. This involves developing networks of personal and professional support within and across various organizations to advocate for the representation of family difference in early childhood education.

Conclusion

This chapter has provided a critical overview of the changing perspectives of family, including the current social, political and economic challenges facing families today. It has argued strongly that in order to be more inclusive of the diversity that exists in families it is imperative that we begin to shift away from normalizing discourses of the nuclear family that perpetuate fixed structural definitions of family based on biological connections. This discourse primarily operates to dismiss family diversity as problematic, reinforcing social inequities in the process. Viewing families as performative social spaces in which similar and different performances of family are possible, as well as being localized and globalized networks of choice, is an important step in the process of acknowledging how families are constantly negotiated and recreated by the individual subjects living within them. Early childhood educators have a critical advocacy role to play in challenging narrow normalizing discourses of family that undermine the vast diversity of family performances experienced by the children and families with whom they work.

Recommended reading

Carrington, V. (2002) *New Times: New Families*. Dordrecht: Kluwer Academic.

Mercier, L.R. and Harold, R.D. (2003) At the interface: Lesbian-parent families and their children's schools. *Children & Schools*, 25(1): 35–47.

Silva, F.B. and Smart, C. (1999). The 'new' practices and politics of family life, in E.B. Silva and C. Smart (eds) *The New Family?* London: Sage Publications.

Weeks, J., Heaphy, B. and Donovan, C. (2001) *Same Sex Intimacies: Families of Choice and Other Life Experiments*. London: Routledge.

BILINGUALISM, IDENTITY AND ENGLISH AS A GLOBALIZED LANGUAGE

Introduction

For much of the world's population, being bilingual or multilingual is the norm and the ability to speak two or more languages is a way of accumulating social capital and good standing within one's own language and cultural group (Singh 2002b). In Australia, more than 2.8 million people (including young children) speak a language other than English at home, and moreover there are at least 50,000 Indigenous language speakers (Australian Bureau of Statistics 2005). However, for children growing up with two or more languages and dialects who attend 'English only' preschool and school settings, the retention of their home language or dialect can be severely thwarted particularly when there is limited institutional and educational support for their use.

The focus of this chapter is an examination of the social and political forces involved in the retention and learning of home languages and dialects in early childhood. A brief overview of the established and dominant theories of child bilingualism are provided, along with a critical discussion of their limitations in understanding the significance of the cultural, social and political processes that affect language retention and language learning in globalized English-speaking nation states such as Australia, the United States and Britain. In particular, this chapter will offer a conceptual reframing of bilingualism, language retention and identity in young bilingual children. Further, data from two research projects will be examined to demonstrate the impact of broader socio-political forces and power relationships, which regularly operate and position young bilingual children, families and educators into marginalized situations in everyday relations and social practices.

English as a globalized language

Power relations that exist between nation states in our society are directly linked to modes of production, trade, commerce and media that operate at global levels. Constituted in these modes of production, communication technologies are paramount, and most of these technologies are transmitted in English. Hence, English is currently considered a globalized and international language, which in the past fifty years has gained much prominence and power over other languages (Crystal 1997; Pennycook 1998).

While the majority of the world's population do not speak English as their home language or dialect, English is the second most widely spoken language, with 5.4 per cent of the world's population having proficiency in its use (Nettle and Romaine 2000). However, Crystal (1997) reminds us that English has not become a powerful language because of its inherent linguistic or grammatical features, or because of the numbers of people who speak it, but rather because of the political, economic and military might of its people. So, because it is a powerful language everyone in the world wants to speak it and gain social and economic power through its use. Anglophone countries, such as the United States and Britain, which dominate global communication technologies, finance, trade and means of production, have 'considerable power relative to those that do not control these resources' (Singh 2002b: 17).

As a consequence of English as a globalized language, in recent years, 'English only' policies and politics in the United States, Britain and Australia have emerged (Crystal 1997; Nettle and Romaine 2000). For example, in education, 'English-only' policies in the United States and Australia have seen the dismantling of bilingual programmes in preference for 'English only' programmes (see, for example, Villenas and Deyhle 1999; Crystal 1997; Gutiérrez et al. 2000). On the other hand, in Asia and Europe, it is common for bilingual schools to teach English at early childhood levels. For example, Sweden recently began teaching English as a foreign language to children, while in China and Japan English-language programmes are offered at pre-school levels. Furthermore, English is now taught as a foreign language in over 100 countries, including China, Russia, Germany, Spain, Egypt and Brazil (Crystal 1997).

While globalization and the dominance of English are on the rise, the fact remains that language is a significant marker of identity, and identity is inextricably linked to the ways in which we understand others and ourselves. Despite the fact that people around the world desire to pass on to their children the language through which local identities are expressed, families are under considerable pressure to abandon their home language or dialect in favour of English. Parents see the benefits in their children speaking English, but this is often at the expense of the home language or dialect. Nevertheless, the disappearance of languages remains a serious threat to human language diversity, and linguists predict that of the 5000–6000 languages spoken in the world, half will be extinct by the next century (Nettle and Romaine 2000).

Learning English at the expense of the home language

Up until the 1950s research on bilingualism was narrowly distorted and incorrectly pointed to intellectual difficulties and emotional problems in bilinguals (Makin *et al.* 1995). Consequently, it was considered to negatively interfere with children's education in the majority language. In English-speaking countries with large non-English-speaking immigrant populations, such as Australia, efforts to equip bilingual children with the majority language as soon as possible were heavily informed by such research (Corson 1993). Subsequently, in Australian schools there was a singular focus on teaching English to migrant children in order to assimilate them into the Australian education system, reflecting assimilationist policies of that time.

Along with widespread institutional racism in the early twentieth century, minority languages and bilingual education were perceived as potential threats to social cohesion and national solidarity (Corson 1998). In Australia, the combination of protectionist and assimilationist social policies legislated up until the mid-1970s heavily encouraged bilingual families to abandon the use of the home language or dialect, along with their cultural identity, in favour of English and Anglo-Australian cultural identity (Clyne 1991). As a result, language shift in many third-generation migrant families was inevitable and subsequently many children acquired at best a limited and receptive understanding of their parents' language (Clyne 1991). This meant that at best many children grew up understanding the home language or dialect but unable to speak it. Even today, families are coerced into abandoning their home language or dialect, as they receive implicit messages from educators, caregivers and community members that the home language or dialect will impede children's proficiency in English, resulting in academic failure.

Nevertheless, in the past thirty years, empirical research has consistently pointed to the social, intellectual and linguistic benefits associated with bilingualism and language retention (Bialystok 1991; Cummins 1991, 1996; Wong-Fillmore 1991). Still, dissemination of these findings and their potential to inform educators and families alike is relatively scant in terms of being accessible and reliable information sources which parents, educators and caregivers can utilize (Jones Díaz 2003a).

Psycholinguistic and sociolinguistic studies have provided us with conceptual frameworks for understanding how the home language or dialect provides a linguistic resource in the transfer of linguistic knowledge and skills in learning a second language (see, for example, Saunders 1982; Fantini 1985; Arnberg 1987; Bialystok 1991; Cummins 1991; Lanza 1992). However, these studies have limited regard for the influence and impact of broader sociological processes and the impact on the home language or dialect of early exposure to dominant English-speaking environments. For example, recent studies into early childhood language shift have revealed that early exposure to dominant 'English only' environments severely inhibits the development of children's home language, often leading to subtractive experiences of bilingualism (Cummins 1991; Siren 1991; Wong-Fillmore 1991). Subtractive experiences of bilingualism occur when English replaces the home (first) language most often at the expense of the home language or dialect. For young bilingual children, the retention of the home language or dialect will most likely be inhibited when they are exposed to dominant English-speaking environments such as day care and school, without sufficient support for the home language or dialect.

There is consistent support in research findings indicating that language shift takes place rapidly in minority communities and that strong institutional support for the home language or dialect is essential in order to slow down the processes of language shift (Cummins 1991). Given the lack of research into early childhood language shift in Australia, where the impact of monolingual or dominant English-speaking environments has been relatively understudied, one can only assume that in bilingual communities the processes of language shift may parallel the processes of linguistic and cultural assimilation. Consequently, the relationship between language shift and cultural shift is of great significance to early childhood educators working closely with children and families, in terms of understanding young bilingual children's construction of bilingual/biliterate identities in diverse socio-cultural communities (Jones Díaz 2003b).

Therefore, the limitations of both psycholinguistic and sociolinguistic frameworks fail to acknowledge the relationship between discourses and social institutions (Jones Díaz and Harvey 2002), as there is a limited regard for the unequal distribution of linguistic resources influenced by more than the use of language. As Jones Díaz and Harvey (2002) point out, these established theories of bilingualism have not fully articulated the intersections between language retention and identity construction in the early years of children's lives, where the formation of identity is constantly negotiated, transformed and changed amidst a background of hegemonic English-speaking social fields such as preschool, school and community contexts. For example, within the social fields of early childhood, the use of language is central to the construction of social relationships, which are often constituted in power relations, discourses and identities. It has only been in recent years that studies, with a focus on childhood bilingualism and languages learning in education, have examined the relationship between power, discourse and identity particularly in relation to how bilingual children and their families negotiate issues of language and identity in educational settings. The few studies that are emerging examine issues of equity and its impact on language retention and bilingualism in childhood (see, for example, Martin-Jones and Heller 1996; Valdés 1996; Schecter and Bayley 1997; Volk 1997). Martin-Jones and Heller (1996) argue that it is essential to examine discursive practices and discourses that are evident in the daily life of educational institutions. They point out that the language practices in multilingual settings are constituted in the legitimization of power relations among cultural groups. Further, these language practices are embedded in the pedagogical discourses informed through such processes of legitimization most often found in early childhood education.

In early childhood education, the preoccupation with Piagetian and developmental frameworks has underpinned and legitimized narrow monolingual pedagogical approaches to language learning. For example, the unintentional exclusion of information about children's use of and development in their home language or dialect is often apparent in the singular use of 'language' rather than reference to the child's languages in observation and assessment procedures in preschool settings where children's developmental profiles draw on observations and interpretations of children's language development. In such exclusions, 'English' becomes synonymous with 'language' as educators draw on normative monolingual developmental pathways with little regard for the complexities in learning and negotiating two or more linguistic codes in the early years of life. This often results in early childhood educators adopting deficit and dismissive approaches towards bilingual children's cognitive and linguistic capabilities, positioning these children as less capable than English-speaking children.

Towards critical understandings of equity in language retention and language learning

Critical frameworks for understanding bilingualism, identity and language learning are essential, particularly in relation to how schooling and early childhood education reproduce inequality and power relations between various cultural and language groups with differing cultural and **linguistic capital**. Bourdieu's (1993: 78) analogy of the **linguistic market** provides a useful framework from which we can understand the production of linguistic inequality in the early childhood field. His model of **linguistic habitus** + linguistic market = linguistic expression can be effectively applied to 'English only' early childhood settings where the singular use of English throughout the day is normalized social practice. Linguistic habitus is the product of social conditions which produce utterances and linguistic behaviours adapted to the requirements of a given social situation, which Bourdieu refers to as social fields or markets. For Bourdieu (1993: 79), the linguistic market exists when 'someone produces an utterance for receivers capable of assessing it, evaluating it and setting a price on it'. This price is the value of the linguistic performance, which depends on the laws that are determined by the market operating in various social fields.

Bourdieu's notion of linguistic capital is the power to control the mechanisms operating within the linguistic price formation to one's advantage and social power. In this way, Bourdieu emphasizes that every linguistic interaction is determined by micro-markets, which are ultimately dominated by broader structures. So, in 'English only' early childhood settings, the micro-market operating is regulated through the broader legitimization of English overriding other languages spoken by children and staff, rendering them with little social power while privileging English. The power relations evident in these settings mean that children and adults are subject to a 'unified price formation', which is embedded in dominant 'English only' environments and social interactions. Bourdieu (1993), then, asserts that the linguistic market is the place where forms of linguistic domination are secured.

In understanding how linguistic markets secure their domination, the notion of 'habitus' provides a significant contribution to the analysis of social and cultural practices in both educational and non-educational settings. Habitus is the 'system of schemes for generating and perceiving practices' (Bourdieu 1993: 87), which involves the durable incorporation of dispositions, practices and perceptions realized both spontaneously and generatively at the moment of social practice within a social **field** (Bourdieu 1990). 'The habitus is an unpredictable yet often systemic representation of the social condition in which it is produced . . ., a transforming machine that leads us to "reproduce" the social conditions of our own production, but in a relatively unpredictable way' (Bourdieu 1993: 87).

More specifically, then, in relation to the use of languages and dialects, the linguistic habitus involves the production of utterances, speech and communication adapted to a particular social field or market. The forces within the linguistic market of daily interactions that allocate social power will regulate this production of meaning through language in a given situation and the dispositions and tendencies to speak in certain ways become congruent with discourses and 'rules' operating with the linguistic market (Bourdieu and Wacquant 1992). Hence, for bilingual children and adults, the linguistic habitus generated in speaking English and the home language or dialect will undergo various adaptations and transformations within the various social fields they encounter, which can either prohibit or promote the development and use of their home language or dialect. As Bourdieu (1993: 87) writes, 'the situation is, in a sense, the permissive condition of the fulfilment of the habitus'. This means, then, that unless the home languages and dialects of children are authorized and legitimated in early childhood settings, the linguistic habitus generated in speaking the home language or dialect will be replaced by English, and the habitus of speaking English may override children's interest and proficiency in using their home language or dialect with their family and community.

Bourdieu's theory of social practice provides a useful framework for understanding the production of educational and linguistic inequality. In particular, his emphasis on cultural capital as cultural currency or social power assists our understanding of the impact of hegemonic monolingual pedagogies on bilingual children's capacity to exchange social and cultural power. For Bourdieu, human activity is conceptualized as 'exchanges' that occur within an 'economy of practices' which can yield or not yield material and symbolic 'profits' (Olneck 2000). These 'profits' constitute three different forms: embodied cultural capital, objectified cultural capital and institutional cultural capital (Bourdieu 1986). Embodied cultural capital includes modes of interaction and expression, cultural preferences and affinities, ways of knowing and reasoning (Olneck 2000). In this sense, language, knowledge and other representational resources inculcated over time through social and cultural practices become 'embodied' by the individual (Carrington and Luke 1997). Objectified cultural capital includes representational and transmissible cultural texts produced and given value through embodied cultural capital, such as books, art and music (Carrington and Luke 1997; Olneck 2000). Finally, institutionalized cultural capital includes titles, qualifications and certificates authorized by institutions, which are legitimized by state, corporate and professional institutions.

Consequently, for young bilingual children, having proficiency in the home language or dialect will generate differentiated forms of cultural capital depending on how the linguistic market accommodates and validates the required linguistic habitus. However, as children enter 'English only' early childhood settings from infancy, their potential for accumulating embodied cultural capital constituted in learning their home language or dialect will be constrained, as their learning of English will transform their linguistic habitus accumulated through the objectified cultural capital represented through curriculum, pedagogy and policy. Conversely, bilingual children can have opportunities to exchange and accumulate embodied and objectified forms of cultural capital transmitted in both English and the home language or dialect. This can occur through their family, cultural and community networks, or within early childhood settings that promote and extend children's home languages and dialects.

Research into staff practices and attitudes towards language retention and second language learning issues

Two recent studies that have investigated adults' and children's practices and perceptions of bilingualism, language retention and language learning from preschool, school and community settings, reveal significant findings relating to questions of identity, bilingualism and language learning. The first study is the research that we conducted with early childhood educators, which investigated perceptions, practices, policies in long day care and preschool settings within the Inner West and South West areas of Sydney, Australia (Robinson and Jones Díaz 2000). Of the five different areas relating to diversity and difference under investigation in this study, questions relating to bilingualism and biculturalism were examined. The second study, conducted by Jones Díaz (2005), which is in progress, investigates educators' work with bilingual children in general and with Latino/a children in particular. The data drawn from the thirty-four teacher/caregiver questionnaires raised issues about bilingual identity and how teacher/caregiver attitudes towards bilingualism and language retention shape children's identity construction. The study also investigates families and children's differing and similar perspectives on growing up and living with two or more languages or dialects in terms of how children and families negotiate and reconstruct identity pivoted against a backdrop of language retention and language learning in everyday social practices of childhood.

Rhetoric but not reality

Within these two studies, significant issues emerge relating to language retention and the impact on the home language or dialect. In both studies, there is a clear demonstration of good will and awareness of the importance of bilingualism, but the rhetoric and strong support for the retention of children's home languages or dialects does not match the reality. For example, in our research, disparities between what educators believe to be

important and what they actually claim to implement in terms of programming and planning for home language retention were evident (Robinson and
Jones Díaz 2000: 76). Similarly, in the second study, the incongruence
between ideology and practice is also evident. For example, while the
majority of the participants are bilingual, less than half report using their
language with children, and only a quarter of the thirty-four participants
report using the home language 'all the time' with children to promote the
children's cultural and linguistic identity. In other situations, the use of the
home language to assist children in the learning of new concepts, and promoting family involvement, receive lower scores.

Further, in the second study, of the fifty-nine languages listed by participants, as spoken by the children in various settings, only seven are identified
as part of the settings' community language or home language support programme. These languages included Spanish, Vietnamese, Arabic, Assyrian,
Chinese, Thai and Italian. Furthermore, of the nineteen participants who
work in preschool settings, the majority indicate that their setting did not
offer any form of bilingual support to children. This contrasted with the
reality that in preschool settings there was a greater proportion of bilingual
educators employed than in primary school settings. Yet, over half of the
participants across both preschool and primary settings indicate that their
setting does not specifically employ bilingual educators for their language
skills.

The depoliticization of linguistic inequality

All the participants across both studies strongly supported bilingualism, with
most respondents demonstrating adequate insights into the socio-cultural,
linguistic and cognitive benefits of bilingualism. In both of these studies, it
was highly evident that participants' frame of reference was informed by a
hybrid of developmentalism, psycholinguistics and sociolinguistics. Concern
for broader sociological issues relating to language rights, access to the home
language, and linguistic inequality were not apparent. Rather, the majority of
participants rated 'self-esteem' as the principle reason for promoting bilingualism with children, rather than other reasons relating to cultural identity,
family cohesion and overseas links with family and community.

This preoccupation with self-esteem is an indication of how developmental
psychology predominates in education, which tends to depoliticize or
downplay the equity issues in not having access to the home language or
dialect, hence masking linguistic inequality. Martin-Jones and Heller (1996)
argue that pedagogical discourses that focus on individual development as a
basis of evaluation undermine the significance of learning and knowledge
production as a social enterprise. This was apparent in these studies, whereby
concerns for children's individual 'self-esteem' were of higher priority than
concerns for children's lack of opportunities to use their home language at
the setting with other children in social interactions to extend their learning.

Critical approaches to linguistic diversity and difference

In both studies, the vast majority of participants considered that children did indeed have understandings of language and cultural differences. Participants identified many reasons for this relating to children's exposure to 'difference' through living in diverse communities, the setting's approach to diversity and children's experiences with diversity in friendships and their subsequent awareness of different cultural practices. Comments from the second study include the following:

> Our school is approximately 95% NESB [non-English-speaking background]. They see constant examples of cultural and linguistic diversity through multicultural events, items and very vibrant LOTE [language other than English] and community language programme which operates within the school.

> English-speaking children label the non-English-speaking children 'naughty' as they use actions to get what they want, not language.

> Children are very smart to notice language and cultural differences. They can distinguish colour, different clothing, worn by cultural groups that are different from their families. They also have the ability to discover whose children speak the same language as them during playtime.

There was clear acknowledgement in both studies that children were not only aware of language, cultural and racial differences, but also capable of constructing negative attitudes based on these differences, as the comments below indicate:

> They mention that they can't understand what a child is saying and will avoid playing with them sometimes.

> Children often laugh and repeat and/or ask what is being said.

> Especially older children [who ask questions such as] 'Why do they talk funny?'

> Children are aware of when adults/children are not using English. [They comment] 'What are they saying?' or 'They don't speak properly'.

However, there was less concern for the need to encourage children to think critically about issues of racism, stereotyping and power. For example, it was apparent that educators were more comfortable promoting positive attitudes towards cultural, linguistic and racial differences than engaging children in deconstruction and critique of dominant discourses associated with linguicism, racism, stereotyping and power.

> I feel if we teach and nurture a love of ourselves for who we are and a love and appreciation of others for who they are the rest falls into place – awareness, acceptance, tolerance, understanding.

> If children consider children from an NESB important as they can speak another language, I feel friendship and respect will follow.

In the first study (Robinson and Jones Díaz 2000), while some educators did consider the significance of critical thinking about linguistic diversity and difference with children, few viewed structural inequalities associated with linguistic difference and discrimination to be an important issue to raise with children. Thus, limited connections were made between structural or societal inequalities and discrimination. In both studies, there was a strong preference to discuss 'safer' issues with children, such as promoting linguistic, cultural and racial diversity and harmony, rather than more contentious issues of inequality, discrimination and power relations in order to challenge children's negative constructions of difference.

Constructing the deficit 'needy' bilingual child

In Australia, throughout the 1950s and 1960s, cultural deprivation or deficit theories directed at working-class, immigrant and Aboriginal communities were largely informed by the work of Talcott Parsons, the well-known structural functionalist. According to Parsons, individuals inherently possess various talents and skills that schooling can develop and refine. Genetic deficiency became a popular explanation for the educational failure of many working-class, immigrant and Aboriginal children (Germov 2004). In Australia, these deficit theories were also driven by assimilationist social policies of monoculturalism, in which cultural difference was equated with cultural deficit. Children from linguistic, cultural and racial minorities were constructed as underachievers and deficient learners. In educational contexts, such pervading assumptions suggested that there was something wrong with the child, the family and the whole community to which the child belongs. The child's cultural and language background was viewed as a deficit and the only way to help this child was to teach him/her English so the handicap would be overcome.

Even today discourses of deficit very often permeate teachers' expectations of bilingual children. This was apparent in our research, where the majority of the participants tended to construct bilingual children's lack of English as a deficit and locate children in discourses of 'need'. Acceptance of other children and integration into the dominant English-speaking setting was of considerable concern:

> Children from NESB have specific needs that affect development based on their previous experiences.

> Any children who are bilingual will have some additional areas of need in their life compared to children with monolingual/monocultural backgrounds.

Further, in discourses of monolingualism, children's ability to mix effectively with other children (in being able to accumulate social capital in an English-speaking dominant environment) is measured against the ability to speak English. Hence, what counts as cultural capital for these children is the ability to 'fit' into the monolingual 'English only' setting.

In our research, participants' preoccupation with 'fitting in' is synonymous with 'survival' in 'English only' settings or environments where languages other than English have little currency and legitimization. The linguistic market of 'English only' constructs language norms based on monolingual English-speaking practices, masking the reality that it is precisely the linguistic market (English only) within which the 'needs' are constructed. This discourse constructs a natural authority embedded in 'English only' monolingualism, rather than subverting or questioning how the monolingual 'English only' environment works to impede children's capacity to accumulate social and cultural capital in their home language or dialect. As Bourdieu reminds us, education is one of the most significant social fields in which the linguistic market determines social and cultural power. Hence, regardless of whether or not bilingual children's language differences are an obstacle to educational achievement, the fact remains that it is precisely 'the local linguistic marketplace and its relationship to material and symbolic marketplaces of a global nature' that determine the outcome of educational achievement (Martin-Jones and Heller 1996: 131).

Bilingual children's negotiation of languages and identity

From poststructural, critical and cultural studies perspectives, the interconnections between language and identity are related to our sense of 'self' (subjectivity) and to cultural practice, which is constituted in discourse. Language is the technology in which meanings about the world are represented and exchanged through discourses. Hence, ways of understanding relationships, meanings and social practices in the world are constituted in language. For bilingual children, this process operates in two or more languages or dialects.

Identity, on the other hand, gives meaning to people's lives, which they take up as part of their subjectivity. Hall (1996) argues that identities are constructed through discourses of language, history and culture constituted through memory, fantasy, narrative and myth. He conceptualizes identity from two distinct but related viewpoints in terms of the relationship between culture and identity. The first position he argues is related to shared culture or a sense of collective culture in which the mutual histories and cultural practices bind together codes of solidarity and imagined homogeneity within individuals and groups. His second position argues that within the constructed forms of shared cultural discourses and practices, there are points of difference which are fragmented, transformative and positional. In this sense, cultural identity is a matter of 'becoming' as well as 'being' and belongs to the future as much as to the past (Hall 1996, 2001).

Cultural identities are formed through historical and contemporary power relations but are subject to the continuous influences of culture, power and history. Consequently, identities are constantly changing, transformative and multiple, often unstable and up for negotiation, contingent upon the discursive positioning of the 'self'. Hall's conceptualization of the transformative and fluid aspects of identity is applicable to our understandings of the impact of English on young bilingual children's identity formation in terms of how they negotiate two linguistic codes.

In the discussion below, we draw on voices of some of the children and families from the findings of the second study (Jones Díaz 2005) to reframe identity construction in terms of how bilingual children and their families negotiate identity in everyday experiences of growing up living with two or more languages. The discussion that follows highlights the significant relationship between language and identity in bilingual children and their families.

Many of the parents and children in this study expressed the importance of belonging to a cultural minority in which shared cultural and language practices are significant. Jenny, whose children are Chinese-Uruguayan Australians, tried to promote their Uruguayan identity and wanted her children to identify with both her partner's Uruguayan side and her family's Chinese heritage, claiming 'You are from China country and eh ... You are from Uruguay ... You are Uruguay China' [Uruguayan Chinese]. However, Jenny's desire for her children to identify with both her partner's Uruguayan side and her family's Chinese heritage is thwarted by her daughter's identity claim, 'I'm Chinese'. Much of Jenny's struggle with identity politics between her partner and her daughter is located in her daughter's construction of her own Chinese identity being contingent upon her proficiency in Chinese. Jenny's efforts in challenging her daughter, 'no you're Spanish but you can't speak', is an attempt to destabilize language as the singular site for identity construction.

Many of the children in this study negotiate multiple identities in which they located their own subjectivities. When asked questions about their identity, many of the children fused their parents' national identities with language and cultural practices, while simultaneously locating themselves as Australians.

> Yeah, I was born in Australia, but my mummy was born in Peru ... So I speak Australian and Spanish. (Barbi, 5 years)

> Si, ella por supuesto se considera Australiana pero se considera Peruana. Se identifica con el país, con las costumbres, con la música ... [Of course she considers herself Australian but she [also] considers herself Peruvian. She identifies with the country, with the customs, with the music ...] (Carol, mother of Barbi)

> ... y pienso que ella es Australiana, su idioma es inglés pero ella también entiende que sus raíces son de Latinoamérica. Somos de sur América de habla español también. [... and I think that she is Australian, her language is English, but she also understands that her roots are from Latin America. We are from South America and we speak Spanish.] (Miryam, mother of 12-year-old Alison)

Parents' awareness of their children's negotiation of two cultural worlds in which identity is mediated across cultural, linguistic and racial lines was skilfully expressed by one parent (Raul) of two boys from an interracial and interethnic family:

parecido ellos saben que hay una cultura en el medio de mama y papa. [It appears that they know that there is a culture in between the mother and father.]

Lola, who is 11 years old, lives with her mother, grandmother and older sisters. Her father lives in Panama and is of Greek background. In the conversation below, I (Jones Díaz) ask Lola what it means to speak Spanish and have a Latin American background.

> Criss: Do you know what your culture is?
> Lola: Maybe, I don't know. My mum's Uruguayan.
> Criss: So what does that make you?
> Lola: Spanish.
> Criss: Spanish?

Lola identifies herself as Spanish and conflates her mother's cultural background with the Spanish language. She positions her own identity in relation to this homogenized category, 'Spanish', which is often applied to all Latin Americans and Spaniards. However, this is a problematic generalization because it works on two distinct levels. Firstly, it implies that the Spanish language is unique to Spain and that Latin American cultures are duplicates of Spanish culture. Secondly, 'Spanish' refers to the generic language group, spoken by both Spaniards and Spanish-speaking Latin Americans. However, Lola's identification as 'Spanish' reifies and homogenizes both Iberian and Latin American languages and cultures as one unified homogeneous category.

In this second study, it was evident that there were significant intersections between language and identity, and while there were differing points of identity positions between the children and their parents, for the most part the parents' perceptions of their children's identity claims included a strong allegiance to their Latin American cultural heritage. Similarly, the educators and caregivers who participated in this study also had perceptions of how children negotiate and identify with their cultural background. Many of the practitioners reported that the Latin American children with whom they work do indeed identify with their cultural heritage:

> [They are] very much part of the family culture and family experiences such as visiting relatives.

> To varying degrees [they identify with their heritage] ... Some are very vocal and full of information. Some sit back, like all children.

> I perceive that many can relate to their Latin American culture and community as many of them discuss things they have done on the weekend. Such as going to Latin parties, Mexican festivals and some children do Colombian and Flamenco dancing.

However, not all participants agreed with the sentiment raised above:

> They usually consider themselves Australian even when they are coming from [a] Spanish-speaking country.

Feelings of shame and reluctance to use the home language

In the second study, participants highlighted a number of difficulties encountered when trying to encourage children to speak their home language. Many of the teachers and caregivers reported that the bilingual children with whom they worked felt ashamed and embarrassed to speak their home language. Some comments were:

> I believe that children are aware that their home language may be a minority language and to some extent feel threatened by that.

> They are not fully fluent in their home language. They are embarrassed. It's not cool!

> Children often display embarrassment about using their native tongue in the classroom. It clearly makes them feel exposed to teasing or ridicule.

> Many children feel shy and embarrassed about speaking in their home language. It's about having confidence, being able to speak in your home language very well.

> Children [are] not confident to speak at all (even preschoolers) to teachers.

Crucial tenets of poststructural, critical and cultural perspectives highlight agency and subjectivity as critical components in the social construction of the 'self'. The 'self' is considered as an active and conscious thinking subject whose understandings, interpretations and meanings about the world and the social relations between people, institutions and social practices influence daily life. Children, like adults, are capable of shifting and changing their thinking and behaviours according to the social context in which they are involved (see Chapter 2). For bilingual children, choices in language use are contingent upon the social context and their subjectivity. Clearly, from the participants' comments above, children's reluctance and shame in speaking their home language is an illustration of children's capacity to locate themselves in normalizing discourses of monolingualism.

The hegemony of English: structural and institutional constraints in the provision of home language or dialect support

Gramsci's concept of hegemony refers to ways in which power operates between dominant and minority groups through various ideologies and consent. Hegemony is achieved through ideological processes in which the dominant group controls and maintains power over minority groups by convincing them that this is in their best interests (Schirato and Yell 2000). Hegemony is 'a dialectical relationship enabling those in power to maintain power, while apparently giving the people exactly what they want' (Davis 2004: 47). We can apply this term to ideological power relations that exist between languages and between speakers of different languages. Hornberger and Skilton-Silvester (2000) suggest the values placed on languages and dialects in any given society are socially constructed. Therefore, the power relations between languages and speakers of languages are constituted in hegemonic relations that subordinate minority languages and speakers of those languages to the dominant language and culture within society.

In Australia, while there is a vast array of community languages spoken and 'tolerated', there appears to be unequal distribution of linguistic resources in educational, political and social fields within the community. Community and Indigenous languages are considered minority languages and hence often afforded a lower status. For example, in many Australian schools, the provision of community languages is marginal, with programmes being offered on an after-school basis or on Saturday mornings. Where community languages are offered during school hours, of the 248 languages spoken in 1996, 'as few as 31 community languages and 16 Indigenous languages were taught in Australian primary schools for a minimum of 2 hours per week' (Jones Díaz 2003b: 315). It is apparent, then, as Skutnabb-Kangas (1988: 41) argues, that '[d]ifferent languages have different political rights, not depending on any inherent linguistic characteristics, but on the power relationships between the speakers of these languages'.

In the study by Jones Díaz (2005), the power relations between languages were apparent and there appeared to be a relationship between the lack of institutional and structural support for community languages and children's interest in using their home language or dialect at the educational setting. This relationship also highlighted the participants' limitations and frustrations in their work, particularly as community language teachers.

Many community language teachers work in community language programmes offered after school by various ethnic communities. These programmes often receive limited support from local, state and federal levels of government. Hence, the day-to-day management and administration operates through the voluntary sponsorship of different ethnic communities. In order for them to provide a teacher to teach the language, they rely on parent fees and volunteer management committees to sustain their viability in meeting the demands of the programme. Further, due to the diversity of language proficiency and retention rates in many bilingual communities, these community language classrooms will often have a diverse range of language levels, from kindergarten to year 6. Hence, teachers in these classrooms encounter many difficulties and limitations in providing effective community language pedagogy. The following comments highlight some of the participant's frustrations:

Teaching the language after school, children are too tired.

Having mixed ages (6–12).

Hence, it is no wonder, as children grow older, that their interest and proficiency in their home language or dialect becomes increasingly limited. In the Jones Díaz (2005) study, participants were asked if they believed that the bilingual children with whom they work were in the process of losing proficiency in their home language:

Some children are beginning to reply to parents in English even though they are spoken to in home language.

Many kids understand but only speak when necessary or encouraged.

Children understand their home language but rarely use it to communicate.

Children that arrived with little or no English, now speak English at school and at home. We no longer hear them speak their home language.

To be able to communicate successfully at school, children often drop their home language.

Implications for practice

As early childhood educators working with children and families in these changing times, characterized by globalization of English and its technologies as well as increased cultural, social and linguistic diversity, our negotiation of difference in personal and professional lives in our local communities calls for greater reflection, knowledge and understandings about children's experiences of growing up bilingual. The following discussion centres around four major areas of practice that can assist early childhood educators working with bilingual children and their families.

Reframing our understandings of bilingualism and language learning

The need to move beyond psycholinguistic and sociolinguistic models of language learning, as well as Piagetian developmental frameworks, will enable our pedagogies to be more inclusive and recognizant of ways in which bilingualism is shaped and mediated by broader societal processes. It is crucial that early childhood educators recognize that 'English only' educational settings produce monolingual and normative approaches to the use of language and language learning, which can limit bilingual children's potential in negotiating cultural and linguistic capital at the setting.

Early childhood educators need to recognize the diverse ways in which children experience language learning and language use, so that discourses of normative monolingualism are challenged. This means in practice, that educators need to include the home language or dialect in assessment and programme planning in which children's bilingual identities are accommodated accordingly, rather than ignored or dismissed as unimportant and irrelevant to children's lives.

Disrupting the power relations between languages: critical thinking with children and adults

It is crucial that we acknowledge the discursive and political use of language, because every time we use language we invoke and reconstruct the broader cultural, social and political meanings of dominant discourses in our globalized society. This realization may assist us in our understandings about the power relations and equity issues that exist between languages in our dominant English-speaking societies. Therefore, as educators we need to be mindful of our own location in monolingual and normalizing language practices particularly in our interactions with speakers of languages 'othered' through English. In communicating with bilingual families and staff, educators need to take time to draw on their experiences with children's home languages or dialects and find ways to include these experiences in the daily programme.

Further, children are capable of producing discriminatory practices when adults are not around. For early childhood educators, working with young children around issues of language and cultural differences, the need to understand how children take up multiple yet contradictory subject positions in discourse is crucial. Hence, going beyond feelgood and fuzzy statements such as 'it is not nice to make fun of the way Raul talks' does little to help children acknowledge that there exist power relations between adults and children, adults and adults, and children and children, particularly in the context of cultural, racial, linguistic and social differences.

Therefore, it is essential that educators have an understanding of the broader contradictory and complex mechanisms operating in children's lives, in relation to language, 'race', ethnicity, class, sexuality, gender, disability and so on. For example, the acknowledgement that issues of **linguicism** and racism are 'collective' experiences of inequality and worthy of discussion and critique with children will lead towards pedagogical practices that go beyond superficial and tokenistic approaches towards linguistic and cultural differences.

Representations and explanations of linguistic, cultural and racial difference need to go beyond oversimplified and individualistic representations. For example, the emphasis on a child's home language or dialect as 'his/her language', 'that's Raul's language', individualizes the child's linguistic difference. Rather, a more appropriate representation of a child's home language or dialect is discussion about the language as a community or Indigenous language that is spoken in our society by various communities. Here the emphasis is on the diversity of languages spoken in our society rather than confining it to the realm of the child's individual ways of speaking. By focusing on the collective use of language, this locates the language in its broader societal context, enabling children to better understand its dynamic and communicative function within the community.

Reframing our understandings of identity construction in the lives of bilingual children

It is essential that early childhood educators recognize that for many bilingual children and their families, 'experiences of identity and the use of the home language are mediated and negotiated against a backdrop of dominant English-speaking contexts' (Jones Díaz 2003b: 331). This brings about constant negotiation and transformation of identity which is intersected across social fields in which the hegemony of English as a dominant and global language affords it greater cultural, linguistic and social capital. Hence, a move away from understandings about identity as fixed and stable will enable us to understand how bilingual children experience their identity as multiple and transformative. For example, meanings about themselves are often shaped by their experiences of growing up with two or more languages or dialects, which may have less cultural, linguistic and social capital in our society.

Consequently, early childhood educators need to take the time to find out about family language and cultural practices that are significant to children outside the setting. In this way, learning experiences for children are more meaningful and connected to their everyday lives. It is crucial to understand that the relationships between culture and language are not stable, and therefore cultural practice is fluid and dynamic. A move away from fixed ideas about culture as celebration, towards an appreciation of cultural practice as an everyday part of daily life will enable educators to implement experiences that enhance and acknowledge diversity across families, cultural groups and communities.

Creating a linguistic marketplace that legitimizes languages other than English

Early childhood settings that promote and extend children's home languages and dialects by making available opportunities for their use with other bilingual children and educators will contribute towards children identifying positively with their language. Hence, their interest and willingness to continue to speak their language or dialect may follow. This means that languages other than English must attain forms of institutionalized cultural capital (at the setting) in which the policies, pedagogies and curriculum approaches provide enabling linguistic markets through the provision of opportunities for the use of languages spoken by children, families and educators. The following suggestions may assist early childhood educators in implementing experiences that go towards creating a linguistic marketplace that legitimizes the use of languages and dialects spoken by children and families at the setting.

Policy direction and implementation

In order to effectively address the socio-cultural and language learning issues affecting bilingual children, early childhood settings (including schools) need to implement language and literacy policies that reflect contemporary theoretical and pedagogical approaches. Such policies may include home language support, full bilingual programmes and learning English as a second language. These policies should be regularly updated and re-evaluated in consultation with staff, families and children at the setting. Further, policies that enable educators to access professional development, in the form of inservice, conferences and resource development, are crucial.

Working with bilingual staff and families

Bilingual caregivers and educators that represent the languages and cultures of the children at the setting should be employed to support children's home languages or dialects. They play a crucial role in observing, planning and implementing experiences collaboratively with other staff members in which their language expertise is valued and integrated across curriculum areas.

It is crucial that families receive encouragement to continue speaking their home language or dialect to their children. This is especially important because as children's proficiency in English increases, their preference to use English at home with parents and siblings will also become apparent. This can also result in English unknowingly 'taking over' family interactions and the work involved in sustaining conversation in the home language or dialect becoming arduous. Therefore, early childhood educators can offer support and encouragement by being sensitive to families' concerns regarding their children's bilingualism.

Furthermore, families (including grandparents and older siblings) are encouraged to contribute their language and cultural expertise through storytelling, conversations, routines and so on, so that bilingual children hear their language spoken by adults and children at the setting, and other children, who don't speak that language, are exposed to the use of languages other than English, as well as their home language or dialect.

Communication practices and interactional strategies

In order for children to maximize opportunities in language learning, quality communication and interactions strategies are crucial. Educators need to ensure that they provide dynamic, fluid and sustained interactions and conversations across a variety of functional and communicative contexts throughout the day in both English and children's home language or dialect. Bilingual educators are encouraged to use their language particularly with children who speak it and develop close relationships with children in it. Families are also encouraged to continue to speak their home language or dialect with their children at home. However, educators need to understand the complexities and difficulties in raising children bilingually, especially in interracial or interethnic families where more than one language or dialect can be used. Educators need to offer ongoing support to families through the provision of up-to-date information about bilingualism and ways to support the home language or dialect in the setting of the home. For example, pamphlets, websites, bilingual retail outlets and newsletters should be available in a range of languages at the setting. These resources can be accessed from local libraries, the Internet and educational resource settings.

It is also vital that bilingual educators read books in their language or dialect in small groups, making sure that there are more children in the group who speak the language or dialect than do not. This strategy encourages those children who do not speak the language to pay close attention to gestures and visual cues that can aid comprehension. For the bilingual children who do speak the language, their engagement with the text will not only model listening skills but also valorize the linguistic capital in that language. Bilingual staff should not rely on translation methods when reading bilingual books; for example, reading one page in the home language and translating the same page into English. This only encourages the children to focus their attention solely on English, distracting them away from attempting to pick up cues and listen to the story in the home language or dialect.

It is also important that bilingual educators are not used solely for the purpose of translating and communicating between parents and other staff members. Their language and cultural knowledge should be seen as a resource for the children's learning, and it is likely that they are not trained as professional translators.

Programming and planning

With careful programming and planning, early childhood educators can provide relevant experiences to children that will enhance their language learning. For example, observations and assessment procedures need to include children's use of their home language or dialect outside the setting, as well as at the setting. By gathering information from families about the different social contexts in which the home language or dialect is used, practitioners can gain a better appreciation of children's experiences with their home language or dialect. The information collected about children's use of language needs to be integrated across different curriculum areas and implemented in daily experiences.

Further, grouping children in language groups based on age and interest can also provide opportunities for both bilingual staff and children to use their home languages or dialects. This not only supports the development of relationships between bilingual educators and children in the home language or dialect, but also enables bilingual children to extend and develop their home language or dialect. It also provides opportunities for children who speak minority languages in the setting to access social and cultural capital in that language.

Posters, books, CDs, images, songs and other resources used in either the classroom or playroom setting need to represent realistic linguistic, cultural and social practices of the children. Stereotypic images should be avoided and there needs to be a careful balance of resources that represent both traditional and contemporary images of cultural and language practices. Texts in children's languages, including books, newspapers, games, electronic media and popular culture texts, and so on, should be used throughout the day across different curriculum areas. These resources should not be confined to book corner or language sessions (Jones Díaz and Harvey 2002).

Conclusion

In globalized English-speaking nation states, there are cultural, social and political processes that significantly impact on children's and families' experiences of bilingualism, language learning and identity construction.

Bilingual children, families and educators are often positioned as marginalized subjects, particularly in 'English only' settings, in which the broader socio-political forces and power relations have a marked impact on negotiating cultural difference, identity and cultural capital. Also, their capacity to use their home language or dialect in functional and communicative contexts can be minimized through discursive pedagogical practices of monolingualism, which can counteract the intellectual, social, cultural gains in being bilingual. Therefore, it is crucial that educators develop critical and contemporary understandings of the relationship between identity negotiation and languages learning and usage in young bilingual children in order for them to provide quality-based and equitable pedagogies representative of all children using early childhood settings.

Recommended reading

Davis, H. (2004) *Understanding Stuart Hall*. London: Sage Publications.
Hall, S. (2001) Foucault: power, knowledge and discourse, in M. Wetherell, S. Taylor and S.J. Yates (eds) *Discourse Theory and Practice*. London: Sage.
Wong Fillmore, L. (1991) When learning a second language means losing the first, *Early Childhood Research Quarterly*, 6: 323–347.

GENDER PERFORMATIVITY IN EARLY CHILDHOOD EDUCATION

Introduction

Gender is generally recognized as an important equity issue to address with young children and has been incorporated into early childhood programmes to varying degrees. In the past decade research has increased awareness and understandings of the process of gender operating in young children's lives (Davies 1989, 1993; Thorne 1993; Alloway 1995; Grieshaber 1998; MacNaughton 2000). Theoretically, there have been major shifts in the way that gender has been viewed, the role that education is perceived to play in the process of gender formation, and the approaches educators have employed to counteract gender discrimination in schooling – see Arnot (2002) for an in-depth overview of these changes. Theoretical explanations of gender and gender formation have primarily shifted from the essentialist and biological perspectives that dominated up until the 1960s, to views that understand gender as a socio-cultural process, in which what it means to be a girl or boy, woman or man, is socially constructed.

In more recent years, feminist poststructuralist perspectives have taken understandings of the process of gender construction further. These perspectives highlight how gender is discursively constituted, how social relations of power between males and females are perpetuated and maintained through the cultural binary male/female that underpins common-sense oppositional thinking around masculinity and femininity, and how children are active agents in the construction of their own gendered identities (Davies 1989, 1993; Alloway 1995; Gallas 1998; Grieshaber 1998; MacNaughton 2000). Despite these theoretical shifts in understandings of gender formation, it seems that for many early childhood educators children are still largely viewed as 'sponges' that soak up the sex roles that they are required to take on as boys and girls (Robinson and Jones Díaz 2000). This perspective is reflected in the pedagogical and curriculum strategies that are often incorporated in programmes dealing with **gender equity** issues.

Over the past thirty years or so, research has highlighted how the institution of schooling (at all educational levels) largely operates to constitute and regulate normalizing discourses that maintain the gendered power relationships that prevail in the broader society (Connell *et al.* 1982; Mahony 1985; Walkerdine 1990; Robinson 1992, 2000; Mac an Ghaill 1994; Arnot 2002). In particular, this research demonstrates how schooling practices, teachers' perceptions and pedagogies, the curriculum, school organization and management structures all operate to construct gendered identities. To date, much of this research has focused on primary (or elementary) and secondary (or high) schooling. The role that early childhood educators and early education play in the process of gender construction in young children's lives has received comparatively less attention than in other eductional sectors. Paramount to an understanding of the process of gender construction in early childhood is the role that early childhood educators can play in the perpetuation or disruption of normalizing discourses of gender in children's early education. This chapter is largely based on the research and work we have done with early childhood educators in Australia and explores how gender is perceived and theorized, what gender equity strategies are employed, and how these are incorporated in curriculum and pedagogy. In undertaking gender equity work with children, it is imperative that educators are reflexive about their understandings and perceptions of gender and how these impact on their daily interactions with children and on their pedagogical practices. That is, it is critical for educators to ask 'Do my pedagogical practices and interactions with children disrupt, or rather regulate and perpetuate, their positioning in normalizing discourses of gender that strictly confine their options of doing gender within rigid, narrow and oppositional understandings of what it means to be a girl or boy?'.

This chapter also argues that the current understandings of the process of gender construction in children's lives that tend to dominate in early childhood education, do not adequately deal with the way in which gender is inextricably constituted within and normalized through the process of 'heterosexualization' (Robinson 2005c) – that is, how through the processes of gendering, children are simultaneously constructed as heterosexual beings (Butler 1990). As Robinson (2005c) argues, the construction of children's gendered identities cannot be fully understood without acknowledging how the dominant discourses of femininity and masculinity are heteronormalized in children's everyday lives, including through their educational experiences. The works of Judith Butler, particularly her concepts of the heterosexual matrix and performativity, are highlighted as being useful in extending current understandings of the process of gender construction in early childhood education.

What is gender? A feminist poststructuralist perspective

Our discussion of the process of gender construction in children's lives is primarily informed by feminist poststructuralist perspectives, which argue that individual subjects identify and make sense of themselves as men and women or boys and girls through the various cultural discourses of gender made available to them. Gender is considered to be socially constructed in discourse and is a dynamic process referring to the cultural inscription of bodies into masculine and feminine characteristics. Thus, gender is not fixed in one's biological sex – that is, male or female – as perceived in biological determinist explanations, but rather woman, man, boy and girl are unstable and contested social categories whose meanings and representations are susceptible to change across and within different cultures over time. For example, what it meant to be a young woman in white, middle-class, Anglo-Celtic Australia or Britain in the 1800s, and the attendant social expectations, are different from those operating today; understandings and representations of what it means to be a boy in Balinese cultures are different from those in Latin American cultures, and can also change within Balinese cultures. There are many different ways of doing masculinities or femininities across and within cultures, and these are influenced by other markers of identity such as social class, 'race', ethnicity and sexuality. However, despite the fact that there are multiple ways of doing masculinities and femininities, some ways of being a boy or a girl are considered more correct and appropriate than others. Dominant cultural discourses of gender operate to normalize particular ways of doing gender over others. For example, the belief that boys enjoy being physically active, like climbing trees or play fighting, while girls are more sedate, like sitting and playing with dolls, reading quietly, or talking with friends, is a discourse that constitutes meanings, representations and expectations of girls and boys, as well as gender differences in childhood, within some cultures. Children learn what society considers the appropriate and correct way of performing their gender and take these discourses up in order to achieve a recognizable identity within the existing social order (Davies 1989).

Feminist poststructuralist perspectives on gender construction have been critical of the way that Western philosophical thought has traditionally divided people into males and females based on the belief that this is a reflection of the natural order of things. This separation of the genders was primarily based on the view that males and females were inherently different from each other due to the fact that they were biologically different. Dominant discourses of gender that prevail today have been constituted within this dualistic oppositional thinking that has emerged from Western philosophical thought. That is, masculinity and femininity have been constituted within a cultural binary – signified as male/female – and primarily represented and defined in opposition to each other (for example, boys are strong and girls are weak). This cultural binary also constructs them in a hierarchical power relationship that is reflective of gendered social relationships operating more broadly in society. Thus, within this binary, women and girls are always constructed as the powerless Other to men and boys. De Lauretis (1987: 5) argues that the process of gender 'is always intimately interconnected with political and economic factors in each society ... [and] systematically linked to the organisation of social inequality ... assign[ing] meaning (identity, value, prestige, location in kinship, status in the social hierarchy, etc.) to individuals in society'. Within this gender binary, male and female are seen to be complementary yet mutually exclusive. Kimmel (1994: 126), based on his research on constructions of masculinity, points out that 'historically and developmentally, masculinity has been defined as the flight from women, the repudiation of femininity'. These perceived differences between the genders have been highly influential in structuring the pathways open to and chosen by men and women, boys and girl in their lives. The gendered division of labour that operates in the home and in the workplace is reflective of these gendered pathways. Child care, for instance, is a career almost entirely made up of women, while motor mechanics is dominated by men. Alsop *et al.* (2002: 3) point out that this gendered division of labour 'is dependent upon our cultural understandings of men and women being different and thus more suited to different types of work'.

Feminist poststructuralists consider that it is critical to disrupt and deconstruct the oppositional thinking constituted in cultural binaries such as male/female in order to initiate social change. They argue that maleness and femaleness do not have to be discursively constructed in the way they currently are. Davies (1989: 12) points out that 'children can take up a range of masculine and feminine positionings if they have access to discourse that renders that non-problematic'. If constructions of masculinities and femininities were not rigidly constituted within the polarized male/female binary, which is currently linked to one's biological body (for example, genitals), this would allow for a shifting nexus of possibilities open to individual subjects based on capabilities and interests. However, normalizing discourses of gender work powerfully on individual subjects, greatly influencing how they perform their gender. As Davies (1989: 13) points out, 'The development and practice of new forms of discourse ... is not a simple matter of choice, but involves grappling with both subjective and social/structural constraints'. Resisting dominant discourses of gender and positioning oneself in different ways of doing gender that are not socially sanctioned generally equate to getting one's gender wrong. The consequences of getting one's gender wrong can be severe and result in social isolation, teasing and bullying, as well as other forms of violence and regulation.

Sex roles and socialization theory: a critique

Most early childhood educators and pre-service teachers we have worked with tend to operate within the theoretical perspective that gender is socially constructed, primarily through the socialization of young children into particular sex-role behaviours. That is, children are socialized to take up stereotypical behaviours and roles associated with their gender that form 'feminine characters' and 'masculine characters'. Within the theory of sex-role socialization, the biological basis of gender difference is assumed, naturalized and fixed; children are taught the 'roles' that are related to 'real' biological differences identified in male and female bodies and dispositions. Those who do not adhere to this strict gendering process and slip from their specified gender roles and characters are generally considered problematic; it is considered to be associated with either a failure in the socialization process, or as a result of individual pathologies (Connell 1987). The family, schooling, media and friends are considered to be the main socializing agents in society.

This perspective of gender construction has met with much criticism from social theorists (Connell 1987; Davies 1989; Walkerdine 1990; Alsop *et al.* 2002). Much of the criticism is focused on issues around socialization, children's lack of agency, resistance and the perpetuation of Western dualistic thinking. This perspective does not recognize the active role that children play as agents in the construction of their own identities, nor in the regulation of the identities of others. In general, it does not acknowledge the active and significant part that children play in the organization of the social world (Davies 1989). The process of socialization operates in such a way that children are viewed as 'clean slates' at birth and become the passive recipients or objects of the social messages that are enforced on them primarily in their early years and largely through their relationships and interactions with adults. In this process, adults become the active agents, not children; and there is perceived to be a straightforward cause-and-effect link that is highly problematic. However, this process not only relies on and reinforces the traditional Western binary associated with cause-and-effect thinking, but is based on the adult/child binary in which children are the dependent and powerless Other to adults. Resistance is problematized in this perspective in two main ways: firstly, children do not always do what adults tell them to do; and secondly, non-conformity is primarily viewed in terms of individual deviance rather than as resistance to the rigid and narrow social boundaries placed on identities, such as gender.

Davies (1989: 6) makes the pertinent point that 'we need to shift the focus away from individual identity to relations of power and to the multiple subjectivities that are available to any one person within discursive practices of our society'. That is, we need to incorporate an understanding in our ways of looking at the world, of the broad social power relations that are operating in society that work to narrowly and rigidly fix identities within socially sanctioned norms. Sex-role and socialization perspectives obscure the multiple discourses operating around gender, for example, that provide individual subjects with a range of different gendered subject positions to take up as their own. Further, as Davies (1989: 6) highlights, 'These theories of the person obscure our recognition of the complex and contradictory ways in which we are continually constituting and reconstituting ourselves and the social world through the various discourses in which we participate'.

'Biology is destiny': the discourse of biological determinism – a critique

Biological determinist explanations dominated understandings of gender formation up until the mid-twentieth century, but are still influential in educational sectors, including early childhood education, today. Biological determinism refers to the way that meanings of woman and man are perceived to be stable and fixed characteristics that stem from one's biological make-up and sexed body (genitals). Inner biological characteristics were also

perceived to determine and fix other psychological and behavioural dispositions that were associated with maleness and femaleness. As pointed out
above, the cultural binary male/female, reflective of Western philosophical
thought, was based on biological differences between males and females.
Biological explanations emphasized and constructed understandings of gender largely within this rigid binary in which male and female characteristics
are constituted as being different from and opposite to each other. With the
emergence of scientific thought as the ultimate authoritative knowledge
during the Enlightenment period, research focused on 'discovering' the 'differences' between men and women, further emphasizing the polarized dualism of masculinity and femininity linked to physical bodies. In this process,
the essence of femininity and masculinity became located in sex hormones,
with testosterone viewed as the driving force behind male domination.
According to Alsop *et al.* (2002: 19), 'This is now one of the dominant modes
of thinking about biology of sex differences, with women's bodies seen as
particularly dominated by the balance or imbalance of hormones, a "fact"
used to justify exclusion from important roles in public life'. For example, in
some countries, such as Australia, women were excluded from driving public
transport such as trams until recent times, due to the belief that their hor-
monal make-up could lead to unpredictable behaviour that could put the
driver and their passengers at risk. In schooling contexts, biological explanations are often utilized to understand gendered behaviour. The phrase
'boys will be boys' is commonly used to understand the aggressive behaviours, including the sexual harassment of girls, engaged in by many boys.
These behaviours are often perceived to stem from boys' competitive, natural
urges that are often considered uncontrollable, arising from 'healthy' levels of
testosterone (Robinson 1996).

Biological explanations of gender have been seriously critiqued over the
years, particularly by feminists. Feminist poststructuralists, as discussed previously, have pointed out that gender is not fixed in one's biological differences, but is culturally and historically changing. Gender is considered to be
much more dynamic, fluid and contradictory both across and within males
and females (Davies 1989; Grieshaber 1998; MacNaughton 2000). Physical
characteristics used to designate the differences between men and women,
such as body hair and voice pitch, are often poor indicators. The perceived
differences between males and females, including physical differences, are
often intensified through socio-cultural values that influence gendered
behaviour. For example, males and females are equally capable of mothering,
nurturing and caring, but cultural values can operate to discourage boys and
men from displaying these behaviours. Body hair, for example, is actually a
characteristic of human bodies, varying across and within males and females
and performing a specific function. However, some cultures go to severe
lengths to dehair female bodies (anyone who uses wax strips to dehair their
legs knows what is meant by this!) in order to emphasize and regulate male
and female bodies within the oppositional thinking that stems from the
Western cultural binary male/female. Biological explanations of gender universalize and essentialize male and female behaviours; for example, aggressive
and competitive behaviours are a characteristic of being male. Those males

who do not display these characteristics are often viewed as 'problematic' in some way. This perspective does not allow for the vast differences that do exist between males – not all men are aggressive or competitive. Feminist poststructuralists have pointed out that there are multiple ways of doing one's gender which can change over time and place. Consequently, they highlight the need to represent gender in terms of masculinities and femininities.

Over the past two decades, biological explanations of gender have decreased in influence, but the nature–nurture debate is one that will continue to surface from time to time. For example, current scientific explorations around male and female brain differences have fuelled the debate in recent years. The limited scope of this chapter does not allow us to do justice to the different perspectives around this issue. However, it is critical to keep in mind that biological determinist explanations of gender have been used to naturalize and normalize the inequitable social, political and economic relationships that have been socially constructed around males and females.

A glimpse of educators' perspectives on gender

According to our research with early childhood educators, educators' perceptions and understandings of gender and gender formation were largely influenced by discourses that naturalize and normalize gender behaviours in the biological differences between males and females. Most had no formal training in gender equity issues, some had discussed gender in their university training, and only a few acknowledged that they had attended in-service training on gender equity in their places of employment. Consequently, understandings and perceptions of gender were highly influenced by their personal experiences. Interestingly, some educators, who tended to view gender as a social construction in the first instance, resorted to biological explanations in the end when they felt that children seemed to naturally take up traditional ways of being girls and boys, despite the significant efforts they made to provide and encourage alternative gendered ways of being for children. Several educators gave similar examples of this related to the ways girls and boys chose to play with traditional gendered toys despite the availability of other non-traditional options. Alsop *et al.* (2002: 35) make the pertinent point that there is a 'naturalizing trick' operating around people's responses to gender. That is, the habitual or 'second nature' of doing gender often leads one to be seduced by the notion that it must be entirely natural and fixed. Thus, most of the educators and pre-service teachers that we have worked with tended to operate within the theoretical framework that perceives gender construction in terms of children's socialization into accepting particular roles in society based on their gender.

Educators generally considered that children have an understanding of gender, particularly in terms of stereotypes and the potential discrimination that can be associated with this type of thinking. However, there tended to be less certainty about whether children understood the concept of power and how it operates in gendered relationships. For some educators, children were considered 'too young' to understand power and how it operated, let alone engage in using power in any way, either as boys or girls. This perspective primarily stems from the oppositional thinking that is constituted in the cultural binary adult/child, in which meanings of childhood are defined and constructed in opposition to what it means to be an adult. Within this thinking, power is considered to be a complex adult concept that only they understand or practise; this is based on the view that power is primarily negative and utilized by overbearing and manipulative individuals. Children, on the other hand, are viewed as being naturally unaware of such behaviours, too developmentally immature to understand the concept, as well as being 'too innocent' to engage in such manipulative practices. This perspective was encapsulated by an early childhood teacher who commented that 'Children aren't aware of these things unless it is pointed out by adults'. Consequently, some educators were concerned that doing gender equity work (or any other social justice work) with children that went beyond increasing children's awareness of the stereotypes perceived to be enforced on them by adults, was entering dangerous territory, in which children's eyes were opened to 'differences' that they would not naturally see.

Some educators were adamant that they treated boys and girls in the same manner, pointing out that they did not have to incorporate a focus on gender equity into their programmes because their everyday philosophy was that 'We are all the same; we are equal'. This philosophical approach to difference often leads to pedagogical practices that deny difference and the politics of power that operate around identities, not just in terms of gender, but around 'race', ethnicity, class, sexuality and so on. Within this perspective, all difference is overshadowed by the shared element of being 'human', perceived to be the equalizing factor across all cultural differences. This approach appeals to children's perceived innocence, inherent goodness, fairness and thus the ability to look beyond difference. However, the notion of being 'the same' becomes synonymous with characteristics associated with the dominant culture. For example, 'human' designates being 'white', 'Western' and 'male'. The more minoritized cultures take up the practices and perspectives of the dominant culture, the more equal 'they' become. Consequently, this approach to dealing with diversity, including gender, does not adequately allow children to critically deal with their knowledge of difference, different messages received, or the power relations that they encounter and participate in every day that are based on difference. Further, it does not provide children with a critical awareness of the broader structural inequalities that exist socially, politically and economically that impact on all children and their families.

The engagement of educators in perpetuating discriminatory practices among children was raised as a significant issue by some early childhood educators. This was often linked to the cultural backgrounds of educators and staff, to their age, to their status as casual untrained carers, or to a lack of training in gender issues. There was a perception held by some educators that gender issues and gender discrimination were primarily linked to specific cultures that were viewed to be more patriarchal in the way that they treated girls and women. This tended to be associated with educators from non-

Western cultures, who were viewed as perpetuating strong messages in their practices that gender differences between boys and girls were natural and 'healthy'. In terms of age, some believed that older members of staff from different generations had traditional stereotyped values and expectations around children's gendered behaviour. From our observations and experiences in dealing with gender equity issues, it is easy to fall into the 'euro/**ethnocentricism**' or 'generation gap' trap that leads one to uncritically equate gender discrimination with the Other, in this case non-Western cultures and older members in society. This perspective is one that tends to operate largely on racialized and aged stereotypes and the process of essentializing groups – that is, certain characteristics are considered to be natural to all who are part of that group, thus defining and fixing them as such; or the tendency to see one aspect of a subject's identity (often the visible parts) and to make that representative of the whole individual. For example, the stereotype of women from non-Western cultures being oppressed by males is generalized to all and seen as a part of what it means to be a non-Western woman. What the process also does is blind one to the everyday practices of gender discrimination that operate through our own practices and those of the dominant culture, hence depoliticizing the power relations that exist in mainstream society.

Current approaches to gender equity in early childhood education

As pointed out in the introduction to this chapter, incorporating gender equity into the early childhood curriculum is generally considered to be an important part of doing social justice work with children, families, teachers and other staff. The importance accredited to this work in our research with educators is generally associated with the need to counteract the narrow and often stereotypical views that children – as well as some educators, staff and families – have around what they consider to be appropriate behaviour for boys and girls. As pointed out by one director of an early childhood setting:

> Children may not verbally express their views about what women and men should do but they certainly make play choices according to gender stereotypes quite often.

However, despite this support for the incorporation of gender equity into programmes, it does not necessarily translate into what individual educators do in practice. In our research, only about half the educators acknowledged that they regularly included a focus on gender issues in their programming and pedagogical practices. In many cases, dealing with gender equity issues was not necessarily seen as a systemic commitment to an ongoing process of initiating individual or institutional change, but rather as addressing problems as they arose or when recognized by educators and other staff. For example, as one educator commented:

We deal with gender discrimination where ever possible; we address issues as they arise.

This was echoed by another educator who pointed out:

We ask children about their views and explain things when we hear discrimination between girls and boys.

Consequently, in many early childhood settings, dealing with gender issues is often unplanned, spontaneous and left to the commitment of individual educators, who have a particular interest in the area. Most settings have a policy that deals with gender equity, but it is often encompassed within a broader 'umbrella' policy, such as an anti-bias policy, dealing with diversity more generally. Specific social justice or equity issues such as gender can often get lost in broader anti-bias policies if they are not generally considered a problem or a focus of interest for individual settings. They also provide an opportunity not to directly address specific controversial issues that settings choose not to deal with, such as gay and lesbian families.

In recent years, critical research has highlighted the need to recognize the relations of power that operate around gender and view children as active agents in the construction of their own gendered identities (Davies 1989, 1993; Alloway 1995; MacNaughton 2000; Robinson and Jones Díaz 2000). Still, many educators in our research rely on gender equity strategies that focus solely on challenging children's stereotypical gendered behaviours and expanding their views about what roles they can take up as boys and girls. This approach was largely facilitated through supporting children to participate in non-traditional play; encouraging both boys and girls to spend time in various gendered spaces or play centres that are usually dominated by one gender or the other; and through different role modelling displayed in posters and books depicting males and females engaging in non-traditional gendered roles. The following examples given by educators highlight this particular approach:

Boys and girls are given the same opportunities and are encouraged to participate and be active in all centres, for example, home corner, beauty salons, dress-ups, woodwork.

Staff challenge children's stereotypes/bias through resources like books and posters showing males and females doing non-traditional activities.

Challenging children with their beliefs that pink and blue are not for girls and boys respectively and that doctors, nurses, teachers, police can be both male and female.

We set up activities in a way that both genders play; if boys do not play with home corner we programme blocks in it.

The last comment above highlights a particular strategy often utilized in this approach. When girls or boys do not take up the option of engaging in non-traditional gendered play areas, traditional gendered toys or equipment are used to entice children into these spaces. In the example given, boys are lured into home corner through the use of blocks; in another example, trucks and cars were placed in the shopkeeping area to encourage boys' participation. As pointed out previously, sex-role and socialization theories, which underpin these approaches, do not provide a framework for informing practices that consider children as being active in the process of gender construction and do not allow for an understanding of the way that power works in children's everyday lives. In these approaches, adults are the agents of the resocialization attempts on children's gendered practices, while children are expected to passively take on the new ways of being with minimal resistance. There is also no consideration of how children actively resist taking up different ways of being masculine or feminine subjects if it is not part of how they see the world and how they fit into this larger picture as gendered, classed, racialized, sexualized beings for instance. Children are constantly negotiating the various gendered discourses that are culturally available to them; either resisting or taking up different meanings of being boys or girls, depending on their perceived investments in taking up particular ways of being over others. I (Robinson) recently encountered an example of the way children use particular discourses to their advantage when looking after a friend's two children, a boy and a girl. They had set up a corner of the lounge room as a hospital and were designating roles, when the young boy indicated that he had to be the doctor, because 'girls cannot be doctors'. His sister tried to resist the claim, but he persisted that girls could only be nurses; in the end his sister gave up and started to play the role of the nurse. When I challenged his claim he became even more agitated and forceful about his position as the doctor. Having some insight into his family relationships, I asked him the name of his doctor, which he quickly replied was Mary! I asked him if Mary was a woman or a man, to which he replied in a rather bemused manner, 'a girl'. He soon realized that his claim was compromised and quickly dissolved the game and ran off to play something else. Ultimately, the young boy wanted to play what he considered to be the powerful role of the doctor and tried to negotiate this through discourse.

A liberal feminist perspective – see Tong (1989) for an explanation – tended to inform many of the educators' approaches to gender equity. This has been the traditional approach underlying gender equity policies and initiatives in girls' education in primary and secondary schooling up until recent times. Within this context, equity between males and females is considered achievable primarily through providing women and men the same access to political, economical, educational and social opportunities and civil rights. It is considered that legislating for equal access and opportunities across these areas will counteract the disadvantages that women have historically experienced.

As the comments above indicate, challenging children's stereotyped perceptions of gender and gender roles was the main means through which gender equity practices were instigated. Some educators pointed out that they often invited parents who were involved in non-traditional gender roles and occupations to talk with children and to act as role models. This approach to gender equity highlights the importance of equal access and opportunities not only in the public spheres of work and politics, but also in the private realm of the family and personal relationships. The sharing of roles associated with caring and nurturing of children and home duties, traditionally perceived as 'women's work', is considered crucial to gender equity in both the public and private realms. The gender equity areas believed to be most important to address with children by the majority of the participants reflected this perspective, and related to gender stereotyping and sharing 'mothering' and household duties.

However, the philosophical and practical approach to gender equity outlined above has been criticized for its lack of recognition of power in gendered relationships, on both the micro everyday interactions and macro structural levels in society. Increasing women's access to non-traditional roles and increasing men's shared involvement in the home through equal opportunity legislation is important but it has not to date changed the overall power imbalances operating between men and women in various contexts. This point is best reflected in the words of a boy aged 5, who commented to one of our early childhood students during her practical experience:

A lady might be able to be a postman on a bike, but they aren't as good or fast as a man.

Many early childhood educators encourage boys into the traditionally female-dominated area of 'home corner' or girls into the male-dominated 'block corner', but do not critically challenge children's gendered ways of making meaning in their everyday interactions in or out of these areas. In some instances, as pointed out earlier, if boys do not actively engage in 'home corner' experiences, then blocks are programmed into that area to encourage their participation. Unfortunately, there seems to be limited deconstruction of the gendered power relations operating in such instances, consequently the status quo reigns despite the change of environment and good intentions.

Deconstructing gender and power at all levels of society is crucial to building children's understandings of gender discrimination and inequality. However, among the participants generally in this research, a dominant perspective prevailed that tended to distance children from the broader social inequities that are experienced by individuals, families or minority groups. The links between the discrimination experienced by individuals and broader structural power relations were viewed as less significant and relevant to children's lives. Consequently, children are not challenged, for example, to critically consider the links between stereotyping, gender roles in the home, violence perpetrated against women, children and some men and the discrimination experienced by women and girls in various contexts, beyond the early childhood setting and the family. Therefore, children do not gain an adequate understanding of the way that gender power relations are intimately inherent in socio-cultural, political and economic structures in society and how individual practices and interactions on a daily level contribute to these gendered structures, including those in which children are engaged. This practice of distancing children from broader social issues is often founded in dominant social discourses that perpetuate developmentalist understandings of children (see Chapter 1), that view and construct them as being 'too young' to understand or 'too innocent' to be subjected to the burdens of what are perceived to be adults' concerns.

The heterosexualization of gender: Butler's performativity and 'hctcroscxual matrix'

A critical aspect of gender formation that tends to receive limited focus in early childhood education is the way that gender is inextricably constituted within and normalized through the process of 'heterosexualization' (Butler 1990; Robinson 2005c). As Robinson (2005c) argues, the construction of children's gendered identities cannot be fully understood without acknowledging how the dominant discourses of femininity and masculinity are heteronormalized in children's everyday lives, including through their educational experiences. What this means is that through the processes of gender formation, children's sexual identities are simultaneously being constructed and normalized as heterosexual. This is interesting when one considers how powerful the discourse is that constitutes children as 'innocent', 'asexual' and 'too young' to understand sexuality (Robinson 2002, 2005b). The process of heterosexualization that operates in children's lives is largely rendered invisible through heteronormative discourses that normalize and naturalize this process within constructions of gender.

Judith Butler's use of performativity and her concept of a heterosexual matrix are particularly helpful in understanding the construction of gender, how it is heteronormalized, and in looking at the ways girls and boys assert their gendered subjectivities. Butler (1994: 33) defines performativity as 'that aspect of discourse that has the capacity to produce what it names ... this production actually always happens through a certain kind of repetition and recitation'. She further elaborates by pointing out that performativity 'is the vehicle through which ontological effects are established' (Butler 1994: 33); that is, how and where masculinities and femininities are played out, culturally and historically, is the way in which hegemonic forms of masculinity and femininity get established, instituted, circulated and confirmed (Butler 1994). According to Butler, it is the repetition of the performance of masculinities and femininities that constructs and reconstructs the masculine and feminine subject. Thus, gendered identities are formed from the performances of subjects and the performances of other subjects towards them. Children repetitively perform their femininity and masculinity in order to 'do it right' in front of their peers and others (Butler 1990), and it is through this repetitive process that the feminine and masculine subject becomes defined and constructed. The repetitiveness of the performance makes it seem natural and real. Individual subjects strive to have their gendered performances considered authentic or real through the judgements of others. As Robinson (2005a) points out, it is important to remember that the concept of gender performance is always one that is enacted within strictly defined cultural boundaries; what counts as a performance of masculinity or femininity is rigidly defined and policed by the socio-cultural context in which one is located over various historical points in time. Thus, for young children, getting their gender performance right is critical, not only in terms of how they see themselves, but also in the way they are viewed and accepted by others, particularly their peers. If they do not get their gender performance right and do not conform to what is generally upheld as appropriate boy or girl behaviour, they run the risk of being ostracized or bullied.

Feminist poststructuralist perspectives of gender formation, as discussed previously, highlight that the knowledge of what it means to be a boy or a girl is constituted within the multiple discourses of masculinity and femininity that are culturally and historically available. These meanings of gender are always defined through their intersections with other sites of identity, such as 'race', ethnicity, class, sexuality and so on. Dominant or hegemonic discourses of gender (those that are most powerful and perceived as 'true' representations) in various cultural contexts operate powerfully at both the macro and micro levels of society to define what are considered 'normal' gender performances. These hegemonic discourses work to police and regulate 'correct' performances of gender. As argued above, 'normal' and 'correct' gender performances of masculinity and femininity are generally heterosexualized. Thus, gender performances are constituted within relations of power; they embody norms of behaviour which subjects aspire to achieve, and reinforce the power of certain groups over others, especially heterosexuals over non-heterosexual or queer identities (Robinson 2005a).

Butler's (1990) concept of a 'heterosexual matrix' helps to explain how the 'correct' gender becomes heterosexualized. The heterosexual matrix is 'a grid of cultural intelligibility through which bodies, genders, and desires are naturalized'. Butler (1990: 151) explains this matrix further as a 'hegemonic discursive/epistemic model of gender intelligibility that assumes that for bodies to cohere and make sense there must be a stable sex expressed through a stable gender (masculine expresses male, feminine expresses female) that is oppositionally and hierarchically defined through the compulsory practice of heterosexuality'. In other words, Butler is arguing that we make sense of gendered bodies and desires through the way that they are discursively unified, naturalized and fixed through compulsory heterosexuality (Rich 1980). The perceived fixed, unified and stable nature of this embodied relationship between gender and sexuality is constituted and perpetuated through the cultural binary male/female, which defines masculinity and femininity as natural opposites.

Alsop et al. (2002: 97) argue that in Butler's theory 'it is the "epistemic regime of presumptive heterosexuality" [(Butler 1990: viii)] which drives our division into male and female, and which itself structures our understanding of biology'. Thus, in Butler's perspective, it is the presumption of heterosexuality that ascribes bodies as gendered, rather than traditional perspectives which uphold that the natural distinction of bodies into male and female signifies the normality and naturalness of heterosexuality. Butler argues that it is the way that the construction of gender is assumed to be a natural process given by biology that is critical to these understandings. The effect of the range of gendered performance is to make it appear that there are two distinct natures, male and female. As pointed out by Alsop et al. (2002: 99), 'What we take to be "nature" is therefore an effect rather than a cause of our gendered acts'. Thus, the repetition of normalized gender performance polarized within the cultural binary male/female, which is socially constituted, renders this behaviour as being a given from nature, or one's biology.

Butler's works, along with feminist poststructuralist understandings of the formation of gender, provide early childhood educators with a useful theoretical framework to inform their practices and gender programmes with children. Feminist poststructuralist perspectives point out that individual subjects are not stable, unified or fixed, but rather are shifting subjects, who are dynamic, contradictory and changing. Gender formation is a continuous, complex and negotiated process in which children actively construct and reconstruct their performances through the socio-cultural discourses they have available to them. Individual boys and girls will locate themselves within certain discourses of masculinities or femininities, taking up these meanings and social relationships as their own. However, one's subjective positioning is not fixed, but can discursively shift as individuals read their locations within relations of power, claiming or resisting discourses according to what they want to achieve (Hollway 1984). Young boys who engage in bullying behaviour as a performance of their masculinity, which is reinforced through a respect from their peers (albeit a respect often based on fear) and societal and media representations of appropriate masculinity associated with aggression (for example, rugby league sporting heroes), will generally not be convinced to change their behaviour based on pleas of hurting another child's feelings. Getting the performance of this form of masculinity correct, especially in front of peers, is often about public displays of aggression over others. The 'realness' of doing gender is the ability to compel belief in the performance. For example, for many young boys, the judgement of their male peers is critical to the measurement of how authentic they are at doing their masculinity.

Thus, how gender and heterosexuality intimately and powerfully intersect in the definition and normalization of each other is critical to an understanding of the construction of individuals, including children, as gendered and sexualized subjects. Although there is an increasing understanding of how gender construction operates in children's lives, the way in which stable notions of gender, sex and desire are constituted, expressed and normalized through compulsory heterosexuality (that is, how gender is heterosexualized and sexuality is simultaneously normalized as heterosexual) needs greater consideration in early childhood education.

Heterosexualization and heteronormativity in early childhood education

Robinson (2002, 2005c) argues that heteronormativity in early childhood education is largely rendered invisible through the hegemonic discourses that constitute understandings of childhood and sexuality. The presumption that children are asexual, 'too young' and 'too innocent' to understand sexuality is contradicted by the fact that the construction of heterosexuality and heterosexual desire is an integral part of children's everyday experiences, including their early education; for example, children's literature widely used in early childhood education constantly reinforces a heterosexual narrative (Cahill and Theilheimer 1999; Theilheimer and Cahill 2001). This process of heterosexualization continues largely unnoticed and unchallenged unless it is perceived to be working ineffectively; that is, when the boundaries of compulsory heterosexuality (Rich 1980) seem to be crossed and when children's heterogendered constructions seem to be unacceptably and inappropriately slipping beyond the norms. It seems that it is through such transgressions that children learn lessons about what is acceptable and what is intolerable. For example, parents are often concerned about their sons dressing in women's clothes, fearing that this behaviour may lead to homosexuality; and educators can problematize and discourage young children's desires for same-sex relations if they transgress from what is perceived to be normalized heterosexual gendered behaviour. Wallis and VanEvery (2000) describe an instance of this, where a young boy was actively discouraged by educators from articulating his wish to 'marry' the person he loved best, which was his best male friend.

Play is a critical site of gender construction, but it is equally a significant site in which heteronormative discourses operate. Mock weddings, mothers and fathers, chasing and kissing games, and girlfriends/boyfriends are all examples of young children's narratives of their experiences in early childhood education. Such activities are often viewed as a natural part of children's everyday lives and are rarely questioned or thought about by educators. Children's play practices are rarely considered part of the normalization of the construction of heterosexual desire and the inscription of heterogendered subjectivities in young children. These heterosexualized activities are not linked to understandings of sexuality, but are seen as 'children being children', a natural part of growing up. Epstein (1995) has argued that the relationship between gender and sexuality is critical to an understanding of sexism and heterosexism in education, pointing out that sexism cannot be understood without an analysis of its relationship with heterosexuality.

The media, popular culture and children's literature play a major role in the perpetuation of heteronormativity in children's everyday lives. Children's literature and films provide numerous examples of the ways in which children's cultures and children's gendered lives are heterosexualized. Giroux (1995: 1) argues that 'Children's culture is a sphere where entertainment, advocacy, and pleasure meet to construct conceptions of what it means to be a child occupying a combination of gender, racial, and class positions in society through which one defines oneself in relation to a myriad of others'. Robinson (2005c) points out that an examination of children's classic books, such as *Beauty and the Beast* (Disney 1994a), *Anastasia* (Krulik 1997) and *The Little Mermaid* (Disney 1994b), demonstrates the pervasiveness of the fantasized heterosexual happy ending that is about not just constructing gendered identities, but a specific type of gender performance that is heterosexual. Thus, deconstructing children's popular cultural texts provides a critical context in which to disrupt normalizing discourses that perpetuate gender inequalities. The construction of heterosexuality is part of children's everyday lives, including what is learnt in their early educational experiences; however, it is rarely ever noticed, and almost never ever thought about (Robinson 2005c). It is important that early childhood educators refocus their critical lens around construction of gender in early childhood in order to understand how gender is heterosexualized through heteronormative daily practices and interactions with peers, family, in schools and other institutions working with children.

Liberatory potentials of non-normative discourses of gender

Why should educators encourage children to take up non-normative dis-courses of gender if children are happy the way they are? This question was asked by an early childhood pre-service teacher in one of our diversity classes, and led to an interesting debate among the students. In the end, all the students including the one who had initially asked the question agreed that challenging discourses that perpetuated gender inequalities was critical for the well-being of all children, and that it went far beyond the early years of their lives; indeed, it was considered critical to the social, economic and political lives of all, regardless of their age. Normalizing discourses of gender that restrict and regulate understandings of what it means to be a girl or boy, woman or man, can impact on individual subjects in many different ways throughout their lives. How children would like to be able to choose to express and embody their genders can be very different from the way they actually do it on a daily basis.

Young children learn quickly that if they do not get their gender 'right' and conform to 'appropriate' gender behaviours they can be ostracized and bul-lied by their peers, and can be punished in different ways by adults, including their parents. For example, young boys who do not like to engage in what are considered typical masculine behaviours, such as aggressive play fighting, or competitive group sports such as rugby, but rather prefer reading, dancing, or even playing with girls, can experience a difficult time in their schooling, which can have long-term affects on their emotional and physical well-being. As pointed out previously in this chapter, not only are their performances of masculinity questioned but also their sexuality. Many young children, youth and adults, who experience homophobia or **lesbophobia** and heterosexist harassment, do so not because they are gay or lesbian, but because they are perceived to be so by others, for not conforming to what is considered 'appropriate' gender behaviours. Even if any of these young boys do choose to identify as gay in their lives, the consequences of non-conformity are already well understood. The association of violence with performances of hege-monic masculinity has implications not just for those who identify as gay or lesbian, or those perceived to be so by others, but also for women, whose lives are emotionally, physically, socially and economically affected by experiences of sexual violence, sexual harassment or domestic violence. Feminist post-structuralist perspectives remind us that there are multiple ways of doing masculinity, but how these are culturally read and interpreted constitutes the inequalities reflected in broad social relationships in society.

Normalizing discourses of gender diminish the options and choices chil-dren have in their lives. Their perceptions of appropriate masculine and feminine behaviours can restrict what they choose to learn, what activities and sports they choose to participate in, how they interact with other chil-dren, the feelings that they perceive they can openly display, what they see to be their choices of potential careers, how they envisage their futures, and so on. The construction of gender is about constructing social relationships that impact on us all.

Implications for practice in early childhood education

The issues raised throughout this chapter have important implications for the way that gender issues and gender equity are approached in early childhood education, as outlined below. Educators are in a positive position to encourage children's location with non-normative gender discourses through the critical work they do with children and their families, thus providing children with far more options for doing gender than they currently perceive they have open to them.

Policy direction and implementation

Gender equity policies in early childhood education are important documents, which provide direction for dealing with gender in settings and for educating staff, children and families about significant issues. It is important to review current policies for sexist language or normalizing discourses that restrict and regulate gendered identities to narrow definitions of what it means to be a girl or boy, woman or man. It is important that settings incorporate a non-sexist language policy that involves staff, children and their families. As with all policies, it is important to include staff, children and their families in developing and revising policies. It is also critical to monitor, evaluate and review policies on a regular basis.

Communicating and negotiating with families

A critical understanding of how gender is culturally constructed is vital, particularly when working in diverse communities. Early childhood educators need to be able to locate their own positions, as well as others', to ensure sensitivity and equity are considered. It is important that educators encourage family involvement in their gender equity strategies. As pointed out in our research, many parents are not familiar with how gender is constructed in early childhood and often resort to biological explanations of the gendered differences that they perceive among their children. It is important that gender education programmes are also designed to meet the needs of parents; for example, it is critical to highlight the liberatory potential of children's positioning in non-normative gender discourses, despite some fears that it can impact on future sexualities. Parents' awareness of gender issues can be fostered through parent–teacher nights, informal meetings, newsletters, information sheets and organization of different displays (for example, domestic violence issues; International Women's Day information), and encouraging parents who are involved in non-traditional gendered employment, activities or sports to give talks to children and their families.

Programming and planning

Viewing children as active participants in the construction of their own gendered identities and in the regulation of how others do gender is an important theoretical framework from which to begin educating children about gender issues. As pointed out above, current approaches that focus on disrupting stereotypical gender roles do not challenge the power relations that operate around gendered identities. Incorporating a deconstructive approach to children's understandings of gender encourages children's critical thinking around the issues and focuses on new and different possibilities of doing gender. Working with children to recognize the liberatory potentials in taking up non-normative discourses of gender is important as it increases the options that they feel they have in their lives and it disrupts the notion of difference as deviance. Deconstructing children's play themes, popular culture texts, and utilizing texts with different storylines provide children with new, liberatory and non-traditional gender subject positions to consider. The latter point may mean increasing the resources that educators have access to that provide storylines with non-normative gender subject positions. Feminist poststructuralist perspectives point out that it is important to begin to give alternative non-normative discourses of gender status and power, so children will see some personal investments in desiring to take them up.

Working with staff, families and children

Social justice education is far more successful if a whole institutional approach is taken to educate management committees, staff, children and families about equity issues. Doing this work is often not easy, especially when individual subjects are located in different discourses of gender. Some of these discourses may not contribute to a different and more equitable understanding of gendered relationships, but rather perpetuate differential treatment for males and females. Different readings of gender may cause some resistance among staff, families and children, but it is important to continue to work through these issues together. Opening up a dialogue that respects different opinions and encourages all to contribute is an important foundation from which to find a point of reconciliation that works in favour of social justice.

Conclusion

This chapter argues that feminist poststructuralist perspectives provide a critical theoretical lens through which to analyse the social construction of gender in society. It has also pointed out that any examination of the construction of gender in young children's lives needs to include a focus on how gender is inextricably constituted within and normalized through the process of heterosexualization that operates through everyday practices, including those in education. As Robinson (2005c) reminds us, within the hegemonic processes of gender construction, children are simultaneously constructed as heterosexual beings, but it tends to be rendered invisible through heteronormativity. Educating children and families around the liberatory potentials of taking up non-normalizing discourses of gender is important for providing children and adults with greater flexibility and options in their lives on many different levels. However, children's transgressions from what is generally perceived to be appropriate masculinity and femininity are most likely to be punished in various ways rather than encouraged. Consequently, children quickly learn what is acceptable and what is intolerable in terms of their gender performances. This brings into critical view the importance of educators' examining their own subject positions in terms of gender and the effects that this can have on children's choices in their early education.

Recommended reading

Alloway, N. (1995) *Foundation Stones: The Construction of Gender in Early Childhood.* Carlton, Vic.: Curriculum Corporation.

Alsop, R., Fitzsimons, A. and Lennon, K. (2002) *Theorizing Gender.* Cambridge: Polity Press.

Davies, B. (1989) *Frogs and Snails and Feminist Tales: Preschool Children and Gender.* Sydney: Allen & Unwin.

Davies, B. (1993) *Shards of Glass. Children Reading and Writing beyond Gendered Identities.* Sydney: Allen & Unwin.

MacNaughton, G. (2000) *Rethinking Gender in Early Childhood Education.* Sydney: Allen & Unwin.

Thorne, B. (1993) *Gender Play: Boys and Girls in School.* Buckingham: Open University Press.

8

THE LION, THE WITCH AND THE 'CLOSET':

Dealing with sexual identity issues in early childhood education

Introduction

Since the late 1980s there has been a steady growth in the literature which highlights the importance and relevance of addressing lesbian and gay issues with children (see Derman-Sparks and the A.B.C. Task Force 1989; Corbett 1993; Wickens 1993; Boldt 1997; Casper *et al.* 1998; Cahill and Theilheimer 1999; Robinson and Jones Díaz 2000; Kissen 2002; Robinson 2002, 2005c, 2005d). It has generally been within the context of the perceived importance of recognizing children's family experiences that the relevance of this area to children's early education has been acknowledged by early childhood educators. It is generally upheld that good early childhood pedagogy reflects and empowers the diverse cultural backgrounds of the children and families with whom they work. This positive representation of the diversity of children's identities in the daily programming and planning of early childhood education is considered to be crucial for developing individual children's positive 'self-esteem', as well as fostering their appreciation for the diversity that exists more broadly in society. Thus, it is primarily through these child-centred discourses that dealing with certain aspects of lesbian and gay people's lives has gained some acceptance within early childhood pedagogy and curriculum.

However, there has been limited incorporation of the social justice and equity issues faced by gay and lesbian people in early childhood education programmes. This is largely due to the fact that this aspect of diversity and difference is often perceived to be irrelevant or inappropriate to address with young children. As Robinson (2002: 416) points out, 'Sexuality and sexual orientation issues are controversial areas that are often fraught with many obstacles and cultural taboos that operate to silence, marginalize, and/or limit any dialogue or representation of this form of difference, especially in the context of children and early childhood education'. Thus, this chapter examines the major barriers that exist in the field of early childhood education that operate to exclude the incorporation of gay and lesbian equity issues in social justice education. These barriers include: the dominant discourses of childhood and sexuality that intersect to constitute sexuality issues as irrelevant to children; the widespread belief that 'the family' is the only legitimate context in which to deal with gay and lesbian issues with children; the pervasiveness of the discourse of compulsory heterosexuality (Rich 1980) and the assumed absence of gay and lesbian families in settings, as well as the assumed absence of significant gay or lesbian adults in children's lives; the prevalence of heterosexism and homophobia in early childhood settings; and the perceived irrelevance of broader social, political and economic issues to the 'child's world' (Robinson 2002).

The relevance of doing social justice education with children around gay and lesbian equity issues goes much further than increasing children's awareness of family diversity. It is important to provide children with the space and skills to deconstruct the stereotypes and myths that prevail about gays and lesbians that underlie much of the discrimination, harassment and violence that they can encounter in their lives. Much of this discrimination begins in the early years of life, as children negotiate the normalizing discourses that operate around gender and sexuality and take up these perspectives as their own 'truths' about the world. They learn quickly through their interactions with adults and other children, as well as through the media, what is considered to be a socially acceptable performance of their gender; and, as pointed out in the previous chapter, these gender performances are strictly heterosexualized. Consequently, children learn to become powerful regulators not only of their own gendered and sexualized identities, but also of those of other children and adults. This process impacts significantly on young children's lives, how they see themselves, what options they feel they have, how they see and interact with their peers and how they engage more broadly with the world around them. Leaving critical discussions of sexuality and sexual orientation until adolescence does not acknowledge how these areas of identity are constructed and negotiated in young children's lives. The consequences of silencing such dialogues among children may be reflected in two critical points: firstly, the high rate of gay and lesbian youth suicide in Western countries, stemming from harassment, alienation, rejection and a lack of positive representation of non-heterosexuals (Hillier and Walsh 1999); and secondly, the alarming fact that much of the harassment, violence and hate crime experienced by people who identify as non-heterosexuals, or are perceived to be so by others, is carried out by adolescent boys and young men (Chasnoff and Cohen 1997; Tomsen 2002).

Feminist poststructuralism and sexual identities

Feminist poststructuralism is the primary theoretical framework that informs the discussion in this chapter. In this perspective, sexual identity is considered to be a social construction, rather than biologically determined.

Sexual identity is viewed as constituted within discourse and as being fluid, flexible and changing. The cultural binary of heterosexual/homosexual is seen to be the foundation of the dominant discourse that normal sexuality is represented by heterosexuality, while non-heterosexuality is defined oppositionally as deviant and abnormal. Utilizing Foucault's concept of 'regimes of truth', the normalization of heterosexuality and its social sanction as a 'truth' is constituted through everyday language, interactions, practices and policies of individuals and social institutions on the micro and macro levels of society; that is, through the taking up of discourses, which constitute heterosexuality as normal and non-heterosexuality as the abnormal Other. Individual subjects constitute, enact and embody their sexual identities through their location within particular discourses of sexuality that are available to them. As active agents in the construction of their own sexual identities, individual subjects reflexively negotiate the different discourses of sexuality available, taking up those that are perceived to propose more personal investments for them at that point in time. However, heteronormativity operates both consciously and unconsciously as a powerful regime of truth, as indicated previously. Notions of 'choice' become problematic, as can be seen from the consequences of taking up a subject position within a discourse of sexuality that is not socially sanctioned. Foucault's *History of Sexuality Volume 1* (1978) provides a critical investigation of the way in which the sexual identities of individual subjects are constituted within and 'governed' by the discourses operating in society. This includes the discursive construction of the homosexual Other and the consequent policing of all sexualities. Foucault argues that powerful techniques of surveillance that are operating in societal institutions, including the government itself, lead to the internalization of self-disciplining techniques by individual subjects. In these ways individuals take up the culturally coded ways of being through their embodiment of the exercise of power at work in and on them through socially sanctioned discourses.

Queer theory and sexual identity

Queer theory has also influenced the approach taken to sexuality in this discussion. This theory stems largely from poststructuralist theoretical perspectives. It reinforces the notion that identities are not fixed or stable, but rather are shifting, contradictory, dynamic and constructed. Queer theory upholds that all identities are performances and challenges normalizing practices, particularly in terms of sexuality and the heteronormative constructions of gender. It challenges the unquestionable, natural and normal positioning of heterosexuality as the superior sexuality and the othering of non-heterosexual identities, which is constituted within the cultural binary heterosexual us/homosexual them (see Jagose 1996; Sullivan 2003). The term 'queer' encompasses those who feel 'marginalized by mainstream sexuality' (Morris 2000: 20), including those who see themselves as heterosexual but challenge the conformity constituted and enforced in hegemonic discourses of heterosexuality. Ultimately, queer theory disrupts the notion that one's gender and sexuality are inherently fixed in one's biological sexed body, upholding the pluralities of sexuality and the multiplicity of gender. Thus, this perspective provides a critical theoretical lens through which one can begin to see the everyday processes of heteronormativity. Judith Butler's (1990, 1993) work on gender and sexuality has been highly influential for queer theorists. Butler's concept of performativity (see Chapter 7) advances the argument that gender is articulated through socially endorsed performances constituted in discourses of what it means to be a girl, boy, woman or man. The very fact that these performances are embodied and repeated so frequently results in the appearance that gender is natural and linked to one's biology. The authenticity of how one does one's gender is linked to how others read one's performance. This operates in the same way for sexuality, which is perceived to be socially constructed rather than linked to biological bodies or fixed gender identities. Performativity opens up the possibility of there being new and different ways of performing gender that operate outside the rigid boundaries of the socially sanctioned cultural binary of masculine/feminine. For queer theorists, it is the visibility of the Other that troubles the normative cultures underpinned by such cultural binaries, allowing a critical space in which individual subjects can take up different ways of being in the world as gendered and sexualized subjects.

Other theoretical perspectives on sexual identity

Biological determinism

This perspective views sexuality as originating from one's biological make-up. Some researchers are currently trying to find evidence of a 'gay' gene and exploring possible brain differences between homosexuals and heterosexuals. However, there is no evidence at this point to support this perspective. Biological determinism is often used to support gay rights inasmuch as people who identify as gay are perceived to not have a choice in their sexuality. Thus, their rights are viewed within the perspective that 'they can't help the way they are' and therefore need support to live their lives in the most equitable ways possible. Feminist poststructuralists are critical of perspectives that fix sexuality in biology, as they view sexuality as a social construction and as being fluid, flexible and changing.

Social constructionism

Within the perspective of social **constructionism** sexual identity is perceived to be primarily influenced by the values and practices of the cultures and society in which we live. As in the social construction of gender identity, individual subjects are 'socialized' into sexual identities that their culture defines as 'normal' and 'appropriate'. Heterosexuality is generally upheld as the norm, while non-heterosexuality is constructed as 'deviant' and 'abnormal'. Sexuality in this perspective becomes a 'choice' in that one can choose to conform to society's values and practices, or resist and engage in non-heterosexual relationships. However, the idea of 'choice' must be problematized in that there are many different social controls, such as discrimination, threats or actual violence, and potential rejections from families and friends, among others, operating to make individual subjects conform to the normalizing practices of the culture.

Freud and psychoanalysis

Freud's theory of sexuality was based on his work, primarily with middle-class women, as a therapist and physician in Vienna in the late 1890s and early 1900s. Freud proposed that infantile sexuality was central in the formation of individual subjects and argued that instinctual drives encountered by the infantile body, essentially from the mother (for example, suckling, kissing, touching), resulted in the child recognizing the origins of and experiencing pleasure and desire, which are then carried unconsciously and consciously by the infant throughout life. Thus, Freud believed that human culture stemmed from our 'convoluted attempts to contain and redirect the energies of sex' (Bhattacharyya 2002: 5). In this process, socialization became focused on redeploying and redirecting our selfish devotion to physical pleasure. Consequently, children's sexuality is interrupted (or becomes latent) and their desires are redirected to more socially accepted practices and objects, learning to achieve satisfaction through other means. However, Freud points out that this disciplining of sexual impulses (or repression) results in multiple and complex neuroses that signify human existence (Bhattacharyya 2002). Freud's theory of sexual identity has been criticized for its heterosexism, through the way he associated neuroses with, among other things, the failure of individuals to conform to the socially sanctioned practices of heterosexuality.

Discourses of childhood and sexuality

Dominant discourses around childhood and sexuality underpin the widespread perception that exists in early childhood education, and in society more broadly, that dealing with sexuality and sexual identity equity issues is irrelevant to children and their lives. In the research we have conducted with early childhood educators on this issue, sexuality – especially gay and lesbian issues – is largely viewed as an 'adults only' concept, with many early childhood educators considering children to be 'too young' to understand; in other words, addressing these issues is often considered to be developmentally inappropriate. The types of comments that we often encounter from early childhood educators are: 'Children are too young to deal with such adult issues'; 'I don't think they are aware of sexuality, but rather friendships, which can be with anyone'; 'They can understand when it is brought to their attention, but it is not something that concerns them'. As one director of an early childhood centre commented:

> Sexuality appears to be an issue that adults have difficulty talking about and very strong religious attitudes about rightness/wrongness. There also

appears to be a lack of developmental knowledge in relation to children and therefore a questioning of the appropriateness. There is a concept of keeping children 'innocent'.

This perceived irrelevance of sexuality and of lesbian and gay equity issues to children's lives is reinforced by theories of child development and child-centred pedagogy that are central to early childhood education. Theories of child development, such as those devised by Piaget, generally underpin early childhood educators' practices and understandings of 'the child' and of 'childhood'. Such theories have perpetuated the view of the 'universal child' in which all children, from birth, are perceived to proceed through a biologically predetermined set of linear cognitive developments that correlate with chronological age. At the end of this process, children reach their destination of 'adulthood', which is identified by the ability to engage in abstract and hypothetical thinking. This dominant discourse of childhood, which perpetuates white, Western and middle-class values, fails to adequately acknowledge the importance of socio-cultural factors such as gender, class and ethnicity, as well as historical contexts. Further, this discourse, constituted within the rigid binary relationship of adult/child, defines 'the child' in opposition to what it means to be an adult (James and Prout 1990; Cannella 1997; Gittins 1998; Dahlberg *et al.* 1999). This oppositional perspective underpins much of the common-sense understandings of childhood and the child as being the antithesis of an adult, and influences the way that children and adults are viewed in the world. Within this context, children are perceived to be the dependent, immature and the powerless Other in relation to the independent, mature, powerful and critically thinking adult. Thus, the cultural binary adult/child perpetuates 'common-sense' understandings that the differences between children and adults are logical, biological and natural. This binary operates to exclude children from the 'world of adults' (Gittins 1998).

However, in recent times, developmentalist understandings of childhood have been challenged by theories that highlight the socio-cultural construction of childhood and the diversity among children. These new perspectives are disrupting fixed common-sense understandings of childhood through acknowledging the way this knowledge has been largely socially and culturally constructed by adults. Mayall (1996: 1) points out that 'Children's lives are lived through childhoods constructed for them by adult understandings of childhood and what children are and should be'; to this we would add adult views of what children should and should not know. This is echoed by Gittins (1998: 111) who comments that 'images of children are invariably constructed *by adults* to convey messages and meanings *to adults*'. However, it is important to point out that even within some of the newer pedagogical approaches that take up postmodern and poststructuralist perspectives of childhood and diversity and difference, such as Reggio Emilia (Dahlberg *et al.* 1999), interventions in terms of sexuality can often still be marginalized or non-existent.

Sexuality, like childhood, has also been traditionally perceived as being fixed, biologically determined and linked to developmentalist theory.

Physiological sexual maturity has represented the boundary between adulthood and childhood (Gittins 1998) and sexuality is generally considered to begin at puberty and to mature in adulthood. Children's sexuality within this discourse is immature or non-existent. However, this reading of sexuality has also been challenged in recent times by theorists who have gained prominence for their arguments around reconceptualizing sexuality as a socially constructed social relationship (Foucault 1978; Weeks 1986; Butler 1990). Sexuality within poststructuralist and queer perspectives, as pointed out previously, is considered to be a fluid, non-linear, multifaceted, complex, contradictory and unstable relationship that can vary across cultures and over historical periods of time, according to the discourses available (Foucault 1978; Weeks 1986; Britzman 1997). This understanding of sexuality informs our discussion and is defined by Weeks (1986: 25) in the following manner:

> Sexuality is something which society produces in complex ways. It is a result of diverse social practices that give meaning to human activities, of social definitions and self-definitions, of struggles between those who have power to define and regulate, and those who resist. Sexuality is not a given, it is a product of negotiation, struggle and human agency.

Similar to the construction of gender, sexuality is socially and culturally constituted, with desire constructed and policed through powerful societal discourses (for example, particular religious and legal discourses) and social practices that are institutionally and individually supported at both the micro and macro levels in society. However, just as gender is made to appear as being from nature and biology, so is sexuality, with the relationship between the two viewed as symmetrical. As Wilton (1996: 127) points out, 'This profoundly ideological notion of complementary gendered polarity – heteropolarity – has become the mystified and naturalised organising principle which saturates Western culture, structuring thought and social organisation around notions of binarism, complementarity, unidirectionality and polarity'. Through this process of normalization, heterosexuality is upheld as the natural, instinctual, desired, appropriate sexuality, with all other deviations from this behaviour considered unnatural and abnormal. Thus, sexuality, like gender, is perceived as shifting, changing, flexible and fluid; it is produced by society in complex ways, through diverse social practices, individual and social definitions; it is about relations of power. As Weeks (1986: 25) points out, 'Sexuality is not a given, it is a product of negotiation, struggle and human agency'.

Therefore, it is in this context of the social construction of sexuality and childhood that we can view the ways in which sexuality has been culturally and historically defined as the exclusive realm of adults, in which children are constituted as the innocent and asexual Other. Children are perceived to be asexual, innocent and 'too young' to be capable of understanding or dealing with such 'adult' concepts as sexuality. This perception is intimately linked with dominant religious and moral values within the social order (Gittins 1998). Sexuality is often narrowly defined by the physical sexual act of having sex, rather than as an aspect of adults' and children's identities. This practice serves to intensify the perspective that sexuality is irrelevant to young children. Consequently, not only has childhood been defined by adults for adults, as indicated previously, but so has children's relationship to sexuality (Silin 1995; Gittins 1998; Robinson 2002). Adults have defined what children should or should not be, and should or should not know.

It is interesting that children who have an understanding of sex and sexuality are often othered as 'unnatural children', with 'unnatural knowledge'. This is particularly so for children who come from lesbian, gay, bisexual or transgender families, or from families where parents or carers have made conscious decisions to inform their children about sex and sexuality issues. There is often the added judgement made about the parents of these children, as being involved in immoral and 'unnatural' sex and who are not fulfilling their roles as 'good' parents by properly sheltering their children from 'deviant' sexual behaviours. Patton (1995) points out that some adults fear that providing children or adolescents with sexual knowledge will directly result in 'causing' youth to have sex prematurely.

What Is heteronormativity?

Heteronormativity is used to designate how heterosexuality is constituted and represented as the natural and normal sexuality. The normalizing discourse of heterosexuality takes on the privileged and unquestionable position of being the 'true' sexuality, or the representation of the natural order of things, primarily through the way it is linked to the male/female biological binary and to procreation. Heterosexuality is also normalized through the way it is 'encoded in language, in institutional practices and the encounters of everyday life' (Epstein and Johnson 1994: 198). For example, religious discourses and practices significantly contribute to the way heterosexuality is normalized and non-heterosexualities are abnormalized and excluded; for example, in terms of the perceived illegitimacy of gay and lesbian marriages and families. The assumption that is often made on enrolment forms in early childhood settings that children come from heterosexual families is another example of heteronormativity in practice. Thus, the normalization of heterosexuality is a social phenomenon that is actively negotiated, with its dominant discourses and narratives primarily constituted within the socially constructed cultural binary of heterosexual us/homosexual them – a powerful hierarchy in which heterosexuality defines and speaks with perceived authority about the Other. Institutionalized heterosexuality thus becomes the definer of 'legitimate and prescriptive sociosexual arrangements' (Ingraham 1994: 204) and the norm by which all other sexualities are defined as different, illegitimate and abnormal. Within this framework, heterosexuality becomes compulsory (Rich 1980). As Letts (1999: 98) points out, heteronormativity is ultimately about power, a reinforcing of a 'culture of power' associated with heterosexuality. Within this culture of power the normalization of heterosexuality is rendered invisible and diverts attention and critique away from the macro- and micro-social, economic and political discursive practices, including those that operate in educational institutions that construct and maintain this hierarchy of difference across sexual identities.

Heteronormativity in early childhood education

There are many contradictions that surround the perception that children are 'too young' to deal with sexuality issues; most are related to the process of heteronormativity. As discussed in the previous chapter, the construction of heterosexuality and heterosexual desire is part of the everyday practices in early childhood settings (Cahill and Theilheimer 1999). The incorporation of mock weddings, the encouragement of various activities in home corner, such as mothers and fathers, and young children's participation in kissing games and girlfriends/boyfriends are common among children. These and many other activities are rarely questioned, but rather are part of the normalization of the construction of heterosexual desire and the inscription of heteronormative gender in young children's lives. For many early childhood educators these activities are considered to be 'children being children', and a natural part of growing up, linked to the process of child development. However, Epstein (1995: 57), based on her work with nursery-age children, reminds us that

> sexism is, by definition, heterosexist and that sexism cannot, therefore, be understood in the absence of an analysis of heterosexuality as both political and institutionalized ... that school is an important locus for the inscription of gender and of heterosexuality and that it is, therefore, also an important locus for challenging dominant discourses of (hetero)sexism.

It seems that for some, sexuality becomes problematic when it transgresses the boundaries of compulsory heterosexuality, with double standards often disguised and perpetuated through discursive practices that constitute children as being 'too young' to deal with sexual differences and discrimination. This perspective is reflected in the following response by the director of a preschool setting:

> I think children are really too young to deal with sexuality issues. They have no understanding of it; it isn't part of their experiences ... Like they do get into playing house, mothers and fathers and getting married, that kind of thing, but that's normal everyday play that children like to get into. They see it all the time on television and in their lives. But beyond that, I don't think it's appropriate and it's not part of their experiences.

Myths about gay and lesbian people

There are many myths surrounding people who identify themselves as gay or lesbian, which operate to diminish their power and to demonize these individuals in the eyes of society. The following are examples of some of the myths that tend to prevail in the early childhood field:

Myth. Gays and lesbians are paedophiles.

Response. Research overwhelmingly indicates that most child sexual abusers are heterosexual men and are largely known to children; they are either members of one's immediate and/or extended family or are friends or acquaintances (Breckenridge and Carmody 1992; Easteal 1994).

Myth. Gays and lesbians are promiscuous.

Response. Sexual promiscuity is behaviour that can be engaged in by any person regardless of their sexual orientation. However, this is a stereotype, largely perpetuated by the media, which is frequently directed at gays and lesbians, especially gay men. Not all lesbians and gays engage in promiscuous behaviour, just as not all heterosexuals engage in promiscuous behaviour; most are in committed monogamous relationships.

Myth. Young boys who dress up in women's clothing will grow up to be gay.

Response. Dressing up in women's clothing does not cause boys to become gay. This fear stems from the rigid representation of hegemonic masculinity as being opposite and distanced from femininity and being inherently heterosexual. If boys take up any form of behaviour that is considered feminine in any way, their sexuality becomes suspect. It is fun to dress up in different clothing; Shakespearian male actors played female roles but their sexuality was never questioned – acting was just not considered appropriate behaviour for women in those times. Since women have entered the theatre many have dressed in men's clothing and played male roles, but ironically the same fears are not expressed about the behaviour compromising females' femininity and becoming more masculine, or the possibility of them becoming lesbian.

Myth. Gays and lesbians are sinful.

Response. Gay and lesbian people are not inherently sinful. Some religious faiths are against same-sex relationships, while other religions embrace the diversity that exists in relation to sexual orientations. What is regarded as sinful changes over time and in different contexts; what is condemned at one point in time becomes accepted in another. 'Living in sin' was a term used to describe unmarried couples living together. As mores and values change, living together before marriage has become normalized. Today, there are very few religious groups who condemn these views. Just as laws condemning same-sex relationships have changed, so too are moral and religious attitudes changing.

Myth. Children who grow up in gay and lesbian families will become gay or lesbian themselves.

Response. The majority of children who grow up in gay and lesbian families identify as heterosexual, but there are some children who do identify as gay, lesbian, bisexual or queer from these families. This is the same in heterosexual families – that is, not all children become heterosexual, some identify as gay, lesbian, bisexual or queer. Most children who identify as gay, lesbian, bisexual or queer have heterosexual parents. Thus, family type does not determine one's sexuality. However, research shows that children growing up in gay and lesbian families tend to have a far greater awareness of different sexualities as possible options in their lives; that is, heterosexuality is not considered the only option and non-heterosexuality is not perceived as deviant or an abnormal choice.

Homophobia and heterosexism in early childhood settings

As pointed out in the previous chapter on gender performativity, how normalizing discourses of gender work to strictly regulate performances of masculinity and femininity within narrow and constricting definitions of what it means to be a boy or girl, man or woman, has important implications for all of us, regardless of our sexual orientation. The consequences of such rigid constructions of gender can have devastating impacts on individuals, particularly children and youths who are actively negotiating the gender discourses available to them within powerful peer groups. Consequently, working with children around the liberatory potentials of taking up non-normative gender positions is an important aspect of doing social justice work with children and their families. However, this work cannot be done successfully without doing sexuality issues and deconstructing how normalizing discourses of gender are heterosexualized, contributing to the perpetuation of homophobia and heterosexism in society.

Discourses of homophobia and heterosexism that prevail in society define all sexualities other than heterosexuality as abnormal and deviant, thus relegating those who identify as other than heterosexual to the margins while simultaneously silencing their experiences of discrimination and inequality. In early childhood settings, as in other educational contexts, dealing with gay and lesbian social justice issues often encounters resistance from educators and parents who are positioned in homophobic and heterosexist discourses, which can be strongly linked to religious, moral and cultural beliefs around same-sex relationships. Many early childhood educators allude to their religious values, and those of children's parents, as an important factor in their not dealing with gay and lesbian issues with children. The intersection between religious discourse and sexuality difference is an area that many find difficult to reconcile or negotiate, as demonstrated in the following comments by early childhood educators:

> I don't feel comfortable with these issues at all and wouldn't discuss them with children. It is against my religious and moral values.

> We have never had children from a family with two parents of the same sex, probably because of our Christian focus. It is not relevant to our setting.

> Children should not have to accept this lifestyle, particularly where it conflicts with the religion taught at home (as in my centre). However,

children need to be taught to accept people. Staff and families need to be aware of this.

As in all educational contexts, educators have a critical role in creating positive learning environments in which all individuals have similar opportunities to reach their potentials, and can feel supported, included and affirmed about who they are. Not only do educators have a 'duty of care' to the children and adults with whom they teach, but there is also a broader role that involves a communal responsibility for fostering social justice within the communities in which we live and teach. This is reflected in the philosophies of Reggio Emilia, which emphasize the liberatory potential of early childhood institutions as 'civil forums', in which important social issues and events are openly discussed with children, and social justice perspectives, policies and practices are paramount. Educators who are positioned in discourses that operate to undermine *respect* for the differences that exist in people's lives may have difficulties negotiating and incorporating social justice pedagogies and philosophies into their daily work with children and their families. Negotiating the different discursive locations that exist among educators and families is not easy work, but it is not impossible to find a point of reconciliation across differences that can lead to respect for difference, rather than just 'tolerance'. It is within this context that it becomes possible to begin doing social justice education with a whole-institution approach, but there is no shifting without education, patience, dialogue, or a willingness to take individual and communal risks (Robinson 2005d).

Sexuality is also largely considered to be a matter that should remain within the privacy of the family and is therefore not perceived to be the responsibility of early childhood educators. As one child-care worker articulated, 'Their private issues áre their private issues'. Britzman (1997) argues that this perception that sexual identity is a 'private' affair, which has little to do with public lives, is a powerful myth. It contributes to heteronormativity and perpetuates the notion that heterosexuality has nothing to do with homosexuality. To the contrary, the cultural binary heterosexual/homosexual operates not just to narrowly and rigidly define the two oppositionally, but what is perceived as possible for those who identify with either of these sexualities. Britzman (1997: 192) points out: 'The fact is that schools mediate the discourses of private and public work to leave intact the view that (homo)sexualities must be hidden'.

Heterosexuality becomes the 'public' voice, definition and representation of 'normal' and 'natural' sexuality. This normalization of heterosexuality is further enforced through powerful gender discourses that operate to constitute socially sanctioned performances of masculinity and femininity as heterosexual and regulate gender conformity among children and youth. Early childhood education is very much part of this normalization process of the construction of the heterosexual public/homosexual private binary. This is reinforced in early childhood education through the process in which lesbian and gay identities are legitimized largely and solely within the privatized context of the family. This point is discussed further at a later stage in this chapter.

Not surprisingly, then, homophobic harassment and violence experienced by some gay or lesbian early childhood educators in their workplace is an issue that has arisen in our research. This harassment is experienced from other staff and/or from parents of children attending their settings. One teacher pointed out that 'We have some gay staff and some positive images, but some heterosexual staff still have a problem with it and there is some tension there'. Research in other areas of the workforce, including various educational contexts, highlights that homophobic harassment, discrimination and violence are widespread and have crucial implications for the well-being of individuals who experience these behaviours (Ferfolja 1998; Irwin 1999). Such harassment is also in breach of anti-discrimination legislation throughout Australia, which raises concerns about employers in the field of early childhood education in the public sector adhering to their responsibilities in providing 'safe' workplaces free from discrimination. Homophobia among educators and parents sends strong messages to children about difference.

Heterosexism and homophobic stereotypes and myths can be perpetuated through daily pedagogical practices and everyday interactions between educators and children (Robinson and Jones Díaz 1999). One highly influential homophobic myth that has been prevalent in early childhood educational settings (and within the broader society) is the perception of 'homosexuals' as paedophiles and sexual predators (Silin 1997; Cossins 1999). Though there is limited research on male early childhood educators' experiences of working in this traditionally female-dominated area, anecdotal evidence seems to suggest that this myth has been partially responsible for keeping men in Western nations, regardless of their sexuality, out of the field of early childhood education (King 1997). Male early childhood educators are located in a range of complex and contradictory discourses. They can be viewed as positive role models for children, through their challenging of hegemonic constructions of masculinity, but, on the other hand, can be seen as potential child molesters and paedophiles. These men are often perceived to be sexually suspicious, as their very employment challenges hegemonic constructions of masculinity and gender roles, which are intimately linked to constructions of heterosexuality. Child care and working with children is considered traditionally to be a 'woman's role' and those men who challenge gender traditions and participate in 'women's work' are often scrutinized by others, particularly by other men, who take up hegemonic masculine, heterosexual identities. Not only is their gender questioned but so too is their sexuality, by association. This process, combined with homophobic myths that associate paedophilia with homosexuals, results in the perception that male early childhood educators are potential child abusers, who need to be watched carefully. This surveillance can be intensified if male early childhood educators openly identify as gay.

Dealing with gay and lesbian equity issues with children is also frequently misconstrued as dealing with sex, rather than about the experiences of communities or about loving or caring relationships. Homophobia operates to define and essentialize non-heterosexuality purely in terms of physical sexual acts. Thus, the focus in non-heterosexual relationships is centralized on the perceived abnormality and deviance of their sexual behaviour – behaviours often mistakenly considered to be absent in the sexual practices of heterosexuals. These sexual practices are largely viewed as deviant when engaged in by same-sex couples (Kitzinger 1994; Ferfolja 2003). What are rendered invisible in this process are the ordinary everyday activities and tasks that are part of the lives of all regardless of sexual orientation. Consequently, the hypersexualization of gay and lesbian identities results in the perception that doing sexuality work with children is developmentally and morally inappropriate behaviour and perpetuates many of the myths about non-heterosexuals.

Out of sight, out of mind: 'compulsory heterosexuality' and the invisibility of sexual Others

Many early childhood educators do see the importance of dealing with gay and lesbian discrimination in early childhood education, but many of them consider the issues to be irrelevant to their respective workplaces and therefore do not address them (Robinson 2002, 2005c). Whether these issues are considered as relevant is primarily based on educators' awareness of gay and lesbian families in their settings, as indicated in the following comments:

> We haven't dealt with these issues because we haven't had gay and lesbian families in our setting. It isn't really a concern to us.

> At the moment I would only address these issues if I had children from homosexual families, if the children were curious.

> I would consider these issues important when/if gay and lesbian parents use my setting.

The above comments reflect a widely held myth that doing anti-homophobia and anti-heterosexist education is only relevant to a 'minority' of people who identify as non-heterosexual and not to those who are heterosexual. However, as pointed out previously, sexuality is a socially constructed social relationship (Weeks 1986; Britzman 1997). The homosexual/heterosexual dualism represents a hierarchical power relationship in which definitions and understandings of homosexuality are defined in opposition to what it means to be heterosexual, and vice versa. Sedgwick (1990) makes the point that gay and lesbian issues are not just relevant to a minority of people who identify as gay or lesbian, but rather the heterosexual/homosexual binary relationship, which largely perpetuates discriminatory thinking towards non-heterosexual identities, is crucial in the way that all people's lives are determined, controlled and regulated across the spectrum of sexualities.

For some, the relevance of dealing with gay and lesbian issues depends on whether the presence of gay and lesbian parents is causing 'problems' for the setting or for the children from these families. Some also perceive it as a potential problem if other children are becoming 'too curious' about other children's same-sex parents. Consequently, it seems that for many, dealing with gay and lesbian issues is only done as a last resort and where it is judged that educators could no longer afford to ignore issues or divert children's curiosity. Such perceptions relinquish educators' responsibilities for validating families parented by gays and lesbians and for providing non-discriminatory educational environments for all children. It also sends a strong message to children that such issues are not to be openly discussed, reinforcing the taboo that already silences discussions in this area. Further, failure to positively intervene in children's discriminatory practices up-front with regard to these issues prolongs the problem, and 'blames the victim'. It can also send the message that educators may condone the discriminatory behaviour of other children, which may result in the child or children believing that they are somehow responsible for the teasing or marginalization that they might be experiencing around these issues.

Early childhood educators often assume that lesbians and gays are not a part of their clientele, community or members of their own staff. Unlike more visible identity differences, sexuality is often not readily recognized and is often assumed to be heterosexual, if not openly stated otherwise. Such assumptions, constituted within the discourse of 'compulsory heterosexuality' (Rich 1980) or 'heterosexual assumption' (Weeks *et al.* 2001), and reinforced through the pervasiveness of heterosexism, are prevalent throughout early childhood education (as elsewhere in society). This results in an assumed absence of gay and lesbian parents or significant adult carers, or even early childhood educators, unless they are publicly 'out' to their children and settings. However, the 'invisibility' and silence of gay and lesbian families are often enforced due to the extent and effectiveness of homophobia and heterosexism within educational settings and in society more broadly. This makes it extremely difficult and potentially risky for gay and lesbian families to 'come out' to their children's educators and/or openly discuss their concerns. Many gay and lesbian families who send their children to daily child care and preschool do not disclose their sexualities and are not out to their children's educators. A failure to acknowledge this possibility can result in the denial of many children's experiences within alternative family structures and reinforces the illegitimacy of gay and lesbian identities. Some gay and lesbian families actively seek out early childhood settings that demonstrate a commitment, through policies and practices, to diversity and difference (hopefully including sexuality) in order to feel more confident that they will be respected and that their children will not be discriminated against. It is important to point out here that in some cases children from gay and lesbian families attending early childhood settings do on occasions experience discrimination from other children and from educators and other staff members.

Another assumption often made by early childhood educators is that children, regardless of their family structure, do not know or interact with adults who openly identify as gay or lesbian. Many educators, often unfamiliar with children's social lives beyond the setting, generally read children's lives from the context of their own experiences of diversity, which may be limited. In addition, the dominant discourse of childhood, as discussed earlier in this chapter, leads to a misconception that all children are naïve and innocent and 'suitably sheltered' from what adults' generally consider to be 'inappropriate' issues, such as sexual orientation.

The inclusion of sexual Others: legitimating difference within 'the family'

It has been highlighted in our research and teaching in this area that the only perceived legitimate and relevant context in which to deal with gay and lesbian issues in early childhood education is within the discourse of family diversity and parenting. As one teacher indicated, 'I think all this comes under family life and shouldn't be separated from that'. As raised in the introduction to this chapter, dealing with family diversity is generally considered important in developing an inclusive curriculum. Understanding the nature and meaning of family and the cultural diversity that exists within families is viewed as being developmentally appropriate and relevant to children's experiences of the world. However, the extent to which educators deal with the diversity of family types, particularly the representation of gay and lesbian families, varies greatly. As discussed previously, the inclusion of gay and lesbian families in the early childhood education curriculum tends to rely on the educator's perception of what they consider relevant and appropriate to the children in their settings, as well as their own personal comfort levels in addressing such issues.

The legitimating of lesbian and gays within the context of 'the family' can be viewed as part of a normalization process, where sexuality and sexual differences can be eclipsed, albeit temporarily, by more familiar, acceptable and comfortable discourses of family diversity and mothering and fathering. This rigidly confined validation of lesbian and gay identities within the family further relegates non-heterosexual identities to the private sector, where power and status are diminished. This perspective is also reflected in the experiences of early childhood education pre-service teachers when they undertake practical experience in the field. For example, one student in the programme in which we teach, chose to produce a pictorial booklet for children on family diversity and wanted to include gay and lesbian parenting. The early childhood centre was enthusiastic about the booklet generally, but was somewhat concerned about the inclusion of gay and lesbian parents. Finally, a compromise was reached and the student was directed not to use the terms 'lesbian' or 'gay', but to use the phrase 'some children have two mummies or two daddies'. Such stories are not unusual and are heard from many pre-service early childhood teachers who are keen to be inclusive of sexual identity in their practices, but learn quickly that it may not be as easy as anticipated.

This example raises some important issues that need to be addressed. It highlights that some early childhood educators consider 'the family' context both a developmentally appropriate and a comfortable vantage point from which to introduce gay and lesbian issues into early childhood education. If this is the case, then it is one way to begin to break down the homophobia and heterosexism that operate in early childhood education and in developing more inclusive practices around diversity. However, it seems that when gay and lesbian families are raised in discussions with children, the focus tends to be limited to how children might experience living in such a family, such as the potential for being teased by other children. Thus, these families are often being constructed as sites of discrimination, rather than sites of celebration. Broader social, political and economic experiences of discrimination encountered by these families are generally considered far less important or relevant. Consequently, the approaches taken to dealing with gay and lesbian issues reflect a range of contradictory positions on the part of educators. For example, in the first instance outlined above relating to the development of the book on families, the issues were depoliticized and desexualized in order to make them less controversial and more 'sanitized' for children; in the last instance, it becomes a case of overpoliticization, where families are primarily constructed as sites of discrimination.

What about children's voices?

There has been limited research focusing on children's perceptions of gays and lesbians or of sexuality generally. The video *It's Elementary: Talking about Gay Issues in Schools* (Chasnoff and Cohen 1997) is an excellent exception and provides a critical glimpse of the perspectives of young children from early childhood through to secondary schooling in the USA. There has been some research that has focused on the experiences of children living with gay or lesbian parents (Tasker and Golomobok 1997). However, the silence in this area is primarily a result of the issues we have discussed previously around sexuality being considered irrelevant and an inappropriate or taboo topic to address with children (Robinson 2002, 2005c).

As pointed out previously, adults often have the perspective that sexuality issues are not part of 'children's worlds' or part of their everyday conversations with each other. However, children are constantly negotiating the discourses associated with gays and lesbians that are spoken and enacted by their families, peers, teachers, media and other popular cultural contexts. Foucault (1978) points out that what is unspoken is as powerful as what is spoken. This is critical in terms of what individual subjects take up as their 'truths' in the world. Chasnoff and Cohen (1997) powerfully demonstrate how these issues are very much part of children's lives and how they look at the world; including how they use derogatory terms associated with gays and lesbians in their everyday conversations to put people down and gain power over others. There is often the perspective that young children use these words but do not know what they mean. However, what is important in this respect is not whether children know the 'exact' meanings of the words they use, which can shift according to who speaks them and in what context, but the way these words take on a particular meaning signifying an insult or an action of gaining power over others, through the ways in which the children use them, as well as how the words and actions are read by those individual subjects at whom they are directed. Such interactions between children become critical sites of the construction of children's gendered and sexualized identities on a daily basis. These interactions also create critical spaces in which educators can explore children's locations within normalizing discourses; disrupting and deconstructing the meaning making that is being constituted in their words and actions. That is, these spaces provide opportunities to re-examine with children the cultural scripts implicit and explicit in the discourses that they are enacting and to encourage different readings.

I (Robinson) recently overheard a conversation between a boy aged 7 and a girl aged 5 in which they were talking about their favourite singers. The young girl asked the boy whether he liked a particular male singer, to which he replied, 'No, he's gay!' Joining in the conversation, I asked what was wrong with him being gay and if that stopped the boy from liking the singer's music. The boy quickly replied, 'Gay men are OK, they are funny, but lesbians are mean'. When I asked how he knew this, he gave several examples of television shows that he had seen in which there were gay characters that were represented as funny and entertaining. Similarly, his perception of lesbians being mean was based on a television show that portrayed a lesbian character, rather fleetingly, as a mean and aggressive individual. Consequently, the young boy had taken on these discursive representations as his 'truth' about gays and lesbians generally. The discourse of gay men as 'funny' and entertaining is a dominant one that prevails in Western societies and is largely perpetuated through popular culture, especially film and television comedies. Interestingly, being the 'jester' or 'entertainer' has been one way in which being a gay male has been accepted in mainstream heterosexual culture. Viewing lesbians in this oppositional manner to gay men reflects the binary gay male/lesbian that underpins the dominant discourse of lesbians that has been largely portrayed in popular culture. This portrayal of lesbians is especially evident in films, where they have been frequently represented as aggressive, mean and manipulating and generally deserving the ill fate that many of them meet in the end – see Epstein and Friedman (1995) for an in-depth review of the depiction of gays and lesbians in films. However, the power of discourse lies not in how 'true' or 'real' the knowledge is, but rather in how it is taken up, embodied, and spoken as 'truth' by individual subjects, popular culture and social institutions.

Implications for practice in early childhood education

The issues raised in this chapter have significant implications for policies, pedagogy and the curriculum in early childhood education. On the whole our research with early childhood educators indicates that most educators do consider dealing with gay and lesbian equity issues in children's early education as a matter of equity and social justice. It is generally seen to be integral to an 'anti-bias' approach and it is generally believed that developing 'tolerance' of all sorts should always be on the agenda. However, from our experience, this strong philosophical perspective is often not borne out in practice, for the various reasons that have been discussed throughout this chapter.

Policy direction and implementation

In our experience and research in this area, early childhood institutions that openly and equally include gay and lesbian equity issues in their social justice and equity agendas along with other areas of difference, do not meet with the parental and community resistance often perceived to follow such as deci- sion. If early childhood institutions are to become 'civil forums' as articulated in the philosophies of Reggio Emilia, it is important to include sexuality issues on the agenda. Social justice philosophies, policies, practices and education are not about picking and choosing which area is more worthy than another, based on personal beliefs. Early childhood education policies need to reflect this philosophy and early childhood institutions, in a whole- setting approach, need to work towards its implementation across everyday practices with children and families. Consequently, naming and including gay and lesbian perspectives in policies is an important part of this process, even if they are perceived not to be part of the family clientele. Broad umbrella policies, such as an anti-bias policy, which are seen to be inclusive of a range of diversity and difference issues, can actually silence and marginalize more controversial issues, such as sexuality. Therefore, it is important to review policies in order to ascertain if they inadvertently perpetuate homo- phobic and heterosexist discourses.

Developing and implementing policies generally involves including staff, children and families in the process. Educating those involved about why it is important to include these perspectives, what the important issues are, and the responsibilities and roles of individuals in the implementation of policies is important to the success of this process. It is also critical that policies are openly displayed in services and are discussed with new families; this is also a critical part of the education of community members. However, the success of such policies will be ultimately reliant on management supporting educators in actively implementing the policies in daily practice, even if resistance arises. The development of supportive procedures for dealing with resistance from various sources, including parents, managers and other staff members, is important.

Communicating and negotiating with families

It is crucial that educators do not assume that gay and lesbian parents are not utilizing their services. Homophobia and heterosexism make it difficult and often impossible for some gay and lesbian parents to come out to their children's educators. Thus, their silence and invisibility should not be per- ceived to be an indicator of their absence. Openly including gay and lesbian perspectives in policies will provide a more supportive environment in which to foster trusting relationships between educators and families. Including gay and lesbian parents in the development of programmes that deal with the social, political and economic issues facing their families and communities is also important in developing positive relationships between educators and families.

Programming and planning

Educators need to encourage children's critical thinking around the nor- malizing discourses of gender and sexuality that operate in their lives. The process of deconstruction is particularly useful for identifying the discursive location of children in these areas, for acknowledging social power relations, for highlighting stereotypes and myths, and for posing different and new questions that encourage non-normative subject positions in discourse. Such an educational programme needs to be founded within a theoretical framework that recognizes that children are active participants in the construction of their own identities and those of others (see Chapter 2). In programmes that are developed around children's interests, sexuality issues can be creatively tapped into through a range of different topic areas that children often raise, especially those that are related to gender identities and families, which both open up discussion possibilities around gay and lesbian equity issues. Ultimately, encouraging children to take an active interest in current affairs issues and engaging them in critical discussions will provide a plethora of interest-based issues that can include sexuality issues.

Working with staff, families and children

Despite the prevalent belief to the contrary, gay and lesbian equity issues are relevant to all children and their families regardless of their sexual orientations. As pointed out in this chapter, normalizing discourses of gender and sexuality operate to regulate and constrain the behaviours of all individuals and to perpetuate homophobia and heterosexism. It is important to initiate and maintain an inclusive and continuous dialogue around the issues, concerns and fears of educators and families in order to provide a more supportive environment for the development of effective social justice policies and practices in this area. This needs to be done in conjunction with the development of an ongoing education programme for management, educators, other staff members, and families on the broad socio-political and economic issues facing gay, lesbian, bisexual, transgender and queer people and how heteronormativity works in early childhood settings. A focus needs to include possible strategies for dealing with these issues in early childhood programmes.

Conclusion

This chapter has stressed the importance of dealing with sexuality and sexual orientation issues in early childhood education. It has particularly focused on how the hegemonic discourses of childhood and sexuality that prevail in early childhood education (as elsewhere in society) intersect to construct the perception that sexuality and sexual orientation issues are irrelevant to children and their early education. However, it has also been argued that these equity issues are as relevant to children's lives as they are to adults. Further, it has been pointed out that regardless of whether early childhood settings have known gay or lesbian families utilizing their services, doing sexuality equity issues need to be a critical component of social justice education for all.

Recommended reading

Boldt, G. (1997) Sexist and heterosexist responses to gender bending, in J. Tobin (ed.) *Making a Place for Pleasure in Early Childhood Education*. New Haven, CT: Yale University Press.

Cahill, B. and Theilheimer, R. (1999) Stonewall in the housekeeping area: gay and lesbian issues in the early childhood classroom, in W.J. Letts IV and J.T. Sears (eds) *Queering Elementary Education: Advancing the Dialogue about Sexualities and Schooling*. Lanham, MD: Rowman & Littlefield.

Casper, V., Cuffaro, H.K., Schultz, S., Silin, J.G. and Wickens. E. (1998) Towards a most thorough understanding of the world: sexual orientation and early childhood education, in N. Yelland (ed.) *Gender In Early Childhood*. London: Routledge.

Kissen, R. (ed.) (2002) *Getting Ready for Benjamin. Preparing Teachers for Sexual Diversity in the Classroom*. Lanham, MD: Rowman & Littlefield.

Robinson, K.H. (2005c) 'Queerying' gender: heteronormativity in early childhood education, *Australian Journal of Early Childhood*, 30(2). In press.

Robinson, K.H. (2005d) Doing anti-homophobia and anti-heterosexism in early childhood education. Moving beyond the immobilizing impacts of 'risk', 'fears' and 'silences'. Can we afford not to? *Contemporary Issues in Early Childhood Education*, 6(2). In press.

Weeks, J., Heaphy, B. and Donovan, C. (2001) *Same Sex Intimacies: Families of Choice and Other Life Experiments*. London: Routledge.

9

THE CHALLENGE OF DIVERSITY AND DIFFERENCE TO EARLY CHILDHOOD EDUCATION

Introduction

Our research and work with early childhood educators and pre-service teachers shows that social justice education is generally considered an important aspect of children's early education. However, throughout this book we have highlighted many of the contradictions and complexities facing early childhood educators in doing this with children, families and communities. We have also acknowledged that doing social justice education in practice can be difficult work, as it frequently involves taking perceived and 'real' personal and professional risks, which can challenge many educators' subjective positions in the world, particularly in relation to their understandings of childhood and in terms of how they view difference (Robinson 2005d).

We started this book with a discussion of what we have called a hierarchy of differences. What is meant by this is that some areas of social justice are considered personally and professionally more relevant and worthy of support and consideration than others. This personal and professional preference for taking up certain areas of social justice over others is primarily based on individual (dis)comfort levels around doing work in various areas of social justice. As pointed out in Chapter 1, how comfortable one feels addressing specific equity areas will be related to a number of different issues, including level of expertise across social justice issues and one's subjective location in discourses of diversity and difference. One's location in these discourses will be influenced by personal experiences and cultural and religious beliefs, among other factors. Social justice education around sexuality issues, for instance, is an area that many early childhood educators feel uncomfortable addressing, primarily due to its controversial status and the perceived risks involved in incorporating these issues into programmes. As some early childhood educators have pointed out to us, it is much easier and personally less risky to take up the discourse of the irrelevance of sexuality issues to young children and to pass the responsibility on to secondary educators working with older children. Furthermore, like sexuality issues, other equity issues faced by single parents, or those associated with family poverty, can also be marginalized and silenced in the discourse that positions these issues as 'private' family matters. Consequently, many equity issues are placed in the 'too hard' basket and are not included in children's early education, even when children bring issues up themselves. Children receive strong contradictory messages from individuals and institutions. Where children discursively locate themselves in terms of difference and equity, and how this is played out in their lives, is very much influenced by educators' discursive practices and the contradictory messages they receive.

In many respects, early childhood education, as a microcosm of the broader society, operates to perpetuate the status quo in society; that is, through everyday practices it maintains the social order or power relations that currently exist in the world. As Kobayashi and Ray (2000) argue, social institutions, such as education, actively participate in defining which social justice issues will be recognized, taken up and challenged and which social inequalities will continue to be publicly tolerated. However, we share Dahlberg *et al.*'s (1999) vision of early childhood institutions as potential 'civil forums', and perceive that through collective community action we can actively foster and create more democratic philosophies and practices between adults and children, as well as across and within different socio-cultural groups throughout the world. Through an awareness of the complexities and contradictions that operate for early childhood educators around diversity and difference, as a community of educators, we can collectively begin to deconstruct the barriers that currently exist and that prevent the full inclusion of socio-cultural Others. Individual early childhood educators are a critical component of this democratic project, as their daily work with children and their families is crucial in terms of disrupting the normalizing discourses that perpetuate power inequalities that are experienced by those who are not part of the dominant culture.

However, it is important that all educators take a reflexive approach to their practice with children and families in order to understand how their subject positions in discourses can perpetuate, consciously or unconsciously, the social inequalities that prevail in society. In other words, as pointed out previously, reflexivity is about developing a critical self-conscious awareness of one's relationship with the Other (McNay 2000). We feel that this is the crucial starting point for anyone who is involved in doing social justice education. A reflexive approach to diversity and difference is primarily about deconstructing the discourse of 'tolerance' in order to refocus more on the discourse of 'respect'. Many educators view tolerance as the reflection of the success of their practices; however, we feel that respect is a far better measure. The concept of tolerance is constraining, as it is always about a precarious hierarchical power relationship that has its limits on how long one can 'tolerate' the existence of someone else, who is often perceived as an annoyance or irritation. In contrast, respect is about accepting people's rights to choose to be who they are in the world that sit equally beside different ways of being, knowing and doing.

In this final chapter, we highlight several critical issues that we feel early childhood educators need to consider when reviewing current approaches to social justice education with children and their families. They are issues that we have addressed at various points throughout this book and include: promoting theoretical understandings of children, childhood, diversity and difference; enhancing links between theory and practice; acknowledging how diversity and difference are often located in the discourse of deficit; encouraging children's critical thinking and learning; deconstructing the adult/child binary; increasing communications with families and communities; developing policies and procedures that incorporate social justice perspectives; building supportive networks at all levels of early childhood education; promoting professional development of educators and other staff; and the need for further research into diversity and difference in early childhood education.

Promoting theoretical understandings of childhood, diversity and difference

Feminist poststructural perspectives, as well as the other cultural and critical theories which have largely informed the theoretical frameworks of our various discussions in this book, provide invaluable understandings of the social construction of childhood through different discourses that are historically and culturally available. These frameworks acknowledge the multiple subjectivities of children across different sites of identity and recognize that children are active participants in the construction of their own identities and in the regulation of the identities of others. For example, through the lens of feminist poststructural perspectives educators can shift their reliance on 'common-sense' oppositional thinking constituted in cultural binaries, such as adult/child, which construct understandings of what it means to be an adult or child. Such knowledge tends to inform many educators' daily practices with children, thus perpetuating the hierarchal relations of power that exist between adults and children.

Incorporating contemporary theoretical and critical perspectives of childhood, diversity and difference into early childhood programmes, policies and practices is a critical foundation for effectively doing social justice education with children and their families. Traditional perspectives of childhood and children's learning, based on developmentalism, are still largely viewed by many educators as the only legitimate and acceptable theoretical tools for understanding children, families and diversity. However, as we have argued throughout this book, modernist perspectives of childhood and children's learning are limited in their potential to inform successful approaches to social justice education. Modernist universalized discourses of childhood do not address children's agency or the multiple experiences of what it means to be a child across different socio-cultural contexts, such as gender, sexuality, class, 'race', (dis)ability, ethnicity and so on. Developmentalism constrains our understandings of children's identity formation, particularly in contexts of diversity in which children's and families' negotiation of their difference is ongoing, complex and often contradictory. Children, like adults, construct multiple identities. Through the entering and re-entering of different discursive fields, children are capable of taking on multiple ways of being, doing, thinking and acting, depending on the power relations operating in a given social field. Children need to be given opportunities to question, analyse, test and critique different versions of 'reality' in ways that are contextually relevant to their daily lives, in order for them to deal with the complexities and contradictions characteristic of a postmodern, globalizing and diverse world.

Early childhood educators' perspectives of childhood and of diversity and difference can impact on the social justice issues considered appropriate to address with children. Children are aware of diversity and difference from very early ages, and this influences their behaviours towards others and their everyday social practices. Like adults, children are acutely aware of the normalizing discourses that operate in society and actively regulate and police their own behaviours and those of others according to these social norms. However, the discourse of childhood innocence is a powerful influence on how many early childhood educators perceive children's experiences and understandings of diversity, difference and social inequalities. Consequently, some aspects of social justice education (for example, poverty, sexuality, death, divorce, domestic violence) are often not raised with children by educators who are located in discourses that construct children as being 'too young' to understand what they perceive to be adult concepts.

The hegemonic discourse of childhood and the cultural binary adult/child continue to perpetuate the oppositional thinking that constitutes traditional understandings of what it means to be a child or an adult. These modernist common-sense perspectives are perceived to be representative of the 'natural order of things' and operate to artificially construct different and mutually exclusive polarized worlds for children and adults. Consequently, many early childhood educators (like other adults) participate in the construction and maintenance of these separate imagined 'spaces', designated as the 'world of adults' and the 'world of children', through their everyday practices and interactions with children. This polarized constructed relationship between adults and children primarily defines childhood in opposition to what it means to be an adult. In this process certain knowledge, practices and roles become designated as associated with adults and thus perceived to be irrelevant to children. Broader social, economic and political issues are generally considered to be irrelevant to the 'world of children'; indeed, they become perceived as adult burdens and responsibilities from which children need to be protected for as long as possible. This protection is generally aimed at maintaining their childhood 'innocence'.

The discourse of childhood innocence, in conjunction with perceptions that children are 'too young' to deal with issues perceived solely as associated with adult lives, impacts on the way social justice education is undertaken with children. For example, as pointed out previously, many educators do not see the relevance or significance of relating individual discrimination to broader social, economic and political inequalities when dealing with equity issues with children. It is often felt that children will have no understanding of these broader concerns. This is also reflected in the way sexual equity issues are perceived as irrelevant to children's lives and understandings.

Yet, children are growing up in an increasingly globalized and competitive world, characterized by accelerated and sophisticated media and communications technologies, such as the Internet, film, television and computers. As these technologies become more integrated into children's entertainment, popular culture and toys, the perceived dichotomy between children's worlds and adults' worlds is blurred. However, despite the fact that children have greater access to 'adults' worlds' through these technologies, hegemonic discourses of childhood prevail, masking the reality that today young children are knowing and less naïve than earlier generations.

In order to support children in voicing their ideas and concerns about different social issues and current events and to contribute as active citizens in society in their own right, there needs to be a disruption of and a shift away from the limitations of traditional perspectives of childhood and children's learning. This will enable both early childhood educators and children to engage in experiences, projects and programmes that can bring about change.

Positioning children and families within discourses of deficit

Some children and their families who come from minority socio-cultural backgrounds or non-nuclear families are often perceived as being culturally or linguistically deprived. Children from language backgrounds other than English are often positioned in deficit discourses if they are perceived by educators as being unable to integrate effectively and adapt to early childhood settings and if they are not speaking English. In terms of bilingualism and language retention, there are greater concerns for children's individual socio-emotional needs and lack of English-language proficiency, than with broader sociological issues associated with home language retention and its connections to bilingual identities.

Families parented by gays and lesbians are often, consciously and unconsciously, positioned within discourses that construct them as being deficient. As pointed out in Chapter 8, homophobia and heterosexism operate in ways that construct these families primarily as sites of discrimination, which results in children being potentially harassed or teased. Thus, they are rarely constructed in positive discourses that view them as sites of celebration.

It is crucial that early childhood educators build on the cultural, linguistic and social capital of children, families and staff from diverse backgrounds, rather than diminishing and dismissing their 'difference' as deficit. Since early childhood educators are at the forefront of young children's educational trajectory, their willingness to challenge normalizing discourses of heterosexuality, femininity, masculinity, childhood, 'race', monolingualism, nuclear family and so on can ultimately transform children's early experiences of education from potential failure to guaranteed success. In this way, 'difference' is able to accumulate equality, rather than be the site of marginalization and subordination.

Fostering children's critical thinking around diversity and difference

Developing children's critical thinking around diversity and difference is an important component of doing social justice education with children. Our research indicates that the development of children's critical thinking is not generally given a central focus in the equity work that educators do with young children. Rather, the focus tends to be on identity stereotypes, with limited acknowledgement of how the politics of difference operates in society to perpetuate inequalities.

While our research indicates that the use of resources is seen to be an effective way of introducing diversity and difference, the focus tends to be mainly superficial. There is a heavy reliance on resources as a means of promoting cultural diversity at the expense of fostering children's critical thinking around the issues. Appropriate use of such resources can aid critical thinking, but there is little evidence in our research to indicate that this is a common practice in the field. Consequently, little emphasis tends to be placed on developing and fostering critical thinking in children (and adults) about racism, sexism, homophobia, racial and cultural differences, monolingualism, inequality and power, for instance. Critical thinking is a crucial aspect of social justice perspectives. There is a tendency to operate in a superficial and 'touristic' manner in terms of diversity in which the provision of resources alone is often considered sufficient enough in reflecting and exploring diversity and difference.

The philosophy that 'We are all the same, we are all equal' is commonly articulated among educators. However, this discursive reading of socio-cultural equity, where understandings of what it means to be 'the same' are standardized on hegemonic cultural values, dismisses the importance of acknowledging power differences among individuals and across different cultural groups. Consequently, the discrimination and inequalities faced by individuals (educators, families or children) are not generally linked to socio-cultural factors. For example, when gay and lesbian issues are dealt with in early childhood they are rarely considered within the broader social issues of homophobia or heterosexism. There seems to be a prevalent perspective that dealing with diversity in early childhood is not relevant or directly related to broader social issues around discrimination or inequality.

Consequently, for many educators, doing social justice education with children does not currently include analysing how discrimination and inequalities are constituted within broader socio-cultural, political and economic relationships in society in terms of their impact on adults and children in daily life. Inequality and disadvantage are becoming more apparent in recent years due to the impact of globalization, which brings increased economic hardship to many low-income and single-parent families, who are most vulnerable to the decreased levels of commitment from governments in providing equitable and affordable health and welfare services, as well as public education (including early childhood education).

This lack of contextualizing and acknowledging inequalities and discrimination in broader socio-cultural, economic and political discourses is most likely influenced by the prevalence of the discourse of childhood that renders these concerns as irrelevant to children's understandings of the world and to their daily lives. In order for children to understand their own discriminatory practices, it is critical for them to be aware of how power and inequality are constituted within the discourses that are culturally and historically available to them in society. Consequently, it is imperative that social justice education with children is extended to include the development of children's critical thinking about the issues. As pointed out in Chapter 2, deconstruction is a valuable teaching tool that can be utilized in everyday activities with children to foster their critical thinking.

However, questions for learning and finding out about the world are culturally and socially embedded (Makin *et al.* 1995). In many middle- to upper-class white Anglo-Australian homes, good problem-solving encompasses thinking critically and verbalizing ideas accordingly. In other cultures, however, encouraging children to question and verbalize their ideas can be considered offensive and thus culturally inappropriate. Therefore, teaching strategies used to facilitate problem-solving and critical thinking may in fact be representative of only one cultural context that is Anglocentric, Western and middle-class, with little regard for how children mediate between different cultural, classed and gendered expectations and discourses. Getting children to locate how their shifting subjectivities are constituted in discourses is critical if adults are going to be effective in assisting to deconstruct dominant discourses which produce inequalities. Hence, it is crucial that critical thinking is not used as yet another tool for marginalizing those children who have less experience of verbalizing, questioning or expressing their opinion.

Unfortunately, there are no 'quick-fix solutions' to dealing with incidences of racism, sexism, homophobia, classism, linguicism and so on, in or out of early childhood settings or classrooms. What works for one person in one context may not be useful to someone else dealing with a similar or different issue in another context. Intervention in these areas of social justice needs to become part of one's daily curriculum and programming, an integral part of how one lives one's life on all levels. In such a context, there is an understanding that disrupting and challenging inequality can be fraught with contradiction and complexity and is ongoing and never ending. Hence, 'quick-fix solutions' may appeal to many as a way of masking or obscuring difficult issues, but ultimately they will not provide a sufficient means for effectively dealing with issues of diversity and difference.

Out of sight, out of mind

The perceived irrelevance of certain social justice issues to particular early childhood settings is problematic in the field. There is a powerful prevailing discourse that perpetuates the belief that there is no need to address areas of social justice that are not perceived to be part of the communities that individual settings cater for. For example, it is often perceived that it is not important to address racism among a predominantly Anglo-Celtic group of children; or that it is irrelevant to deal with homophobia or gay and lesbian issues if there are perceived to be no gay or lesbian families utilizing the service. The relevance of doing social justice education is largely based on the presence of visible and audible differences, such as skin colour, language and cultural practices. Other differences that are not so readily obvious tend to be considered as being absent from settings. Assumed absences can result in perpetuating further invisibility, silencing and marginalization of minority groups. For example, if gay or lesbian parents are not known to educators, they are assumed not to be there. Consequently, in settings where there are many children with obvious physical and language differences, doing social justice education is considered more relevant to these children and their families, than in settings that have more homogeneous clientele groups. Interestingly, the justification for intervention is frequently based on the fear of potential conflicts or on necessity when problems arise. This is particularly so in the case of children who are learning English, in which transitional approaches to the home language are utilized to help 'settle the child'. The language is not the focus in this strategy, rather the child's need to integrate into the 'English only' setting is the priority.

There is a need to recognize that all areas of social justice education are relevant to all children and families, regardless of their backgrounds. Indeed, they may be even more relevant In less culturally heterogeneous settings, where dominant cultural values and perspectives prevail and where interactions with minority groups may be more limited. In culturally homogeneous settings, racializing practices or heteronormative assumptions may be more explicit. Furthermore, in homogeneous contexts, where the absence of cultural and social diversity and difference does not always give children opportunities to develop understandings about diversity, negative generalizations and stereotypes can often result. Derman-Sparks and the A.B.C. Task Force (1989: 9), echoing the sentiments of the social theorist Foucault, express this sentiment aptly, in the suggestion that 'Children are as vulnerable to omissions as they are to inaccuracies and stereotypes. What isn't seen can be as powerful a contributor to attitudes as what is seen'. It is equally crucial that the normalizing discourses operating in the lives of children from homogeneous environments are disrupted and challenged, even in the absence of obvious cultural diversity.

Further, Sedgwick (1990) points out in the context of sexuality (but also in other areas of difference) that it is crucial to understand that difference and its consequences not only are the concern of a minority of people who share such difference, but also have highly significant implications for the way others live their lives, including the 'majority' culture. For example, the heterosexual/homosexual cultural binary that underpins much of the inequalities and common-sense knowledge of sexual differences that prevail in society, not only restricts the lives of those who identify as gay or lesbian, but also impacts on others, including heterosexuals. The young boy who wishes to challenge the boundaries of his gender and enjoys dressing up in women's clothing is no doubt familiar with the consequences of not conforming to the rigid and narrow definitions of what is generally considered to be appropriate masculinity, which are highly influenced by such binaries as heterosexual/homosexual.

Developing inclusive policies and procedures around diversity and difference

There is a need for early childhood settings to develop policies and practices that reflect a broad range of contemporary diversity issues. These policies are more effective when they are developed in consultation with staff, families, communities and relevant stakeholders so that different perspectives are included. It is important that policies and procedures specifically address the complexity of issues relevant to the communities, children and families using the setting. It is also important that policies and procedures are inclusive of areas often perceived by early childhood educators as 'irrelevant' to their setting or assumed to be absent, as discussed above. Generic 'one glove fits all' procedures often indicated in multicultural and anti-bias policies do not allow for diversity of practice and the complexity of issues to be well understood. For example, strategies in providing gender equity in settings which have culturally diverse families require approaches which may differ to those undertaken with middle-class, white professional families.

Communicating with families and communities

Doing social justice work in early childhood education involves working with families as well as with children. The perspectives of families can impact significantly on how diversity and difference are addressed in different early childhood settings. We have found that families that are representative of the dominant culture tend to have more power and control over the everyday policies and practices in early childhood settings. This is not surprising since they tend to have more cultural and linguistic capital to negotiate formal and informal interactions in educational contexts than families from minority cultures. It is important that all families are encouraged to participate in their children's early education. However, this may mean that educators will have to actively develop a supportive and trusting environment in order for this to happen.

Families can make valuable contributions on many different levels. They can be encouraged to be involved in policy development, decision-making and programming. However, it is critical to foster the involvement of those families whose perspectives are rarely acknowledged or are only given tokenistic consideration. As pointed out above, it is most often the parents who represent the dominant culture that tend to have their perspectives reflected in the discursive practices of early childhood settings. Families can be a valuable resource for educators in terms of understanding the children with whom they work. However, we have found in our research that communications with families tend to be limited and often one-way, that is, educators advising families. For example, educators often advise families regarding the importance of home language retention, but few educators are able to report on family perspectives in relation to language retention. Families are often not encouraged to provide information about their children's experiences at home or in the community, and educators seldom seek out families as a resource for increasing their awareness of diversity issues.

The relationship between families and educators is a complex and often potentially volatile one. It appears that for many educators the family should take prime responsibility for particular issues related to children's education around diversity and difference, such as sexuality issues and home language retention. This raises some important points around the perceived responsibilities of educators and parents when it comes to difficult and controversial areas associated with social justice education that are often considered 'private' family matters. However, we feel that educators have a responsibility to foster community and social values that are about upholding human rights across the social justice spectrum. It is our view that there needs to be more in-depth dialogue between families and early childhood educators around controversial social issues, in order to shift these debates to a more productive level, with the aim of reaching a point of reconciliation. Currently, the perceived threat of parental and community resistance is enough to immobilize educators around dealing with more controversial social justice issues, such as gay and lesbian equity concerns. Consequently, these issues continue to be avoided. However, this does little to deal effectively with the inequities and discrimination that surround these areas and only serves to perpetuate the silencing and marginalization of 'minority' groups.

The role of management bodies

Management organizations in early childhood education have a critical role to play in supporting educators to develop and implement inclusive social justice policies and programmes. However, we have found that despite federal and state government policies and programmes relating to access and equity issues, there is often a lack of support or leadership direction provided by management bodies in the areas of social justice education. This further exacerbates the constraints associated with incorporating diversity and equity into programming and teaching practices. Building positive support networks across all levels of early childhood education is crucial to the successful implementation of inclusive social justice education programmes. This becomes especially important when educators need the institutional support in order to tackle more controversial issues. Thus, incorporating a social justice education programme is about fostering a communal courage and sharing the responsibility by promoting a perspective towards social justice, which involves a whole-setting, institutional and community approach.

The importance of professional development for early childhood educators

Pre-service early childhood education courses provided by universities and technical colleges are in a key position to address contemporary emerging frameworks and approaches around social justice in early childhood. For example, this may include an understanding of how feminist post-structuralism, cultural and critical theory can effectively inform practice. It is essential that in-service and pre-service agencies recognize the need to provide updated theoretical and practical frameworks for effectively working with contemporary social issues of whiteness, sexuality, globalization and class. Further, in order for graduates to fully grasp the complexities associated with diversity, pre-service education courses need to provide subjects that include professional experiences that focus on issues of diversity and difference. These need to go beyond anti-bias and multicultural perspectives.

To this end, pre-service and in-service providers need to address and evaluate the manner in which current resources associated with diversity are utilized in settings. It is apparent from our research that resources tend to be utilized on a superficial level. In order to make full use of the variety and quality of resources that are available to early childhood settings, critical reflection and evaluation of the use of resources would enable educators and children to make realistic connections to children's and families' everyday life situations and practices.

Further research into diversity and difference in early childhood education

Our research is unique in its aim to locate educators' perceptions and practices in contexts of diversity and difference. However, there is a need to juxtapose educators' perspectives with the voices of children and their families in order to obtain a picture of how current discourses of difference in early childhood settings operate to locate diverse socio-cultural groups in everyday social practices. Peak early childhood organizations involved in accreditation and professional development can make a significant contribution by collaborating with universities to conduct research to bring about innovative pedagogical practices that benefit all children and their families.

Still, there are a number of specific areas of diversity in which further study would be useful. In particular, research investigating children's voices as they negotiate aspects of identity and power relations in everyday social practices in early childhood settings would provide significant insights into the different ways in which children locate themselves in various mainstream discourses of diversity and difference. Moreover, research that investigates how new graduates negotiate and implement pedagogies of difference and diversity in their first year of practice would effectively inform undergraduate university courses, which specifically focus on issues of diversity and difference and on educators' work in early childhood education. Finally, collaborative research opportunities should be promoted and encouraged between university teams and peak early childhood organizations and resource agencies, in order to investigate the outcomes of current professional development strategies employed to enhance approaches to diversity and difference in early childhood settings.

Conclusion: taking personal and professional risks for social justice

Dealing with diversity and social justice issues in the lives of children and their families, as well as making a positive contribution to this area in the community more generally, is certainly a priority area for many early childhood educators. The focus on this agenda continues to intensify in a rapidly changing world where the complexities of identities, played out on a global scale, impact severely on local communities throughout the world. Consequently, the lives of children and adults are challenged, disrupted and changed by broad social, political and economic issues that seem, for many, irrelevant and far removed from the 'world of children'. In order to make a significant difference in terms of social justice, educators and educational institutions need to engage more actively in taking risks in this area, challenging and disrupting everyday relations of power that underpin the various forms of inequality that operate.

To make a difference in social justice, we must *all* engage in taking risks around challenging inequalities; this includes disrupting the normalizing discourses around controversial issues such as sexuality (Robinson 2005d). However, as Robinson (2005d) argues, taking risks should be a thoughtful process involving individual agency and community responsibility in the pursuit of a different, but positive future for ourselves, children, families and future generations. Further, Robinson (2005d) points out that in order to be successful in this process on any level, the first risk is to deal with the contradictions around social justice that operate in everyday interactions, which continue to disrupt and undermine this work.

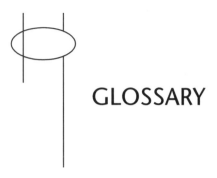

GLOSSARY

Agency is the power of individuals to actively participate in the construction of their self through the process of subjectification.

Affirmative action Policies and formal programmes developed to redress past discrimination and structural inequalities through the preferential treatment of disadvantaged groups.

Assimilation A process by which immigrants are expected to adopt the language, culture, religion and values of the dominant group by surrendering their own language, culture and religious values.

Authoritative knowledge The privileging of certain knowledge and understandings as being representative of ultimate 'truth'.

Binary Two opposite terms defined against each other, generally representative of a hierarchical power relationship in which one is subordinated to the other – for example, the binaries of male/female, adult/child, Western/Eastern, mind/body.

Biological determinism A perspective that considers one's identity, behaviours and actions as being fundamentally determined by biology.

Capitalism An economic system that has prevailed since the Industrial Revolution in the eighteenth century, which has impacted on the structure of social relations of power operating in society. It is an economic system that is based primarily on private ownership of property and on private enterprise; it perpetuates notions of individualism, competition, supply and demand, the profit motive, and neoliberalism.

Constructionism A perspective that considers identity as being historically and socially constructed across different cultures, rather than being essentialized in human biology.

Cultural capital A set of resources such as knowledge, language and literacy practices which have value in a particular cultural field. It includes representational and symbolic knowledge systems. Like other forms of capital (for example, economic and social capital), it accumulates social power and can be exchanged and distributed across various social fields.

Deconstruction is a process of critical analysis that focuses on investigating the cultural and political meanings hidden in texts, which are representative of broader social relations of power.

Diaspora signifies the movements of groups of people from an original 'home' to many other locations and the networks of affiliation that are formed between these communities (Grewal and Kaplan 2002: 458).

Ethnocentrism is the perception that one's own culture is superior to another.

Essentialism The perspective that characteristics of persons or groups are largely similar in all human cultures and historical periods, as they are fundamentally influenced by biological factors.

Field is a social context which authorizes specific social practices which can determine and regulate what constitutes cultural, social and economic capital.

Gender equity aims for legal, social, political and economic equality between males and females.

Habitus is a set of dispositions to act and think in certain ways, which is influenced by one's cultural pathways – that is, practices, habits, perceptions and attitudes generated in early childhood socialization.

Hegemony stemming from the works of the Italian Marxist, Antonio Gramsci (1891–1937), the concept refers to the way that one powerful social group imposes its particular perspectives, beliefs or political and economic conditions upon another group.

Heteronormativity is the way that everyday interactions, practices and policies construct individuals as heterosexual; this process of 'compulsory heterosexuality', as termed by Adrienne Rich (1980), is integral to the way that heterosexuality is normalized and naturalized and non-heterosexual relationships are rendered deviant, abnormal and unnatural.

Heterosexism is the belief that heterosexuals are superior to non-heterosexual identities. This perspective is demonstrated through the exclusion of non-heterosexual subjects in policies, curricula, events and activities.

Homophobia is the prejudice, discrimination, harassment or acts of violence against sexual minorities, such as gays and lesbians, or those perceived by others to be gay or lesbian, based on the non-conformist ways in which they act as boys and girls, men and women. Homophobia is generally used as a term that encompasses the experiences of lesbians, but it is important to identify lesbophobia as it often gets silenced and marginalized in this overarching term.

Hybridity is a two-way borrowing and lending between cultures, which involves fusion and creation of a new form.

Identity is the social categories of the subject – that is, 'race', class, gender, sexuality, ethnicity and so on.

Ideology Stemming from the philosophy of Karl Marx, the nineteenth-century German political and economic philosopher, ideology refers to a system of beliefs or ideas perpetuated by dominant classes and imposed on less powerful people, which influence their perspectives and outlooks on the world.

Imagined communities describe the national identities created through media representations of people in diverse geographical locations (Grewal and Kaplan 2002).

Imperialism A policy of expansion where one country exerts its power and domination over another, taking over its territory and controlling its social, political and economic life.

Individualism The perspective that the interests of the independent, unique individual ought to be paramount.

Intersectionality The importance of recognizing the multiplicity of identity – for example, the way that sexism, lesbophobia and racism intersect in the lives of lesbian women of colour.

Lesbophobia is the prejudice, discrimination, harassment or acts of violence against lesbians, or those perceived by others to be lesbian, based on the non-conformist ways they act as girls or women.

Liberalism A political and social philosophy that stresses the rights and freedoms of the individual.

Liberal humanism A social and political philosophy that stresses the importance of humanist ideals, such as individualism, universalism, objective scientific knowledge and linearity, to understandings of societal and human progress.

Linguicism Ideologies structures, and practices which are used to legitimate, effectuate, regulate, and reproduce an unequal division of power and resources (both material and non-material) between groups which are defined on the basis of language (on the basis of the mother tongues) (Skutnabb-Kangas, 1988: 42).

Linguistic capital Language resources, including speech, communication and utterances that have the potential to accumulate social power in particular cultural fields in which they are legitimized and authorized.

Linguistic habitus Linguistic utterances, behaviours, expressions and interactions are produced in the linguistic habitus. Derived from Bourdieu's concept of habitus, it includes the dispositions, practices and perceptions in the various technologies and articulations of speech, language and communication that are adapted to and reproduced in the requirements of a given social situation.

Linguistic market The social situation or field where the value or 'price formation' of the linguistic utterance is determined by rules and regulations operating within a given situation.

Oppression is the exploitation, marginalization, violence, cultural imperialism and powerlessness experienced by individuals and groups.

Other This term relates to those groups that have been marginalized, silenced, denigrated or violated, and defined in opposition to, and seen as other than, the privileged and powerful groups that are identified as representing the idealized, mythical norm in society.

Postcolonial A term used to refer to the period following formal European colonization; however, it can also depict the continuing influence and power of the former colonizers over the economies and cultures of decolonized states (Grewal and Kaplan 2002).

Postmodernism A late 1960s cultural movement originally associated with the arts, architecture and music. In more recent times it has been incorporated into the humanities and social sciences, questioning the humanist focus on universalism and human progress. Grewal and Kaplan (2002: 290) indicate that in the arts, this movement resulted in 'the rejection of the idea of newness and individual genius in favour of inquiring into methods and styles of the past'. In the humanities and social sciences, this perspective 'led to questioning the dominant narratives produced in the West and to decentering the powerful centres of knowledge and culture'.

Poststructuralism A perspective that emerged in the 1970s in response to the universal systems proposed by an earlier movement, structuralism. Structuralism, based on universalizing classifications of human society and culture, influenced the modern disciplines of social sciences (for example, sociology and anthropology) and the humanities. Poststructuralism argues that there is no one universal structural system that can apply to every place, culture and time; and that universal explanations or one dominant view leads to the suppression or invisibility of important differences (Grewal and Kaplan 2002). It questions the possibility of objectivity of authoritative knowledge, on which individual subjects construct their 'truths' about the world.

Reflexivity is individual awareness of one's own biases and prejudices that underpin the way that one operates in the world.

Social reproduction The process through which the social order and hierarchies of power are perpetuated through institutions such as the family, schools and the military.

Stereotype A set of behaviours or qualities that are believed to be fixed and unchanging and that influence the way that one thinks about a group or person.

Subjectivity encompasses the unconscious and conscious thoughts and emotions of the individual, or one's sense of self and how one relates to the world. In Foucauldian terms, subjectivity is constituted in discourses.

REFERENCES

Aboud, F. (1988) *Children and Prejudices*. Oxford. Basil Blackwell.

Albrow, M., Eade, J., Dürrschmidt, J. and Washbourne, N. (1997) The impact of globalization on sociological concepts: community, culture and milieu, in J. Eade (ed.) *Living the Global City: Globalization as Local Process*. London: Routledge.

Alloway, N. (1995) *Foundation Stones: The Construction of Gender in Early Childhood*. Carlton, Vic.: Curriculum Corporation.

Alloway, N. (1997) Early childhood education encounters the postmodern: what do we know? What can we count as 'true'? *Journal of Early Childhood Education*, 22(2): 1–5.

Alsop, R., Fitzsimons, A. and Lennon, K. (2002) *Theorizing Gender*. Cambridge: Polity Press.

Anthias, R. and Yuval-Davis, N. (1991) Contextualizing feminism, gender, ethnic and class divisions, in L. McDowell and R. Pringle (eds) *Defining Women: Social Institutions and Gender Divisions*. Cambridge: Polity Press and the Open University.

Appadurai, A. (1996) *Modernity at Large: Cultural Dimensions of Globalization*. Public Worlds, Volume 1. Minneapolis: University of Minnesota Press.

Apple, M.W.A. (1999) *Power, Meaning and Identity: Essays in Critical Educational Studies*. New York: Peter Lang.

Apple, M.W. (2001) *Educating the 'Right' Way: Markets, Standards, God, and Inequality*. New York: RoutledgeFalmer.

Arnberg, L. (1987) *Raising Children Bilingually: The Pre-school Years*. Clevedon: Multilingual Matters.

Arnot, M. (2002) *Reproducing Gender? Essays on Educational Theory and Feminist Politics*. London: Routledge/Falmer.

Ashcroft, B. (2001) *Post-colonial Transformation*. London: Routledge.

Ashcroft, B., Griffiths, G. and Tiffin, H. (1995) *The Post-colonial Studies Reader*. London: Routledge.

Australian Bureau of Statistics (2003) 4442.0 Family characteristics, Australia. http://www.abs.gov.au (accessed 16 March 2005).

Australian Bureau of Statistics (2005) *Yearbook Australia: Population: Languages.* http://www.abs.gov.au/ausstats/abs@.nsf/ 94713ad445ff1425ca25682000192af2/dfd8c90c1a541efeca256 f720083300a!OpenDocument (accessed 4 September 2005).

Averhart, C.J. and Bigler, R.S. (1997) Shades of meaning: skin tone, racial attitudes, and constructive memory in African American children. *Journal of Experimental Child Psychology*, 67: 363–388.

Ball, S.J. (ed.) (1990) *Foucault and Education: Disciplines and Knowledge.* London: Routledge.

Beck, U. and Beck-Gernsheim, E. (1995) *The Normal Chaos of Love.* Translated by Mark Ritter and Jane Wiebel. Cambridge, MA: Blackwell.

Best, S. and Kellner, D. (1991) *Postmodern Theory: Critical Interrogations.* New York: Guilford Press.

Bhabha, H. (1994) *The Location of Culture.* London: Routledge.

Bhabha, H. (1998) Culture's in between, in D. Bennett (ed.) *Multicultural States. Rethinking Difference and Identity.* London: Routledge.

Bhattacharyya, G. (2002) *Sexuality and Society. An Introduction.* London: Routledge.

Bialystok, E. (1991) Metalinguistic dimensions of bilingual language proficiency, in E. Bialystok (ed.) *Language Processing in Bilingual Children.* Cambridge: Cambridge University Press.

Boldt, G. (1997) Sexist and heterosexist responses to gender bending, in J. Tobin (ed.) *Making a Place for Pleasure in Early Childhood Education.* New Haven, CT: Yale University Press.

Bourdieu, P. (1986) The forms of capital, in J.G. Richardson (ed.) *Handbook of Theory and Research for the Sociology of Education.* New York: Greenwood Press.

Bourdieu, P. (1990) *The Logic of Practice.* Translated by R. Nice. Cambridge: Polity Press.

Bourdieu, P. (1991a) *Outline of a Theory of Practice.* Translated by R. Nice. Cambridge: Polity Press.

Bourdieu, P. (1991b) *Language and Symbolic Power.* Edited by J.B. Thompson and translated by G. Raymond and M. Adamson. Cambridge, MA: Polity Press.

Bourdieu, P. and Wacquant, L.J.D. (1992) *An Invitation to Reflexive Sociology.* Chicago: University of Chicago Press.

Bourdieu, P. (1993) *Sociology in Question.* Translated by R. Nice. London: Sage Publications.

Bourdieu, P. (1998) *The Essence of Neoliberalism.* http://www.analitica.com/ bitblioteca/bourdieu/neoliberalism.asp.

Brah, A. (1996) Diaspora, border and transnational identities, in A. Brah (ed.) *Cartographies of Diaspora: Contesting Identities.* London: Routledge.

Breckenridge, J. and Carmody, M. (eds) (1992) *Crimes of Violence: Australian Responses to Rape and Child Sexual Assault.* Sydney: Allen & Unwin.

Bredekamp, S. and Rosegrant, T. (eds) (1991). *Reaching Potentials: Appropriate Curriculum and Assessment of Young Children.* Washington, DC: NAEYC.

Britzman, D.P. (1997) What is this thing called love? New discourses for understanding gay and lesbian youth, in S. De Castell and M. Bryson (eds) *Radical In<ter>ventions: Identity, Politics, and Difference/s in Educational Praxis.* Albany: State University of New York Press.

Britzman, D.P. (1998) *Lost Subjects, Contested Objects: Toward a Psychoanalytic Inquiry of Learning.* New York: State University of New York Press.

Britzman, D.P. (2003) *Practice Makes Practice: A Critical Study of Learning to Teach,* 2nd edn. New York: State University of New York Press.

Burr, V. (1995) *An Introduction to Social Constructionism.* London: Routledge.

Butler, J. (1990) *Gender Trouble: Feminism and the Subversion of Identity*. New York: Routledge.

Butler, J. (1993) *Bodies that Matter: On the Discursive Limits of 'Sex'*. New York: Routledge.

Butler, J. (1994) Gender as performance: An interview with Judith Butler, *Radical Philosophy*, 67: 32–39.

Cahill, B. and Theilheimer, R. (1999) Stonewall in the housekeeping area: gay and lesbian issues in the early childhood classroom, in W.J. Letts IV and J.T. Sears (eds) *Queering Elementary Education: Advancing the Dialogue about Sexualities and Schooling*. Lanham, MD: Rowman & Littlefield.

Cannella, G.S. (1997) *Deconstructing Early Childhood Education: Social Justice and Revolution*. New York: Peter Lang Publishing.

Cannella, G.S. and Kincheloe, J.L. (eds) (2002) *Kidworld: Childhood Studies, Global Perspectives, and Education*. New York: Peter Lang.

Cannella, G.S. and Viruru, R. (2004) *Childhood and Postcolonization: Power, Education, and Contemporary Practice*. New York: RoutledgeFalmer.

Carrington, V. (2002) *New Times: New Families*. Dordrecht: Kluwer Academic.

Carrington, V. and Luke, A. (1997) Literacy and Bourdieu's sociological theory: a reframing, *Language and Education*, 11(2): 96–112.

Casper, V., Cuffaro, H.K., Schultz, S., Silin, J. and Wickens, E. (1998) Towards a most thorough understanding of the world: sexual orientation and early childhood education, in N. Yelland (ed.) *Gender in Early Childhood*. London: Routledge.

Cass, B. (1995) Cultural diversity and challenges in the provision of health and welfare services towards social justice: Employment and community services in culturally-diverse Australia, in *1995 Global Cultural Diversity Conference Proceedings, Sydney*. Department of Immigration and Multicultural and Indigenous Affairs, Australian Government. http://www.immi.gov.au/multicultural/_inc/publications/confer/03/speech11a.htm (accessed 10 May 2005).

Castles, S. (2000) *Ethnicity and Globalization: From Migrant Worker to Transnational Citizen*. London: Sage.

Castles, S. and Miller, M.J. (1998) *The Age of Migration: International Population Movements in the Modern World*, 2nd edn. Basingstoke: Macmillan.

Castles, S., Cope, B., Kalantzis, M. and Morrissey, M. (1988) *Mistaken Identity: Multiculturalism and the Demise of Nationalism in Australia*. Sydney: Pluto Press.

Chasnoff, D. and Cohen, H. (1997) *It's Elementary: Talking about Gay Issues in Schools* (film). San Francisco: Women's Educational Media.

Clyne, M. (1991) *Community Languages: The Australian Experience*. Melbourne: Cambridge University Press.

Cohen, R. (1999) *Global Diasporas. An Introduction*. London: UCL Press.

Collins, P.H. (1990) *Black Feminist Thought: Knowledge, Consciousness, and the Politics of Empowerment*. Boston: Unwin Hyman.

Connell, R.W. (1987) *Gender and Power*. Sydney: Allen & Unwin.

Connell, R.W., Ashenden, D.J., Kessler, S. and Dowsett, G.W. (1982) *Making the Difference: Schools, Families and Social Division*. London: Allen & Unwin.

Corbett, S. (1993) A complicated bias, *Young Children*, 48(3): 29–31.

Corson, D. (1993) *Language, Minority Education and Gender: Linking Social Justice and Power*. Clevedon: Multilingual Matters.

Corson, D. (1998) *Changing Education for Diversity*. Buckinghan: Open University Press.

Corteen, K. and Scraton, P. (1997) Prolonging 'childhood', manufacturing 'innocence' and regulating sexuality, in P. Scraton (ed.) *'Childhood' in 'Crisis'*. London: University College London Press.

Cossins, A. (1999) A reply to the NSW Royal Commission Inquiry into paedophilia: Victim report studies and child sex offender profiles – a bad match? *The Australian and New Zealand Journal of Criminology*, 32(1): 42–60.

Crystal, D. (1997) *English as a Global Language*. Cambridge: Cambridge University Press.

Cummins, J. (1991) Interdependence of first and second language proficiency in bilingual children, in E. Bialystok (ed.) *Language Processing in Bilingual Children*. Cambridge: Cambridge University Press.

Cummins, J. (1996) *Negotiating Identities: Education for Empowerment in a Diverse Society*. Ontario, CA: California Association for Bilingual Education.

Curthoys, A. (1999) An uneasy conversation: multicultural and Indigenous discourses, in G. Hage and R. Couch (eds) *The Future of Australian Multiculturalism. Reflections on the Twentieth Anniversary of Jean Martin's 'The Migrant Experience'*. Sydney: Research Institute for Humanities and Social Sciences, University of Sydney.

Dahlberg, G., Moss, P. and Pence, A. (1999) *Beyond Quality in Early Childhood Education and Care: Postmodern Perspectives*. London: Falmer Press.

Davies, B. (1989) *Frogs and Snails and Feminist Tales: Preschool Children and Gender*. Sydney: Allen & Unwin.

Davies, B. (1993) *Shards of Glass. Children Reading and Writing beyond Gendered Identities*. Sydney: Allen & Unwin.

Davies, B. (1994) *Poststructuralist Theory and Classroom Practice*. Geelong, Vic.: Deakin University Press.

Davies, B. (1996) *Power, Knowledge and Desire: Changing School Organisation and Management Practices*. Canberra: Department of Education, Employment, Training and Youth Affairs.

Davies, B. and Petersen, E.B. (2005) Neoliberal discourse in the Academy: the forestalling of collective resistance, *Learning and Teaching in the Social Sciences*, 2(2). In press.

Davis, H. (2004) *Understanding Stuart Hall*. London: Sage Publications.

De Lauretis, T. (1987) *Technologies of Gender: Essays on Theory, Film, and Fiction*. Bloomington: Indiana University Press.

Deleuze, G. and Guattari, F. (1987) *A Thousand Plateaus: Capitalism and Schizophrenia*. Translated by Brian Massumi. Minneapolis: University of Minnesota Press.

Derman-Sparks, L. and the A.B.C. Task Force (1989) *Anti-Bias Curriculum: Tools for Empowering Young Children*. Washington DC: National Association for the Education of Young Children.

Disney, Walt (1994a) *Beauty and the Beast*. Loughborough: Ladybird Books.

Disney, Walt (1994b) *The Little Mermaid*. Loughborough: Lady Bird Books.

Dudley, J. (1998) Globlization and education policy in Australia, in J. Currie and J. Newson (eds) *Universities and Globalisation: Critical Perspectives*. Thousand Oaks, CA: Sage.

Easteal, P. (1994) *Voices of the Survivors*. Melbourne: Spinifex.

Edmund Rice Centre for Justice and Community Education and the School of Education, Australian Catholic University (2001) Debunking the myths about asylum seekers, *Just Comment*, September. http://www.chilout.org/files/erc DebunkingMyths1.doc (accessed 18 August 2005).

Elliott, M. (1992) Images of children in the media: 'soft kiddie porn', in I. Itzin (ed.) *Pornography: Women, Violence and Civil Liberties. A Radical New View*. New York: Oxford University Press.

Engels, F. (1974) *The Condition of the Working Class in England*. Moscow: Progress Publishers.

Epstein, D. (1995) 'Girls don't do bricks': gender and sexuality in the primary classroom, in J. Siraj-Blatchford and I. Siraj Blatchford (eds) *Educating the Whole Child*. Buckingham: Open University Press.

Epstein, R. and Friedman, J. (1995) *The Celluloid Closet* (film). Telling Pictures.

Epstein, D. and Johnson, R. (1994) On the straight and narrow: The heterosexual presumption, homophobias and schools, in D. Epstein (ed.) *Challenging Lesbian and Gay Inequalities in Education*. Buckingham: Open University Press.

Erickson, P.A. and Murphy, L.D. (2003) *A History of Anthropological Theory*, 2nd edn. Peterborough, Ontario: Broadview Press.

Fantini, E.F. (1985) *Language Acquisition of a Bilingual Child: A Sociolinguistic Perspective*. Clevedon: Multilingual Matters.

Fass, P. (2003) Children and globalization, *Journal of Social History*, 36(4): 963–977.

Ferfolja, T. (1998) Australian lesbian teachers – a reflection of homophobic harassment of high school teachers in New South Wales government schools, *Gender and Education*, 10(4): 401–415.

Ferfolja, T. (2003) Mechanisms of silence: sexuality regulation in New South Wales high schools. Perspectives from lesbian teachers. Doctoral dissertation, University of New South Wales, Australia.

Foucault, M. (1974) *The Archaeology of Knowledge*. London: Tavistock.

Foucault, M. (1977) *Discipline and Punish: The Birth of the Prison*. New York: Pantheon.

Foucault, M. (1978) *The History of Sexuality, Volume 1: An Introduction*. Translated by Robert Hurley. New York: Vintage Books.

Foucault, M. (1980) *Power/Knowledge*. Translated by Colin Gordon. New York: Pantheon Books.

Frankenberg, R. (1993) *The Social Construction of Whiteness: White Women, Race Matters*. New York and London: Routledge.

Frankenberg, R. (1997) *Displacing Whiteness. Essays in Social and Cultural Criticism*. Durham, NC: Duke University Press.

Fuss, D. (1989) *Essentially Speaking: Feminism, Nature and Difference*. New York: Routledge.

Galbally, F. (1978) *Review of Post-arrival Programs and Services for Migrants. Migrant Services and Programs*. Canberra: Australian Government Printing Service.

Gallas, K. (1998) *'Sometimes I Can Be Anything': Power, Gender and Identity in a Primary Classroom*. New York: Teachers College Press.

Gandhi, L. (1998) *Postcolonial Theory: A Critical Introduction*. Sydney: Allen & Unwin.

Genesee, F. (1989) Early bilingual development: One language or two? *Journal of Child Language*, 16: 161–179.

Germov, J. (2004) Which class do you teach? Education and the reproduction of class, in J. Allen (ed.) *Sociology of Education: Possibilities and Practices*, 3rd edn. Southbank, Vic.: Social Science Press.

Giddens, A. (1992) *The Transformation of Intimacy: Sexuality, Love and Eroticism in Modern Societies*. Cambridge: Polity Press.

Giroux, H. (1988) *Schooling and the Struggle for Public Life: Critical Pedagogy in the Modern Age*. Minneapolis: University of Minnesota Press.

Giroux, H. (1992) *Border Crossings: Cultural Workers and the Politics of Education*. New York: Routledge.

Giroux, H.A. (1995) Animating youth: The distinction of children's culture. http://gseis.ucla.edu/courses/ed253a/Giroux/Giroux2.html (accessed 8 August 2005).

Giroux, H. (1997) *Pedagogy and the Politics of Hope: Theory, Culture and Schooling*. Boulder, CO: Westview Press.

Gittins, D. (1998) *The Child in Question*. London: Macmillan.

Glover, A. (1991) Young children and race: a report of a study of two and three year olds. Paper presented at the Communities Evolution and Revolution Conference, Australian Catholic University, Sydney, 11–12 October.

Green, R. (1996) Creating an anti-bias environment, in B. Creaser and E. Dau (eds) *The Anti-bias Approach in Early Childhood*. Pymble, NSW: Harper Educational.

Greig, A., Lewins, F. and White, K. (2003) *Inequality in Australia*. Cambridge: Cambridge University Press.

Grewal, I. and Kaplan, P. (2002) *An Introduction to Women's Studies: Gender in a Transnational World*. New York: McGraw-Hill.

Grieshaber, S. (1998) Constructing the gendered infant, in N. Yelland (ed.) *Gender in Early Childhood*. London: Routledge.

Grieshaber, S. (2001) Advocacy and early childhood educators: identity and cultural conflicts, in S. Grieshaber and G. Cannella (eds) *Embracing Identities in Early Childhood Education: Diversity and Possibilities*. New York: Teachers College Press.

Gutiérrez, K., Baquedano-López, P. and Asato, J. (2000) 'English for the children': the new literacy of the old world order, language policy and educational reform, *Bilingual Research Journal*, 24 (1&2): 78–216.

Hage, G. (1998) *White Nation: Fantasies of White Supremacy in a Multicultural Society*. Annandale, NSW: Pluto Press.

Hall, D.E. (2004) *Subjectivity*. New York: Routledge.

Hall, S. (1992) New ethnicities, in J. Donald and A. Rattansi (eds) *'Race', Culture and Difference*. London: Sage.

Hall, S. (1996) Introduction: who needs 'identity'? in P. Du Guy (ed.) *Questions of Cultural Identity*. London: Sage Publications.

Hall, S. (1997) The work of representation, in S. Hall (ed.) *Representation: Cultural Representation and Signifying Practices*. London: Sage, in association with the Open University.

Hall, S. (2001) Foucault: power, knowledge and discourse, in M. Wetherell, S. Taylor and S.J. Yates (eds) *Discourse Theory and Practice*. London: Sage.

Henry, H., Lingard, B., Rizvi, F. and Taylor, S. (1999) Working with/against globlization in education, *Journal of Education Policy*, 14(1): 85–97.

Hillier, L. and Walsh, J. (1999) Abused, silenced and ignored. Creating more supportive environments for same sex attracted young people, *Youth Suicide Prevention Bulletin*, 3: 23–27.

Hollinsworth, D. (1998) *Race and Racism in Australia*. Sydney: Social Science Press.

Hollway, W. (1984) Gender difference and the production of subjectivity, in J. Henriques, W. Hollway, C. Urwin, C. Venn and V. Walkerdine (eds) *Changing the Subject: Psychology, Social Regulation and Subjectivity*. London: Methuen.

hooks, b. (1997) Whiteness in the black imagination; in R. Frankenberg (ed.) *Displacing Whiteness: Essays in Social and Cultural Criticism*. Durham, NC: Duke University Press.

Hopson, E. (1990) *Valuing Diversity: Implementing a Cross-cultural Anti-bias Approach*. Sydney: Lady Gowrie Child Centre.

Hornberger, N.H. and Skilton-Silvester, E. (2000) Revisting the continua of bi-literacy: international and critical perspectives, *Language and Education*, 14(2): 96–22.

Human Rights Equal Opportunity Commission (2004) A last resort? Summary guide. A summary of the important issues, findings and recommendations of the national inquiry into children in immigration detention. http://www.humanrights.gov.au (accessed 25 April 2005).

Human Rights Watch (2004) Refugees and displaced persons. http://www.hrw.org/doc/?t=refugees&document_limit-0,2 (accessed 25 April 2005).

Imhof, I. (2000) Guatemalan massacre survivor demands reparations from World Bank/IADB. http://www.nadir.org/nadir/initiativ/agp/free/imf/america/_guatem.htm (accessed 25 April 2005).

Ingraham, C. (1994) The heterosexual imaginary: Feminist sociology and theories of gender, *Sociological Theory*, 12(2): 203–219.

Irwin, J. (1999) 'The Pink Ceiling Is Too Low': Workplace Experiences of Lesbians, Gay men and Transgender People. Report of a collaborative research project undertaken by the Australian Centre for Lesbian and Gay Research and the New South Wales Gay and Lesbian Rights Lobby. Sydney: Australian Centre for Lesbian and Gay Research.

Jagose, A. (1996) *Queer Theory*. Melbourne: Melbourne University Press.

Jakubowicz, A. (1994) *Ethnicity, Racism and the Media*. Sydney: Allen & Unwin.

James, A. and Prout, A. (eds) (1990) *Constructing and Reconstructing Childhood: Contemporary Issues in the Sociological Study of Childhood*. London: Falmer Press.

James, A., Jenks, C. and Prout, A. (1998) *Theorizing Childhood*. London: Polity Press.

Jenkins, H. (ed.) (1998) *The Children's Culture Reader*. New York: New York University Press.

Jones Díaz, C. (2003a) Growing up bilingual and building identity: a reframing of bilingualism in early childhood. Paper presented to the University of Western Sydney Education Research Conference, Parramatta, 11–12 October.

Jones Díaz, C. (2003b) Latino/a voices in Australia: negotiating bilingual identity, *Contemporary Issues in Early Childhood*, 4(3): 314–336.

Jones Díaz, C. (2005) Intersections between language retention and identities in young bilingual children. Unpublished doctoral thesis, University of Western Sydney.

Jones Díaz, C. and Harvey, N. (2002) Other words, other worlds: bilingual identities and literacy, in L. Makin and C. Jones Díaz (eds) *Literacies in Early Childhood: Changing Views, Challenging Practices*. Sydney: MacLennan & Petty.

Jones Díaz, C. and Robinson, K. (2000) Diversity and difference in early childhood education in Western Sydney, in J. Collins and S. Poynting (eds) *The Other Sydney: Communities, Identities and Inequalities in Western Sydney*. Altona, Vic.: Common Ground Publishing.

Jones Díaz, C., Robinson, K.H. and Skattebol, J. (2001) Negotiating identities of difference in early childhood settings. Paper presented at the Australian Early Childhood Association Conference, Sydney, 2–7 July.

Jones Díaz, C., Beecher, B. and Arthur, L. (2002) Chilren's worlds and critical literacy, in L. Makin and C. Jones Díaz (eds) *Literacies in Early Childhood: Changing Views Challenging Practices*. Sydney: MacLennan & Petty.

Kaomea, J. (2000) Pointed noses and yellow hair: deconstructing children's writing on race and ethnicity in Hawai'i, in J. Jipson and R. Johnson (eds.) *Identity and Representation in Early Childhood*. New York: Peter Lang.

Kasturi, S. (2002) Constructing childhood in a corporate world: cultural studies, childhood, and Disney, in G.S. Cannella and J.L. Kincheloe (eds) *Kidworld: Childhood Studies, Global Perspectives, and Education*. New York: Peter Lang.

Katz, P.A. (1982) Developmental foundations of gender and racial attitudes, in R.L. Leahy (ed.) *The Child's Construction of Social Inequality*. New York: Academic Press.

Kell, P. (2004) A teacher's tool kit: sociology and social theory explaining the world, in J. Allen (ed.) *Sociology of Education: Possibilities and Practices*, 3rd edn. Southbank, Vic.: Social Science Press.

Kimmel, M.S. (1994) Masculinity as homophobia: fear, shame, and silence in the construction of gender identity, in H. Brod and M. Kaufman (eds) *Theorizing Masculinities*. Thousand Oaks, CA: Sage Publications.

Kincheloe, J.L. and Steinberg, S.R. (1997) *Changing Multiculturalism*. Buckingham: Open University Press.

Kincheloe, J.L. and Steinberg, S.R. (1998) Addressing the crisis of whiteness. Reconfiguring white identity in a pedagogy of whiteness, in J.L. Kincheloe, S.R. Steinberg, N.M. Rodriguez and R.E. Chennault (eds) *White Reign. Deploying Whiteness in America*. London: Macmillan.

King, J.R. (1997) Keeping it quiet: gay teachers in the primary grades, in J. Tobin (ed.) *Making a Place for Pleasure in Early Childhood Education*. New Haven, CT: Yale University Press.

Kissen, R. (ed.) (2002) *Getting Ready for Benjamin. Preparing Teachers for Sexual Diversity in the Classroom*. Lanham, MD: Rowman & Littlefield.

Kitzinger, C. (1994) Anti-lesbian harassment, in C. Brant and Y.L. Too (eds) *Rethinking Sexual Harassment*. London: Pluto.

Kitzinger, J. (1990) Who are you kidding? Children, power and the struggle against sexual abuse, in A. James and A. Prout (eds) *Constructing and Reconstructing Childhood: Contemporary Issues in the Sociological Study of Childhood*. London: Falmer Press.

Kobayashi, A. and Ray, B. (2000) Civil risk and landscapes of marginality in Canada: a pluralist approach to social justice, *Canadian Geographer*, 44(4): 401–417.

Krien, A. (2004) Concern over 'Gay School', *The Age*, 3 June.

Krulik, N. (1997) *Anastasia*. Adapted by Nancy Krulik; illustrated by the Thompson Brothers. New York: Golden Books.

Kumashiro, K.K. (2002) *Troubling Education: Queer Activism and Antioppressive Pedagogy*. New York: RoutledgeFalmer.

Kutner, B. (1958) *Patterns of Mental Functioning Associated with Prejudice in Children*. Psychological Monographs, 72(406). Washington, DC: American Psychological Association.

Lacroix, M. (2003) Canadian refugee policy and the social construction of the refugee claimant subjectivity: understanding refugeeness, *Journal of Refugees Studies*, 17(1): 147–166.

Langer, B. (1998) Globalisation and the myth of ethnic community: Salvadoran refugees in multicultural states, in D. Bennett (ed.) *Multicultural States: Rethinking Difference and Identity*. London: Routledge.

Lanza, E. (1992) Can bilingual two-year-olds code-switch? *Journal of Child Language*, 19: 633–658.

Larbalestier, J. (1999) What is this thing called white? Reflections on 'whiteness' and multiculturalism, in G. Hage and R. Couch (eds) *The Future of Australian Multiculturalism. Reflections on the Twentieth Anniversary of Jean Martin's 'The Migrant Experience'*. Sydney: Research Institute for Humanities and Social Sciences, University of Sydney.

Lareau, A. and McNamara-Horvat, E. (1999) Moments of social inclusion and exclusion. Race, class and cultural capital in family-school relationships, *Sociology of Education*, 72(Jan.): 37–53.

Letts IV, W. (1999) How to make 'boys' and 'girls' in the classroom: the heteronormative nature of elementary-school science, in W. Letts IV and J.T. Sears (eds) *Queering Elementary Education: Advancing the Dialogue about Sexualities and Schooling*. Lanham, MD: Rowan & Littlefield.

Lewin, E. (1998) *Recognizing Ourselves: Ceremonies of Lesbian and Gay Commitment*. New York: Columbia University Press.

Long, S. (2000) The divided nation: Australia's work revolution, in Kevin McDonald (ed.), *Pressing Questions. Explorations in Sociology*, Issue 2. Sydney: Pearson.

Lubeck. S, (1998) Is DAP for everyone? A response, *Childhood Education*, 74(5): 299–310.

Luke, C. (1994) White women in interracial families: reflections on hybridization, feminine identities and racialized othering, *Feminist Issues*, 14(2): 49–71.

Luke, C. and Luke, A. (1998) Interethnic families: difference within difference, *Ethnic and Racial Studies*, 21: 728–754.

Lundeberg, M.A. (1997) You guys are overreacting: Teaching prospective teachers about subtle gender bias, *Journal of Teacher Education*, 48(1): 55–61.

Mac an Ghaill, M. (1994) *The Making of Men: Masculinities, Sexualities and Schooling*. Buckingham: Open University Press.

MacNaughton, G. (1993) Gender, power and racism: A case study of domestic play in early childhood, *Multicultural Teaching*, 11(3): 12–15.

MacNaughton, G. (1998) *Techniques for Teaching Young Children: Choices in Theory and Practice*. Melbourne: Longman.

MacNaughton, G. (2000) *Rethinking Gender in Early Childhood Education*. Sydney: Allen & Unwin.

MacNaughton, G. (2001) Silences, sex-roles and subjectivities: 40 years of gender in the Australian Journal of Early Childhood, *Australian Journal of Early Childhood*, 40(4).

MacNaughton, G. and Davis, K. (2001) Beyond 'othering': Rethinking approaches to teaching young Anglo-Australian children about Indigenous Australians, *Contemporary Issues in Early Childhood*, 2(1): 83–93.

Mahony, P. (1985) *Schools for the Boys: Coeducation Reassessed*. London: Hutchinson.

Makin, L., Campbell, J. and Jones Díaz, C. (1995) *One Childhood, Many Languages: Guidelines for Early Childhood Education*. Pymble, NSW: Harper Educational.

Marginson, S. (1999) After globalisation: emerging politics of education, *Education Policy*, 14(1): 19–31.

Martin-Jones, M. and Heller, M. (1996) Introduction to the special issues on education in multilingual settings: discourse, identities, and power. Part 1: Constructing legitimacy, *Linguistics and Education*, 8(1): 3–16.

Marx, K. (1967) *Capital. Vol 1*. New York: International Publishers.

May, S. (1999) Critical multiculturalism and cultural difference, in S. May (ed.) *Critical Multiculturalism: Rethinking Multicultural and Antiracist Education*. London: Falmer Press.

Mayall, B. (1996) *Children, Health and the Social Order*. Buckingham: Open University Press.

McChesney, R.W. (1999) Noam Chomsky and the struggle against neoliberalism, *Monthly Review*, 50(11): 40–47.

McLaren, P. (1998) Whiteness is ... The struggle for postcolonial hybridity, in J.L. Kincheloe, S.R. Steinberg, N.M. Rodriguez and R.E. Chennault (eds) *White Reign. Deploying Whiteness in America*. London: Macmillan.

McNay, L. (2000) *Gender and Agency: Reconfiguring the Subject in Feminist and Social Theory*. Cambridge: Polity Press.

Mercier, L.R. and Harold, R.D. (2003) At the interface: Lesbian-parent families and their children's schools, *Children & Schools*, 25(1): 35–47.

Mills, S. (2003) *Discourse*. London: Routledge.

Moodley, K. (1999) Antiracist education through political literacy: the case of

Canada, in S. May (ed.) *Critical Multiculturalism: Rethinking Multicultural and Antiracist Education*. London: Falmer Press.

Morgan, D.H.J. (1996) *Family Connections: An Introduction to Family Studies*. Cambridge: Polity Press.

Morris, M. (2000) Dante's left foot kicks queer theory into gear, in S. Talburt and S.R. Steinberg (eds) *Thinking Queer: Sexuality, Culture, and Education*. New York: Peter Lang.

Nettle, D. and Romaine, S. (2000) *Vanishing Voices: The Extension of the World's Languages*. Oxford: Oxford University Press.

Nguyen, K. (2004) Two mums episode sparks row, *The Age*, 4 June.

Office of Multicultural Affairs (1989) *National Agenda for a Multicultural Australia: Sharing Our Future*. Canberra: Australian Government Printing Service.

Olneck, M. (2000) Can multicultural education change what counts as cultural capital? *American Educational Research Journal*, 37(2): 317–348.

Ow, J. (2000) The revenge of the yellowfaced cyborg: The rape of digital geishas and the colonization of cyber-coolies in 3D Realms' *Shadow Warrior*, in B. Kolko, L. Nakamura and G. Rodman (eds) *Race in Cyberspace*. New York: Routledge.

Palmer, G. (1990) Preschool children and race: an Australian study, *Australian Journal of Early Childhood*, 15(2): 3–8.

Papastergiadis, N. (1998) Ambivalence in identity. Homi Bhabha and cultural theory, in *Dialogues in the Diasporas: Essay and Conversations on Cultural Identity*. London: Rivers Oram Press.

Parker, I. (1992) *Discourse Dynamics: Critical Analysis for Social and Individual Psychology*. London: Routledge.

Patton, C. (1995) Between innocence and safety: epidemiologic and popular constructions of young people's need for safe sex, in J. Terry and J. Urla (eds) *Deviant Bodies: Critical Perspectives on Difference in Science and Popular Culture*. Bloomington: Indiana University Press.

Penn, H. (2002) The World Bank's view of early childhood, *Childhood*, 9(1): 118–132.

Pennycook, A. (1998) *English and the Discourses of Colonialism*. London: Routledge.

Pettman, J. (1992) *Living in the Margins: Racism, Sexism and Feminism in Australia*. Sydney: Allen & Unwin.

Piaget, J. (1964) *The Early Growth of Logic in the Child*. New York: Harper.

Piaget, J. (1968) *The Psychology of Intelligence*. Totowa, NJ: Littlefield Adams.

Pickering, S. (2001) Common sense and original deviancy: news, discourses and asylum seekers in Australia, *Journal of Refugee Studies*, 14(2): 169–186.

Rattansi, A. (1992) Changing the subject? Racism, culture and education, in J. Donald and A. Rattansi (eds) *'Race', Culture and Difference*. London: Sage Publications, in association with Open University Press.

Reay, D. (1998) Cultural reproduction: mothers' involvement in their children's primary schooling, in M. Grenfell and D. James (eds) *Acts of Practical Theory. Bourdieu and Education*. London: Falmer Press.

Reay, D. (2003) Shifting class identities? Social class and the transition to higher education, in C. Vincent (ed.) *Social Justice, Education and Identity*. London: Routledge and Falmer Press.

Reddy, M. (1994) *Crossing the Color Line: Race, Parenting and Culture*. New Brunswick, NJ: Rutgers University Press.

Rhedding-Jones, J. (2001) Shifting ethnicities: 'Native informants' and other theories from/for early childhood education, *Contemporary Issues in Early Childhood*, 2(2): 135–155.

Rich, A. (1980) Compulsory heterosexuality and lesbian existence, *Signs: Journal of Women in Culture and Society*, 5: 631–660.

Rizvi, F. (1993) Children and the grammar of popular racism, in C. McCarthy and W. Crichlow (eds) *Race, Identity, and Representation in Education*. New York and London: Routledge.

Robinson, K.H. (1992). Class-room discipline: power, resistance and gender. A look at teacher perspectives, *Gender and Education*, 4(3): 273–289.

Robinson, K.H. (1996) Sexual harassment in secondary schooling. Unpublished doctoral dissertation, University of New South Wales, Australia.

Robinson, K.H. (2000) 'Great tits miss!' The sexual harassment of female teachers in secondary schools. Issues of gendered authority, *Discourse: Studies in the Cultural Politics of Education*, 21(1): 75–90.

Robinson, K.H. (2002) Making the invisible visible: gay and lesbian issues in early childhood education, *Contemporary Issues in Early Childhood*, 3(3): 415–434.

Robinson, K.H. (2005a) Reinforcing hegemonic masculinities through sexual harassment: issues of identity, power and popularity in secondary schools, *Gender and Education*, 17(1): 19–37.

Robinson, K.H. (2005b) Childhood and sexuality: adult constructions and silenced children, in J. Mason and T. Fattore (eds) *Children Taken Seriously: in Theory, Policy and Practice*. London: Jessica Kingsley.

Robinson, K.H. (2005c) 'Queerying' gender: heteronormativity in early childhood education, *Australian Journal of Early Childhood*, 30(2): 19–28.

Robinson, K.H. (2005d) Doing anti-homophobia and anti-heterosexism in early childhood education. Moving beyond the immobilizing impacts of 'risk', 'fears' and 'silences'. Can we afford not to? *Contemporary Issues in Early Childhood Education*, 6(2). In press.

Robinson, K.H. and Ferfolja, T. (2001) 'What are we doing this for?' Dealing with lesbian and gay issues in teacher education, *British Journal of Sociology of Education*, 22(1): 121–133.

Robinson, K.H. and Jones Díaz, C. (1999) Doing theory with early childhood educators: Understanding difference and diversity in personal and professional contexts. *Australian Journal of Early Childhood*, 24(4): 33–41.

Robinson, K.H. and Jones Díaz, C. (2000) *Diversity and Difference in Early Childhood: An Investigation into Centre Policies, Staff Attitudes and Practices. A Focus on Long Day Care and Preschool in the South West and Inner West of Sydney*. Newcastle, NSW: Roger A. Baxter, OAS Engineering Pty. Ltd. and The University of Newcastle Research Associates – TUNRA Ltd.

Rutter, J. (2004) Review: Educational interventions for refugee children: theoretical perspectives and implementing best practice, *Journal of Refugee Studies*, 17: 488–489.

Sánchez, R. (1998) Mapping the Spanish language along a multiethnic and multilingual border, in A. Darder and R. D. Torres (eds) *The Latino Studies Reader: Culture, Economy and Society*. Malden, MA: Blackwell Publishers.

Saunders, G. (1982) *Bilingual Children: Guidance for the Family*. Clevedon: Multilingual Matters.

Sawicki, J. (1991) *Disciplining Foucault: Feminism, Power, and the Body*. New York: Routledge.

Schecter, S.R. and Bayley, R. (1997) Language socialization practices and cultural identity: case studies of Mexican-descent families in California and Texas, *TESOL Quarterly*, 31(Autumn): 513–541.

Schirato, T. and Yell, S. (2000) *Communication and Cultural Literacy: An Introduction*. St Leonards, NSW: Allen & Unwin.

Sedgwick, E.K. (1990) *Epistemology of the Closet*. Berkeley: University of California Press.

Silin, J. (1995) *Sex, Death and the Education of Children: Our Passion for Ignorance in the Age of AIDS*. New York: Teachers College Press.

Silin, J. (1997) The pervert in the classroom, in J. Tobin (ed.) *Making a Place for Pleasure in Early Childhood Education*. New Haven, CT: Yale University Press.

Silva, E.B. and Smart, C. (1999) The 'new' practices and politics of family life, in E.B. Silva and C. Smart (eds) *The New Family?* London: Sage Publications.

Singh, M.G. (2000) Review essay. Changing uses of multiculturalism: Asian-Australian engagement with white Australia politics, *Australian Educational Researcher*, 27(1): 115–130.

Singh, M.G. (2002a) Rewriting the ways of globalising education? *Race Ethnicity and Education*, 5(2): 217–230.

Singh, M.G. (2002b) The sustainability of the earth's people and their cultures. Risks and opportunities: the multilingual knowledge economy. Paper presented to RMIT, 12 September.

Siren, U. (1991) *Minority Language Transmission in Early Childhood: Parental Intention and Language Use*. Stockholm: Institute of International Education, Stockholm University.

Skattebol, J. and Ferfolja, T. (2005) Voices from the ghetto: lesbian mothers speak out. Manuscript under review.

Skutnabb-Kangas, T. (1988) Multilingualism and the education of minority children, in T. Skutnabb-Kangas and J. Cummins (eds) *Minority Education: From Shame to Struggle*. Clevedon: Multilingual Matters.

Spender, D. (1983) *Women of Ideas (and What Men Have Done to Them)*. London: Ark Paperbacks.

Spivak, G.C. (1990) *The Post-Colonial Critic: Interviews, Strategies, Dialogues*. New York: Routledge.

Spivak, G. C. (1999) *A Critique of Postcolonial Reason: Toward a History of the Vanishing Present*. Cambridge, MA: Harvard University Press.

Steinberg, S. and Kincheloe J.L. (1997) *Kinderculture. The Corporate Construction of Childhood*. Boulder, CO: Westview Press.

Stephens, S. (1995) *Children and the Politics of Culture*. Princeton, NJ: Princeton University Press.

Stratton, J. and Ang, E. (1998) Multicultural imagined communities: cultural difference and national identity in the USA and Australia, in D. Bennett (ed.) *Multicultural States: Rethinking Difference and Identity*. London: Routledge.

Sullivan, N. (2003) *A Critical Introduction to Queer Theory*. New York: New York University Press.

Tasker, F. and Golombok, S. (1997) *Growing Up in a Lesbian Family*. New York: Guilford.

Tate, T. (1992) The child pornography industry: International trade in child sexual abuse, in I. Itzin (ed.) *Pornography: Women, Violence and Civil Liberties. A Radical New View*. New York: Oxford University Press.

Theilheimer, R. and Cahill, B. (2001) A messy closet in the early childhood classroom, in S. Grieshaber and G.S. Cannella (eds) *Embracing Identities in Early Childhood Education: Diversity and Possibilities*. New York: Teachers College Press.

Thorne, B. (1993) *Gender Play: Boys and Girls in School*. Buckingham: Open University Press.

Tierney, W. (2004) Globalization and educational reform: the challenges ahead, *Journal of Hispanic Higher Education*, 3(1): 5–20.

Tobin, J. (2000) *'Good Guys Don't Wear Hats'. Children's Talk about the Media*. New York: Teachers College Press.

Tomsen, S. (2002) *Hatred, Murder and Male Honour: Anti-homophobia Homicides in New South Wales, 1980–2000*. Canberra: Australian Institute of Criminology.

Tong, R. (1989) *Feminist Thought. A Comprehensive Introduction*. Boulder, CO: Westview Press.

Troyna, B. and Hatcher, R. (1992) *Racism in Children's Lives: A Study of Mainly White Primary Schools*. London: Routledge.

Usher, R. and Edwards, R. (1994) *Postmodernism and Education*. London: Routledge.

Valdés, G. (1996) *Con Respeto. Bridging the Distances between Culturally Diverse Families and Schools: An Ethnographic Portrait*. New York: Teachers College Press.

Villenas, S. and Deyhle, D. (1999) Critical race theory and ethnographies. Challenging the stereotypes: Latino families, schooling, resilience and resistance, *Curriculum Inquiry*, 29(4): 413–445.

Vincent, C. and Martin, J. (2002) Class, culture and agency. Researching parental voice, *Discourse: Studies in Cultural Politics and Education*, 23(1): 109–128.

Volk, D. (1997) Continuities and discontinuities: teaching and learning in the home and school of a Puerto Rican five year old, in E. Gregory (ed.) *One Child, Many Worlds: Early Learning in Multicultural Communities*. London: David Fulton.

Wade, R. (2001) Showdown at the World Bank, *New Left Review* (second series), /: 124–137.

Walkerdine, V. (1990) *School Girl Fictions*. London: Verso.

Wallis, A. and VanEvery, J. (2000) Sexuality in the primary school, *Sexualities*, 3(4): 409–423.

Waters, M. (1995) *Globalization*, 2nd edn. New York: Routledge.

Way, N. (1997) . . . And the poor get more numerous, *Business Review Weekly*, May.

Webb, J., Schirato, T. and Danaher, G. (2002) *Understanding Bourdieu*. Sydney: Allen & Unwin.

Weedon, C. (1997) *Feminist Practice and Poststructuralist Theory*. 2nd edn. Oxford: Blackwell.

Weeks, J. (1986) *Sexuality*. London: Routledge.

Weeks, J., Heaphy, B. and Donovan, C. (2001) *Same Sex Intimacies: Families of Choice and Other Life Experiments*. London: Routledge.

Wickens, E. (1993) Penny's question: 'I will have a child in my class with two mums – What do you know about this?' *Young Children*, 48(3): 25–28.

Wilton, T. (1996) Which one's the man? The heterosexualisation of lesbian sex, in D. Richardson (ed.) *Theorising Heterosexuality*. Buckingham: Open University Press.

Wong Fillmore, L. (1991) When learning a second language means losing the first, *Early Childhood Research Quarterly*, 6: 323–347.

Yelland, N. (ed.) (1998) *Gender in Early Childhood*. London: Routledge.

Young, R.J.C. (1990) *White Mythologies: Writing History and the West*. London: Routledge.

Young, R.J.C. (1995) *Colonial Desire. Hybridity in Theory, Culture and Race*. London: Routledge.

Young, R.J.C. (2001) *Postcolonialism: An Historical Introduction*. Oxford: Blackwell.

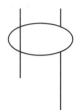

INDEX